Study Guide

Karen Van L
Lourdes A.D
Sheridan Instit

Fundamentals of Nursing

The Nature of Nursing Practice in Canada

Canadian Edition

Barbara Kozier, RN, MN

Glenora Erb, RN, BSN

Audrey Jean Berman, PhD, RN, AOCN

Karen Burke, RN

D. Shelley Raffin Bouchal, RN, PhD
University of Calgary

Sandra P. Hirst, RN, PhD, GNC(C)
University of Calgary

PEARSON
Prentice Hall

Toronto

Dedicated to Thadd, Claudette, and Rene de la Cruz

Vice President, Editorial Director: Michael J. Young
Executive Acquisitions Editor: Samantha Scully
Executive Marketing Manager: Cas Shields
Supervising Developmental Editor: Maurice Esses
Production Editor: Judith Scott
Copy Editor: Rohini Herbert
Production Coordinator: Janette Lush
Page Layout: Deanne Walle
Art Director: Julia Hall
Cover Design: Amy Harnden
Cover Image: The Stock Illustration Source

0-13-126684-5

Printed in Canada.

10 9 8 7 6 5 4

CONTENTS

PREFACE

Learning is not compulsory... neither is survival.

W. Edwards Deming

Welcome to Canadian nursing. Nursing is a profession that requires one to be a lifelong learner because of the myriad changes in health and health care. Recently, Canadian nurses have courageously faced multiple challenges and opportunities that provided lessons for nurses globally. We gratefully acknowledge their contributions.

This study guide has been prepared to accompany *Fundamentals of Nursing: The Nature of Nursing Practice in Canada*, Canadian Edition, by Kozier, Erb, Berman, Burke, Bouchal, and Hirst. Assisting you to learn the relevant concepts and enhance your application of principles is the aim of this guide. A variety of activities is provided to help you recall, analyze, apply, and synthesize, and integrate knowledge and skills.

Each chapter of this study guide corresponds to a chapter in the textbook and includes the following elements:

- An **Overview** that succinctly summarizes the scope of the textbook chapter.
- A list of the **Key Topics** discussed in the textbook chapter.
- **Matching Questions** to assist you in reviewing definitions of important terms and descriptions of important concepts.
- **Multiple-Choice Questions** that ask you to make decisions and solve problems.
- **True-False Questions** to help you test yourself on material in the textbook chapter. In the case of those statements that are false, you are asked to alter them to make them true.
- **Completion Questions** that provide you with additional opportunities to review important concepts and also to complete a table or mark up a figure.
- **Case Studies** that ask you to apply your knowledge in simulated practical situations.

Answer Keys at the end of this book serve as your feedback mechanism by giving the answers to all the study guide questions.

I hope that this study guide supports your learning journey toward becoming a nurse who exemplifies caring and lifelong learning.

Acknowledgements

Sincere thanks to Samantha Scully, Maurice Esses, and Judith Scott of Pearson Education Canada.

Lourdes A. D. de la Cruz

CHAPTER 1

Historical and Contemporary Nursing Practice

This chapter provides you with a concise summary of the state of professional nursing. It analyzes the forces that have helped shape nursing and discusses your role as an evolving professional. The chapter also highlights professional organizations that are active in shaping your profession.

KEY TOPICS

This study guide chapter reinforces the following topics discussed in the textbook chapter:

- history of nursing
- nursing role
- nursing values
- nursing practice
- professionalism
- nurses' associations
- nurse practice acts

Matching

Match each person or group with one of the following definitions of nursing:

a. Leininger
b. Canadian Nurses Association
c. Florence Nightingale
d. Virginia Henderson

___ 1. The unique function of the nurse is to assist sick or well individuals in the performance of those activities contributing to health or its recovery (or to peaceful death) that they would perform unaided if they had the necessary strength, will, or knowledge, and to do this in such a way as to help them gain independence as rapidly as possible.

___ 2. The act of utilizing the environment of the patient to assist him in his recovery

___ 3. The identification and treatment of human responses to actual or potential health problems, including the practice of and supervision of functions and services that, directly or indirectly, have as their objectives the promotion of health, prevention of illness, alleviation of suffering, restoration of health, and optimum development of health potential and include all aspects of the nursing process.

___ 4. Caring is described as the "essence of nursing."

Match each condition of the Canada Health Act *with the appropriate description.*

a. comprehensiveness
b. accessibility
c. universal coverage
d. portability
e. public administration

___ 5. All Canadians are entitled to essential health services, regardless of age, culture, gender, language, income, education.

___ 6. The health-care system must ensure that Canadians have the ability to enter or contact essential health services without user fees.

___ 7. Authorities are appointed by the federal, provincial, and territorial governments to operate the nonprofit insurance programs.

___ 8. The full continuum of health services is covered by the federal, territorial, and provincial health insurance acts.

___ 9. Canadians are entitled to health services wherever they are in the country.

Match each of the nursing values with the appropriate description.

a. accountability
b. choice

___ 10. Nurses promote the autonomy of persons and assist them to gather information to enable them to make informed decisions.

___ 11. Nurses act in a way that is consistent with their professional responsibilities and are answerable for their own actions.

Match the following titles with their appropriate definition:

a. clinical specialist
b. nurse administrator
c. nurse educator
d. nurse midwife
e. nurse practitioner
f. nurse researcher

___ 12. manages the delivery of care through budgeting, staffing, and planning of programs

___ 13. provides prenatal, perinatal, and postnatal care to women experiencing normal pregnancy

___ 14. provides client care and consultation in a specialized area of care

___ 15. investigates client care issues to improve nursing care and expand knowledge

___ 16. provides primary ambulatory care in a variety of settings

___ 17. provides sessions/courses in educational institutions or practice settings.

Multiple Choice

Circle the correct response for each question.

18. Which of the following statements best describes standards of practice?
    a. They reflect the values of the profession, define the expectations of the public, and clarify what the profession expects of its members.
    b. They describe the activities that the members of the profession are licensed to perform.
    c. They design the educational expectations for the practitioners and provide accreditation to the programs.
    d. They reflect the legislation's perspectives of their expectations of the practitioners.

19. Which of the following areas of focus are involved in nursing practice?
    a. hospital care, home care, occupational health and community care
    b. health promotion and disease prevention
    c. wellness promotion, illness prevention, health restoration, and care of the dying
    d. holistic care of clients experiencing alterations in health

20. Marta is a nursing student enrolled in her first clinical course. In the clinical unit, she is most likely functioning at which level of nursing practice?
    a. Advanced Beginner
    b. Competent
    c. Expert
    d. Novice
    e. Proficient

21. Marta's nursing education prepares her for licensure and work as a Registered Nurse. As a new graduate, she is still acquiring clinical skills and knowledge, organizational techniques, and confidence. Marta is functioning at which level of nursing practice?
    a. Advanced Beginner
    b. Competent
    c. Expert
    d. Novice
    e. Proficient

22. After two years of practice, Marta has begun to feel comfortable in her role. She is adept at handling her patient load and prioritizing situations. She is beginning to take on unit leadership responsibilities. Marta is functioning at which level of practice?
    a. Advanced Beginner
    b. Competent
    c. Expert
    d. Novice
    e. Proficient

23. Marta has become a resource for newer nurses on the unit. She is beginning to case-manage clients and coordinate services to meet long-term goals. At an evaluation marking her fourth year of employment, the manager compliments Marta on her ability to see the unit as a whole and to set priorities for care at this higher level. Marta's manager believes she is functioning at which level of practice?

a. Advanced Beginner

b. Competent

c. Expert

d. Novice

e. Proficient

24. Marta's unit receives a thank-you note from the family of a recently deceased client. The family says of Marta, "Marta knew just what to do. She is very special. She was able to size up the situation instantly and handle things efficiently. She always knew what was right for Dad." This family has described Marta as a(n) __________ nurse.

a. Advanced Beginner

b. Competent

c. Expert

d. Novice

e. Proficient

25. Which of the following statements best describes the Canadian Nurses Association?

a. It is a mandatory organization for all Canadian nurses to join in order to be licensed to practise.

b. The Canadian Nurses Association is a federation of 11 provincial and territorial nursing associations.

c. It is a voluntary organization that serves as an authoritative voice for nurses globally.

d. It is an independent group that operates all the provincial nursing organizations.

Case Study

26. 8:00 a.m. Monday: Home health nurse Eduardo Salazar is reviewing his caseload for the day. He has five clients to visit today. The home health agency is holding a staff meeting this morning. In order to attend the meeting, Eduardo plans to see two clients before lunch and the remaining three in the afternoon.

Eduardo schedules his first visit with Jason Essex. Jason is terminally ill with AIDS. His partner cares for him at home. Jason is failing rapidly. His weight has dropped 25 pounds in three months, and his activity level is severely diminished. Jason is receiving parenteral antibiotics. Eduardo will need to inspect the IV site and administer the medication. He will begin teaching Richard, Jason's partner, how to administer the medication. During the time the medication is infusing, Eduardo plans to assess the need for additional home services and to provide emotional support for Jason and Richard.

Eduardo will visit Bridget Coan, only four blocks from Jason's home. Bridget is a 58-year-old woman with severe cognitive impairment secondary to Alzheimer's disease.

Eduardo needs to meet with Bridget's family to discuss ongoing care. Bridget has begun to wander, and her family fears for her safety A family conference has been scheduled for 11 a.m. to discuss Bridget's ongoing care.

a. What role is Eduardo fulfilling when he inspects Jason's IV site and administers the medication?

____

b. What role is Eduardo fulfilling when he assesses the need for additional home services for Jason?

____

c. What role is Eduardo fulfilling when he provides emotional support for Jason and Richard?

____

d. What role is Eduardo fulfilling when he coordinates a conference with the Coan family?

____

CHAPTER 2

Nursing Education in Canada

This chapter offers you a concise view of the pathways to nursing practice and the importance of continuing education. It exposes you to the issues that influence nursing in Canada.

KEY TOPICS

This study guide chapter reinforces the following topics discussed in the textbook chapter:

- nursing education programs
- continuing education for nurses
- nursing associations and their influence upon education
- issues facing nursing education

Matching

Match the following terms with their definitions:

a. certification

b. licensed practical nursing program

c. in-service education

d. computer-mediated distance education

e. entry to practice

___ 1. the educational requirement for a nurse to practise nursing is the successful completion of a baccalaureate degree in nursing.

___ 2. the program that prepares an individual to practise under the supervision of a registered nurse

___ 3. a program to upgrade the skills of employees that is administered by the employer

___ 4. a voluntary and periodic process for a specialty group to demonstrate competence

___ 5. a program that is offered using a computer network

Multiple Choice

Circle the correct response for each question.

6. Which of the following statements is true of the Canadian RN exam?
   a. The national RN exam is administered by a private consortium.
   b. Only graduates from Canadian schools can take the RN exam.
   c. The RN exam is criterion referenced and made up of multiple-choice questions.
   d. The RN exam can be written by any registered nurse who lives in Canada.

7. Which of the following statements best describes the role of the Canadian Association of Schools of Nursing?
   a. It ensures that minimum standards of education are met.
   b. It forms partnerships among the different schools, colleges, and universities.
   c. It approves the curricula of all the schools of nursing.
   d. It grants accreditation based on optimum standards.

8. Which of the following statements best describes graduate education in nursing?
   a. Graduate education prepares nurses to function in advanced practice roles.
   b. Graduate education is required for practice in special care units.
   c. Graduate education prepares nurses to function outside of the hospital.
   d. Graduate education generally requires completion of a diploma.

9. Which of the following statements is true of continuing education for nurses?
   a. Continuing education assists nurses in maintaining currency in practice.
   b. Continuing education is required by all the Canadian provinces.
   c. Continuing education is mandated by employers.
   d. Continuing education may be accomplished completely through home study programs.

10. Who of the following applicants meets the requirement for a graduate nursing education?
   a. An applicant who is a registered nurse and has a baccalaureate degree from another country.
   b. An applicant who has a baccalaureate degree and is licensed to practise nursing.
   c. An applicant who has a baccalaureate degree from an approved university, is licensed to practise within the program's province, and has evidence of scholastic ability.
   d. An applicant who has scholastic ability and has proven research skills.

11. Which of the following statements best exemplifies the changing demographics affecting student populations in nursing?
   a. The number of younger students attracted to the profession has increased dramatically.
   b. There is an increase in the number of students who work throughout the program to obtain funds for tuition fees.
   c. The number of students who are nontraditional learners is decreasing.
   d. There is a decrease in the number of male students.

12. Which of the following statements is true of the shortage crisis in Canada?
   a. There is a disproportionately low number of educational spaces for nursing students.
   b. Nursing is not an attractive profession for young women.
   c. The work conditions for nurses prevent nurses from staying in their jobs until retirement.
   d. The number of graduates from schools of nursing remains low at this time.

Completion

13. Continuing education is a strategy to maintain competency. What are the three needs that arc met by continuing education?

____

____

____

____

14. At the present time, provincial laws in Canada recognize the following three types of nurses:

____

____

____

Fill in the blanks with the appropriate responses.

15. Janice Trodden is a high school student interested in becoming a nurse. She asks you to explain the difference between an LPN and an RN. You explain that an LPN is a (a) ____________________ and an RN is a (b) ____________________. An LPN, also known as a Registered Nursing Assistant (RNA), Certified Nursing Assistant (CNA), or Registered Practical Nurse (RPN), works under the direction of a(n) (c) ____________________ to deliver bedside nursing care. The educational program for an LPN/RNA/CNA/RPN usually lasts (d) ____________________ months.

An RN has the knowledge and skills to make sophisticated nursing judgements; therefore, RN education is more extensive than LPN education. Entry into RN practice is generally achieved by two pathways: (e) ____________________ or (f) ____________________.

Once in practice, RNs may further their education in several ways. Diploma and Associate Degree nurses may return to school for a Bachelor of Science in Nursing (BSN) degree. BSN graduates may return to school for (g) ____________________ ____________________. All nurses may gain further knowledge or skills through (h) ____________________ or (i) ____________________.

Case Study

16. Your neighbour is a high school student who is interested in pursuing a career in nursing. His mother suggested he talks with you. He asks you, "How can I prepare myself to get into the field of nursing?" What would be your response?

____

____

____

____

CHAPTER 3

Nursing Research in Canada

This chapter presents a summary of concepts related to research in nursing. It highlights the ways that you can participate in research endeavours and analyzes your role in protecting the rights of human subjects.

KEY TOPICS

This study guide chapter reinforces the following topics discussed in the textbook chapter:

- evidence-based decision making
- approaches to nursing research
- research process
- protecting the rights of human subjects

Matching

Match the following terms with the appropriate descriptions:

a. feasibility
b. reliability
c. research design
d. significance
e. validity

___ 1. the plan for obtaining answers to the research question

___ 2. the potential to improve client care, test or generate theory, or resolve a clinical problem

___ 3. the availability of time and resources required to investigate a research question

___ 4. the degree to which an instrument measures what it is supposed to measure

___ 5. the degree of consistency with which an instrument measures a variable

Multiple Choice

Circle the correct response for each question.

6. Which of the following best describes the professional responsibility of nurses related to research?
   a. Nurses incorporate appropriate results into their practice.
   b. Nurses attend research meetings regularly

c. Nurses have only a very minor role in research activities.

d. Nurses can only do clinical research with the aid of the interdisciplinary team.

7. Which of the following best exemplifies a qualitative research design?

a. The researcher administers an intervention of interest to a group while withholding it from another group.

b. The researcher interviews a group of individuals and collects their views about an experience.

c. The researcher conducts a survey to find out the differences between two groups of clients receiving care.

d. The researcher compares the results of tests of several groups of clients.

8. What is the best definition of "range"?

a. a measure of variability that consists of the difference between the highest and lowest values in a distribution of scores

b. a measure of central tendency that represents the average score

c. a measure of variability that indicates the average to which the scores deviate from the mean

d. a measure of central tendency that is computed by taking the sum of all of the scores

9. Which of the following is a methodological dimension that needs to be included in a research critique?

a. appropriateness of the research design

b. ethical problems or concerns

c. conceptual framework of the study

d. research results presentation

10. Dr. Sara Roberts, a prominent nurse researcher, is conducting a study on the effectiveness of a falls prevention program. She informs a client on the clinical unit about the study and his right to choose whether to participate in the study. Which of the following rights is she safeguarding for the human subject?

a. right not to be harmed

b. right to full disclosure

c. right of self-determination

d. right to privacy and confidentiality

11. What is the employer's responsibility regarding evidence-based practice?

a. to provide funding for the dissemination of research findings

b. to encourage and support evidence-based practice

c. to provide the tools necessary to implement evidence into practice

d. to ensure that nursing curricula include evidence-based practice guidelines

12. When formulating a research problem, which of the following criteria should the nurse consider?

a. reliability and validity

b. operational definitions of variables

c. experimental, quasi-experimental, and nonexperimental design
d. significance, researchability, and feasibility

Completion

13. All clients must be informed about the consequences of participating in a research study. The nurse must serve as a client advocate in safeguarding the subject's rights. What rights does a research subject have?

____

____

____

14. Which step of the research process is missing from the following list?
Start a research question or problem.
Define the study's purpose or rationale.
Review the related literature.
Formulate hypotheses and define variables.
Select the population, sample, and setting.
Conduct a pilot study.
Collect the data.
Analyze the data.
Communicate conclusions and implications.

Fill in the blanks with the appropriate responses.

15. If you want to find out if a research article is interesting, you might want to read the ______________.

16. If you want to know what data were collected in a research study, you examine the ______________ and ______________.

True or False

Read the following statements to determine if they are true or false. If a statement is false, alter the statement to make it true.

17. Both research and problem solving have the same steps and therefore are the same.
True False

____

____

____

18. Quantitative research is defined as the study of phenomena that lend themselves to precise measurement and quantification, often involving a rigorous and controlled design.
True False

19. Descriptive statistics are used to show patterns and trends.
True False

Case Study

20. Before doing a research study in a pediatric unit, the nurse researcher makes a proposal to the Research Ethics Board of the hospital. How would the nurse propose to obtain informed consent?

Chapter 4

Nursing Philosophies, Theories, Concepts, Frameworks, and Models

This chapter examines the beliefs and philosophies of the most influential nursing theorists. It exposes you to the thoughts that have guided the development of modem nursing.

KEY TOPICS

This study guide chapter reinforces the following topics discussed in the textbook chapter:

- nursing theories
- conceptual frameworks and models
- philosophy in nursing

Matching

Match the following terms with the appropriate definitions:

a. concept
b. conceptual framework
c. conceptual model
d. paradigm
e. ontology
f. philosophy
g. theory

___ 1. an area of inquiry that investigates the nature of being
___ 2. an illustration or diagram of a conceptual framework
___ 3. a scientific discipline that explores and attempts to answer questions about the world and experiences
___ 4. a particular way of thinking based on a specific set of beliefs, values, and assumptions
___ 5. a system of ideas that explains phenomena
___ 6. the basic building block of theory; generates mental images of phenomena
___ 7. a group of related concepts

Match the idea, belief, or philosophy with the appropriate nursing theorist.

a. Henderson
b. Allen
c. Leininger
f. Campbell
g. Parse
h. Peplau

d. Roach i. Roy

e. Nightingale j. Watson

___ 8. The role of the nurse is nurturing individuals who are experiencing critical periods so they may develop methods to meet their basic needs.

___ 9. Nurses need to be a partner with the client, a helper to the client, and, when necessary, a substitute for the client.

___ 10. Nurses' professional caring is an essential ingredient in human development and survival.

___ 11. The theme for nursing is the nature of healthy living.

___ 12. The nurse–client relationship evolves in four phases: orientation, identification, exploitation, and resolution.

___ 13. Health is linked with five environmental factors: fresh air, pure water, efficient drainage, cleanliness, and light.

___ 14. Both the individual and the environment are sources of stimuli that require modification to promote adaptation.

___ 15. The practice of caring is central to nursing.

___ 16. Differences in caring values and behaviours lead to differences in the expectations of those seeking care.

___ 17. The role of the nurse consists of illuminating meaning, synchronizing rhythms, and mobilizing transcendence.

Multiple Choice

Circle the correct response for each question.

18. Which of the following statements best describes the interpretive way of understanding the world?
    a. Knowledge can be obtained by observations and experimentation.
    b. Knowledge is derived from objective measures of what is happening.
    c. Knowledge is derived from creating meaning from experiences.
    d. Knowledge can be obtained through argumentation.

19. Nursing theory is used to:
    a. improve the image of nursing.
    b. differentiate among RN, LPN, and support worker.
    c. provide direction and guidance for practice, education, and research.
    d. make nursing distinct from medicine.

20. The four major concepts of nursing are:
    a. person, environment, family, and caring.
    b. health, illness, recovery, and nursing.
    c. person, environment, health, and nursing.
    d. practice, education, research, and theory.

21. Which of the following exemplifies a phenomenological approach to the study of nursing practice?

a. a study of ethical dilemmas

b. a study of the economics of nursing

c. a study of the art of nursing

d. a study of the experience of grief

Completion

22. Which nursing model(s) guides your nursing education program?

____

____

____

23. Which nursing model(s) do you most identify with? Why?

____

____

____

24. Explain the relationship between nursing theory and research.

____

____

____

____

Case Study

25. Several guest speakers are presenting how they use nursing theories in their practice. The theories they are presenting are Sister Simone Roach's professional caring, Margaret Campbell's UBC Model of Nursing, and Peplau's Interpersonal Relations Model. Your professor suggested that the class think of at least one question to ask of these guest speakers. Identify the questions that you will ask these presenters.

____

____

____

____

____

____

Chapter 5

The Individual—The Client of Care

This chapter explores the relationship of individuality and holism. It presents a discussion of the components of a health status assessment.

KEY TOPICS

This study guide chapter reinforces the following topics discussed in the textbook chapter:

- human needs
- developmental stage theories
- systems theories
- assessing the health of individuals

Matching

Match the following terms to their definitions:

a. holism
b. homeostasis
c. negative feedback
d. perception
e. positive feedback
f. self-identity
g. self-regulation

___ 1. Human beings are more than the sum of their parts.

___ 2. This feedback mechanism stimulates change.

___ 3. Healthy bodies have the tendency to maintain a state of equilibrium while continually changing.

___ 4. The perception of self as a distinct entity in interaction with others.

___ 5. The process of selecting, organizing, and interpreting sensory stimuli into a meaningful and coherent picture of the world.

___ 6. The process by which homeostatic compensatory mechanisms come into play in a healthy person.

___ 7. This feedback mechanism inhibits change.

Multiple Choice

Circle the correct response for each question.

8. The major homeostatic regulators of the body are the:
   a. central nervous system and cardiac system.
   b. autonomic nervous system and endocrine system.
   c. endocrine system and sympathetic nervous system.
   d. cardiac system and respiratory system.

9. Which one of the following statements about human needs is true?
   a. People meet their needs on the basis of societal priorities.
   b. All needs can be deferred, if so desired.
   c. Homeostasis is achievable only if physiological needs are met.
   d. A person chooses ways to meet needs on the basis of learned experiences, lifestyle, personal values, and culture.

10. Which of the following best exemplifies a boundary of a system?
   a. heart
   b. nerves
   c. skin
   d. extremities

11. Why are the developmental stage theories useful in nursing practice?
   a. They allow nurses to predict the different non-normative life events that will occur.
   b. They describe the typical behaviours that occur within an age group.
   c. They explain the inter-relationships between the individual and their significant others.
   d. They allow the nurses to assist the clients in meeting their needs.

True or False

Read the following statements to determine if they are true or false. If a statement is false, alter the statement to make it true.

12. A nurse must recognize the individuality of the client. Dimensions of individuality include one's personality or character and self-identity.
   True False

   ____

   ____

   ____

13. The individual's coping mechanisms are consistent over time. These are behaviours used to deal with stress.
   True False

   ____

   ____

   ____

14. Psychologic homeostasis is learned through the experience of living and interacting with others.
True False

____

____

____

15. When planning nursing care, safety and security interventions will always take precedence over physiological care.
True False

____

____

Completion

16. Identify the major prerequisites for achieving psychologic homeostasis.

____

____

____

____

17. Identify at least two ways in which knowledge of human needs helps the nurse in practice.

____

____

18. Label the hierarchy of human needs according to Maslow.

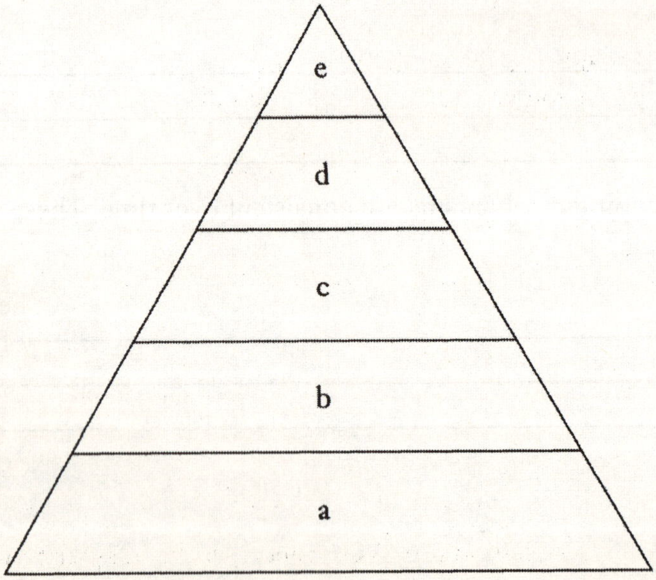

19. When examining your own coping mechanisms, you also need to look at your resources. Examine both your internal and external resources.

20. Analyze your risk for health problems by looking at developmental factors, hereditary factors, gender, and race.

21. Using Maslow's characteristics of a self-actualized person, describe someone you know who meets most of the identified examples.

22. Examine how the cultural variables of decision making and health-care practices influence your nursing practice.

Case Study

23. Luz is a 16-year-old high-school student. Her family migrated to Canada two years ago, and she has adjusted well to the climate and educational system. She comes to see you, the school nurse, because she feels "stressed" as she does not have any friends and misses her old friends. What coping mechanisms would you assess?

CHAPTER 6

Nursing Care of Families

This chapter highlights the development of family nursing and provides a demographic snapshot of Canadian families. It presents ways of exploring family structures and dynamics. The chapter also offers examples of family nursing practices.

KEY TOPICS

This study guide chapter reinforces the following topics discussed in the textbook chapter:

- definitions of "family"
- development of family nursing
- understanding families
- nursing care of families

Matching

Match each term with the appropriate description of a nurse's relational practice.

a. curious listener
b. compassionate stranger
c. nonjudgmental collaborator
d. mirror of family strengths

___ 1. The nurse focuses on the resources and possibilities and collaborates to deal with the challenges faced by the family.

___ 2. Families value the nurse who balances listening and asking good questions to deal with significant perspectives.

___ 3. The nurse is objective yet is interested in the family's issues and is able to offer a new and impartial point of view.

___ 4. Families appreciate a nurse who avoids blaming and criticism so the family members can be more open.

Multiple Choice

Circle the correct response for each question.

5. "When your son bangs the door while you are still talking, what do you do?" This is an example of a:

   a. triadic question.

   b. hypothetical question.

c. difference question.
d. behavioural effect question.

6. When a nurse asks a question of the family members about the way they express anger, she/he is assessing:
   a. coping patterns.
   b. interaction patterns.
   c. family roles.
   d. family values.

7. Which of the following questions best explores the impact of a family member's illness?
   a. How helpful has your family members been during your illness?
   b. How might you want your family to be involved in your care?
   c. How might you successfully implement your treatment options?
   d. Of all your family members, who do you think has had the most difficulty since your hospitalization?

8. Which of the following statements best describes family nursing?
   a. Relational practices that involve the family members in care, respond to their concerns, provide them with information, and offer emotional support.
   b. Practice of nursing that focuses on family members.
   c. A collaborative nursing practice involving individuals, families, and communities.
   d. Practice of nursing that involves family members in providing care to their family members.

9. In what way can the nurse best evaluate nursing care of families?
   a. by reflecting on ways that the family expressed gratitude to the nurse
   b. by reflecting on how the family was involved in decision making
   c. by sending end a survey questionnaire to the family post discharge
   d. by asking the client for feedback about the care received

True or False

Read the following statements to determine if they are true or false. If a statement is false, alter the statement to make it true.

10. Canadian families are characterized by low mobility.
    True False

    ____
    ____
    ____

11. Nursing care of families is implemented through relational practices.
True False

___

___

12. An ecomap depicts the family's connection to the larger systems in its life.
True False

___

___

Completion

13. A statement of praise that emphasizes the strengths and supports movement of the nurse–patient–family system in a manner that the family's needs are met is a ____________________.

14. Nurses care for families through the relationship they form with the clients and their families. Name five examples of family nursing practices.

___

___

___

___

___

15. Describe your own family. Which one of the eight types of families does your family most resemble?

___

___

___

___

16. Is your current family different from your family of origin? If so, describe your family of origin.

___

___

___

___

Case Study

17. Millie, 19 years old, and Ray, 26 years old, are worrying about their mother Maria who was discharged from the convalescent home after a series of mild strokes. Maria assures them that she can take care of herself with the help of her own sisters, Helena and Rita. In addition, a home care nurse visits twice a week and a neighbour from their church has volunteered to look in on Maria every day when the children are out of the house. Maria's former co-workers had been very helpful while she was recovering and they regularly drop by to provide any housekeeping and grocery needs.

    a. From the information, draw an ecomap.

    b. What further questions do you need to ask?

    ____

    ____

    ____

    ____

    ____

CHAPTER 7

Ethics, Morality, and Values

This chapter examines the roles of ethics, and morality values, as they relate to client care. It presents several frameworks for moral decision making and explores the relationship between your views as a nurse and those of the clients to whom you provide care. Numerous clinical examples illustrate the relevance of ethical decision making to nursing practice.

KEY TOPICS

This study guide chapter reinforces the following topics discussed in the textbook chapter:

- moral development
- values clarification
- professional codes of ethics
- contemporary ethical issues
- strategies to enhance ethical decision making and practice

Matching

Match the following key terms with the appropriate descriptions:

a. attitudes	d. law
b. beliefs	e. morality
c. ethics	f. values

___ 1. freely chosen, enduring beliefs or attitudes about the worth of a person, object, idea, or action

___ 2. a reflection of the moral values of a society

___ 3. mental positions or feelings toward a person, object, or idea

___ 4. a method of inquiry that helps people understand the morality of human behaviour

___ 5. personal standards of right and wrong

___ 6. interpretations or conclusions that people accept as true

Match the moral theories and framework with the appropriate descriptions.

a. relational ethics

b. deontology

c. utilitarianism

___ 7. the morality of decisions not determined by consequences; emphasizes duty, rationality, and obedience to rules

___ 8. emphasis on the act bringing the most good and least harm to the greatest number of people

___ 9. stresses responsibility, commitment to others, and caring

Match the moral principle terms with the correct definitions.

a.	autonomy	e.	nonmaleficence
b.	beneficence	f.	caring
c.	fidelity	g.	veracity
d.	justice		

___ 10. fairness; a decision based on facts, fairness, and equity

___ 11. the right to make one's own decisions; recognizes the individual's uniqueness and the right to choose personal goals

___ 12. the ability to tell the truth

___ 13. the quality of being faithful to agreements and responsibilities that one has undertaken

___ 14. the duty to do no harm; the basis of most codes of nursing ethics

___ 15. the duty to do good; to implement actions that benefit clients and their support persons

___ 16. a virtue that nurses must possess to make ethical decisions in practice

Multiple Choice

Circle the correct response for each question.

17. Which of the following statements is true of moral issues?
    a. They are often concerned with issues of right and wrong, good and bad, or should and ought.
    b. They always require the nurse to change the thinking of the client.
    c. They are the same as ethical issues.
    d. They require action on the part of the nurse.

18. When the nurse acts as a client advocate, she:
    a. is an advocate for what is right.
    b. is always in an active role protecting those who cannot speak for themselves.
    c. allows the client to decide what is right and supports the client's decision.
    d. is attempting to protect the status quo.
    e. must always agree with the client.

19. Which of the following is true of nurses and ethical decision making?
    a. Nurses rarely encounter ethical dilemmas.
    b. Nurses always defer to the physician in the case of an ethical dilemma.

c. Nurses frequently encounter ethical issues around use of technology and conflicting loyalties.

d. Nurses must always treat the client aggressively, regardless of medical orders or client wishes.

True or False

Read the following statements to determine if they are true or false. If a statement is false, alter the statement to make it true.

20. Values are learned at an unconscious level through observation and experience; as such, they are greatly influenced by a person's sociocultural environment.
True False

____

____

____

21. A code of ethics is a formal statement about how a group actually behaves.
True False

____

____

22. It is important that nurses be consciously aware of their own values and avoid undue influence of personal values when caring for clients.
True False

____

____

23. Advocacy in nursing is focused on protecting the public's rights through information, negotiation, and influence.
True False

____

____

Completion

24. List four important professional values for nursing according to Watson.

____

____

____

____

25. Is there an ethics committee at your clinical facility? Who belongs to the ethics committee? How often does the committee meet? Are you allowed to attend a meeting?

26. Catherine Pardee is a 22-year-old college student who presents to the OB/GYN clinic requesting pregnancy testing and an abortion if she is pregnant. As the nurse working in the clinic, you obtain a nursing history from Catherine. Catherine informs you that she has had four prior pregnancies. Each of the prior pregnancies had been terminated by an abortion. During the interview she tells you, "I'm terrible about birth control. I just can't remember it, and besides, if I get pregnant, I can always have an abortion."

How do you feel about Catherine's views and clinic presentation?

Would your views affect your ability to provide care to Catherine?

Case Study

27. Nan Motto is a 35-year-old mother of three children, aged 4, 7, and 9. Her younger sister has developed renal failure and is being considered for renal transplantation. Nan's sister has asked her to be the kidney donor. You are the Nurse Coordinator for the Renal Transplant Program. Nan arrives at the clinic for an appointment with you to evaluate her status as a potential donor. In your discussion, Nan admits that she is very uncomfortable about her decision. In assisting Nan to work through her decision-making process, you need to clarify her values. Review some questions that you may ask to help Nan.

28. Jedi Annihi is a 37-year-old man who has undergone a craniotomy and debulking procedure (removal of mass) for a malignant brain tumour. During his initial hospitalization, he is informed by the neurosurgeon that the tumour is a vigorously growing carcinoma. Treatment options are presented. However, the surgeon tells Jedi that he will probably only live another 12 to 18 months. Jedi opts for minimal treatment. During his hospitalization, he prepares a living will with the assistance of a friend who is an attorney. You are a witness to this event. Jedi asks to be discharged home as soon as possible. He plans on taking a vacation with his family and enjoying the remainder of his life. Approximately nine months later, Jedi is brought to the emergency department by his family. He is markedly thinner and confused. An MRI scan demonstrates that the tumour has advanced rapidly. Jedi's family insists that he be admitted and that "everything should be done" including surgery. The family believes that this is what Jedi would want done. They deny the existence of a living will.

a. Identify three appropriate questions for ethical decision making.

b. How do you apply the Canadian Nurses Association Code of Ethics for Registered Nurses?

c. Apply Storch's ethical decision-making framework to the situation. Choose several plans of action and anticipated consequences.

CHAPTER 8

Legal Aspects of Nursing

This chapter provides you with a vast amount of information on the legal aspects that affect your role as a student nurse and your future role as a licensed nurse. The emphasis is on application to the clinical setting and your responsibility for providing safe care.

KEY TOPICS

This study guide chapter reinforces the following topics discussed in the textbook chapter:

- functions of the law in nursing
- process of action
- informed consent
- selected legal aspects of nursing practice
- negligence
- torts
- strategies to minimize liability
- dependent and independent interventions
- incident reports
- reporting crimes, torts, and unsafe practices
- legal responsibilities of students

Matching

Match the type of law with the appropriate description.

a. civil law
b. common law
c. contract law
d. criminal law
e. public law
f. statutory law
g. tort law

___ 1. law that deals with actions against the safety and welfare of the public

___ 2. law used to enforce duties and rights among individuals that are not formalized in a contract

___ 3. decisional law that generally adheres to the doctrine of *stare decisis*, which means "to stand by things decided"

___ 4. law that involves the enforcement of agreements between private individuals

___ 5. the body of law that deals with relationships between individuals and the government or governmental agencies

___ 6. type of law exemplified by state or provincial /territorial nurse practice acts

___ 7. law that deals with the relationship between private individuals

Match each of the following legal terms with its definition or example:

a.	battery	e.	malpractice
b.	false imprisonment	f.	sexual harassment
c.	invasion of privacy	g.	negligence
d.	assault	h.	unprofessional conduct

___ 8. Practice below the standard expected of an ordinary prudent practitioner.

___ 9. A category of offences discussed in most nurse practice acts that serves as grounds for action against the nurse's registration.

___ 10. This act prohibits use of name or likeness without consent, unreasonable intrusion, public disclosure of private facts, and putting in a false light.

___ 11. Four elements must be present for it to be proven: duty, breach, harm, and causation.

___ 12. The client tells the student nurse that she is too dizzy to walk independently. The student believes that the client is not being truthful and insists that she get out of bed immediately. The student grabs the client and drags her out of bed against her wishes.

___ 13. While attending a continuing education course, you are inappropriately touched and propositioned by a colleague.

___ 14. An 85-year-old woman awakens from anesthesia to find herself restrained. The nurse charts that the client is alert and oriented, but the nurse refuses to remove the restraints because she states she is very busy and does not have time to watch the client.

___ 15. A nurse threatens to administer an injection to a client who refuses to take an oral medication.

Multiple Choice

Circle the correct response for each question.

16. You are a nurse assigned to provide care for a client recovering from knee replacement surgery. The client is alert and oriented and able to bathe and feed himself. After breakfast, you place his bed in the lowest position (relative to the floor), raise all four siderails, provide him with the call bell, and instruct him to call for help before getting out of bed. An hour later, when you enter the room to administer his medications, you find him trying to climb out of bed over the siderails. He states that he wants to use the bathroom and does not want to bother you because he knows you are busy. On examination, there is no evidence of injury. The physician who is making rounds agrees with your assessment and reminds the client that he needs assistance getting out of bed. Later in the day, the client's wife threatens to sue you for malpractice, claiming that you have inadequately protected her husband. Which of the following is true of her claim of malpractice?
    a. She has just cause to sue you. You have breached the standard of care.
    b. She must demonstrate that your actions resulted in endangerment for her husband.
    c. The client has not been harmed. Without evidence of harm, malpractice cannot be proven.
    d. She would need to sue the physician rather than the nurse.

17. Which of the following is true of *Nurse Practice Acts*?
   a. They legally dictate the relationship between the nurse and the institution.
   b. They identify the scope of nursing practice.
   c. They legally control nursing practice through certification.
   d. They specify nursing role at a federal level.

18. The *Good Samaritan Act* protects health-care providers:
   a. who render aid in an emergency against liability for any damages or injury.
   b. who render aid in a health-care facility.
   c. who render aid in an emergency against liability unless there is a gross departure from the standard of care.
   d. against liability for damages or injury if they render aid to victims who may not be able to give consent for care due to physical or mental limitations.

19. Which of the following is true of an incident report?
   a. It should be filed within 48 hours of the incident.
   b. It should be incorporated into the medical record.
   c. It should be filed immediately with the hospital attorney.
   d. It should be completed as soon after the incident as possible.

20. Which of the following orders does not have to be questioned by the nurse?
   a. an order that the client questions
   b. any order if the client's condition has changed
   c. a treatment that the nurse believes will cause harm to the client
   d. an order that is written concisely and completely

21. The nurse has many day-to-day roles, including caregiver, client advocate, researcher, among others. However, from a legal perspective, the three roles of the nurse are:
   a. caregiver, case manager, and confidential counsellor.
   b. provider of service, employee or independent contractor, and citizen.
   c. client advocate, family advocate, and institutional advocate.
   d. provider of services, receiver of services, and payor for services.

22. Collective bargaining is a formalized:
   a. process recommended by the CNA for negotiation of wages and benefits.
   b. plan for handling and settling disputes.
   c. relationship between employees and employers, which is widely accepted in nursing.
   d. process that dictates wages, conditions of employment, and the relationship between employee and employer.

23. Etta Nichols is a 79-year-old woman recently admitted to the surgical unit with a fractured hip. She has a history of Alzheimer's disease associated with severe cognitive impairment. Can Etta give informed consent for the surgical repair of her hip?
   a. She may give informed consent.
   b. She may not have the capacity to give consent.

c. Her presence at the hospital implies consent.

d. Her children must give consent.

24. Jason Pulaski is a 42-year-old airline pilot who suffered a 10-cm laceration of the right lower leg while playing rugby with friends. He drove himself to the urgent care clinic. The nurse practitioner determined that the laceration required suturing. Can Jason give informed consent for the laceration repair?

    a. He may give informed consent.
    b. He may not have the capacity to give consent.
    c. His presence at the clinic implies consent.
    d. His wife must give consent since he has been injured.

25. Four-year-old Scott Branch has been seen repeatedly in the pediatric clinic for tonsillitis. The pediatrician recommends a tonsillectomy. Can Scott give consent for the tonsillectomy?

    a. He may give informed consent.
    b. He may not have the capacity to give consent.
    c. His presence at the clinic implies consent.
    d. His parent or guardian must give consent.

26. Your client's family asks you to serve as a witness to a will. Upon witnessing the will, you should:

    a. make an entry in the client's chart noting that a will was made and also note your perception of the client's physical and mental capacity.
    b. complete an incident report detailing the creation of the will and your role; do not make a notation in the chart.
    c. excuse yourself from further client care with this individual; your role as a witness requires dissolving this relationship.
    d. notify the physician that the client has made a will and advise the physician of the nature of the client's wishes.

True or False

Read the following statements to determine if they are true or false. If a statement is false, alter it to make it true.

27. Nurse–client communication is always protected as a privileged communication.
    True False

    ____

    ____

28. On the basis on the legal doctrine of *respondent superior*, the employer is always responsible for the conduct of the employee.
    True False

    ____

    ____

29. For a will to be valid, the person making the will must be of sound mind and must not be unduly influenced by anyone.
True False

30. Torts can result from acts of omission or commission.
True False

Completion

31. The physician orders Demerol 1000 mg IM q4h PRN pain. The nurse examines the order and notes that the dosage is 10 times the dose he anticipated. What should he do?

32. How do you feel about nurses participating in collective bargaining?

33. Imagine that there is a nursing strike at the hospital that you are scheduled to use for your next clinical experience. The nurses at the facility are on strike demanding better staffing ratios. They believe that the safety of client care has been compromised by recent staff layoffs. Management contends that layoffs were necessary due to the financial situation of the facility. Your nursing instructor has asked you to cross the picket line in order to report for your clinical experience. The striking nurses believe that the school is undermining their position by staffing the hospital while they are out on strike. Would you cross the picket line to continue to attend clinical? Explain your answer.

34. There are four elements of proof for nursing negligence and malpractice. First, it must be shown that the nurse was duty-bound to the client. Then, it must be shown that there was a (a) ______________________________.
Third, there must have been an injury to the client, and finally, it must be demonstrated that (b) ______________________________.

35. Identify at least five situations in which a nurse may be charged with malpractice.

____

____

____

____

____

36. Identify the three elements that must be present for informed consent to occur.

____

____

____

37. Imagine that you are caring for a 14-year-old boy who was hit by a truck while riding his bicycle home from school. The physician has determined that the boy has a flat EEG and is "brain dead." Would you be comfortable approaching the family with an organ donation request? Describe how you would handle this situation.

____

____

____

____

38. Does your province/territory have right-to-die and living will statutes? ______________

39. What is an "implied consent"?

____

____

____

40. Does your school provide liability insurance? If so, what is the extent of coverage? Is it advisable for you to have your own personal coverage?

____

____

____

____

Case Study

41. Sheryl is a fellow student in your clinical group. One day when you are both preparing pain medications for administration, you observe that Sheryl signs out two tablets of Oxycodone but places only one tablet in the medicine cup and the other tablet in her pocket. Later in the day, you overhear her telling the physician that the client is not getting relief from his pain medication. She reports that she has administered two tablets of Oxycodone every three hours, but the client is still complaining of severe pain. Sheryl asks the physician to prescribe an injectable opioid for pain relief.

    What would you do in this circumstance?

CHAPTER 9

Health, Wellness, and Illness

This chapter explores a variety of definitions and meanings of health, wellness, illness, and disease. You are exposed to different ways of thinking about health. Your role in promoting health is emphasized.

KEY TOPICS

This study guide chapter reinforces the following topics discussed in the textbook chapter:

- health, wellness, illness, and disease
- models of health
- population health

Matching

Match the model of health with the appropriate description.

a. adaptive model
b. clinical model
c. health field concept
d. eudaemonistic model
e. role performance model

___ 1. People who can perform their roles are healthy, even if they appear clinically ill.
___ 2. Health is a condition of actualization or realization of a person's potential.
___ 3. Illness is a result of interaction among agent, host, and environment.
___ 4. Biology, lifestyle, environment, and health-care organizations determine health.
___ 5. Good health is a flexible adaptation to the environment and an interaction with the environment to maximum advantage.

Match the appropriate classification of illness with the descriptions.

a. acute illness
b. chronic illness

___ 6. severe symptoms of short duration
___ 7. often associated with long-term disease process
___ 8. osteoporosis is an example
___ 9. a cold is an example
___ 10. associated with periods of remission and exacerbation
___ 11. usually has sudden onset

Multiple Choice

Circle the correct response for each question.

12. Numerous authors have identified the components of wellness. In general, they all agree that wellness is:
    a. the absence of disease or illness and is synonymous with health.
    b. the subjective perception of balance, harmony, and vitality.
    c. a process by which an individual can maximize personal potential and enhance quality of life.
    d. a goal that an individual should work toward but may not attain.

13. What are the external factors that affect health status and beliefs?
    a. geography, job status, pollution, race, and gender
    b. family and cultural beliefs, environmental conditions, and support network
    c. living conditions, occupation, and lifestyle
    d. race, gender, education, and family beliefs

14. Your client tells you that he believes diet, exercise, and medications have limited ability to control his high blood pressure and chest pain. He believes that he has been cursed and must suffer the consequences. This thinking is consistent with:
    a. adoption of a sick role.
    b. lack of compliance with medical therapy.
    c. an internal locus of control.
    d. an external locus of control.

15. Which of the following statements about population health initiatives is true?
    a. Community action research provides the foundation for action.
    b. The environmental supports are crucial for starting initiatives.
    c. Strategies for health promotion ought to have been empirically proven.
    d. Innovative ways have to be cost-effective before their implementation.

16. Which of the following statements best describes the concept of wellness?
    a. Wellness is a state of being that incorporates the relationship between the person and the environment.
    b. Wellness is a lifestyle designed by the individual to achieve the highest potential for well-being.
    c. Wellness is the integration of the physiological and role adaptation to the environmental demands.
    d. Wellness is the opposite of illness, and it is always subjective.

Completion

17. How do you define *health?* Evaluate your health status on the basis of your own definition.

____

____

____

18. Complete the following table. Identify an example for each of the following determinants that influence health:

Determinant that influences Heath	Example
Income and Social Status	____________
Education	____________
Social Environment	____________
Physical Environment	____________
Personal Health Practices	____________
Social Support Network	____________

19. Illness is defined as (a) ____________________, whereas disease is (b) ____________________.
Major advances in health care have resulted from the determination of the etiology or (c) ____________________ of some diseases.

20. Identify four measures that the nurse can use to assist clients to make lifestyle changes following an illness.

____

____

____

____

____

____

____

____

Case Study

21. Fanny Yan, a 42-year-old physical education teacher, was to be discharged from the hospital after a mitral valve repair. In preparation for discharge, she participated in rehabilitation group sessions. This group work permitted the participants to work through some of their concerns. During one particular session, Fanny became tearful because she

felt that she would not be able to cope with the physical demands of her job and was fearful that she would be fired. In what ways can you and the group help Fanny?

____

____

____

____

____

22. According to the Health Belief Model, there are four factors that modify a person's perceptions. Demographic variables include age, gender, and race.
    a. _______________ variables include social pressure or influence from peers or other reference groups. Structural variables consist of ____________________.
    b. _______________ of the disease and prior contact with it.

23. Niki Mack is a 27-year-old paralegal who has been hospitalized for evaluation of pre-term labour. She is 27 weeks pregnant (normal term is 40 weeks) but having frequent contractions. Niki has one other child, Scott, aged 3. Her husband travels frequently on his job. Evaluate the effect this hospitalization will have on Niki and her family.

____

____

____

____

____

CHAPTER 10

Health Promotion

This chapter discusses goals, models, strategies, and your role in health promotion of individuals, families, and communities. Several health promotion assessment tools and programs are discussed.

KEY TOPICS

This study guide chapter reinforces the following topics discussed in the textbook chapter:

- health promotion and health promotion programs
- the nurse's role in health promotion

Matching

Match the following terms with the appropriate description:

a. health promotion
b. health hazard appraisal
c. primary prevention
d. secondary prevention
e. tertiary prevention

___ 1. focuses on health promotion and protection against specific health problems
___ 2. directed toward increasing the level of well-being for individuals and communities
___ 3. focuses on restoration and rehabilitation to an optimal level of functioning
___ 4. focuses on early identification and prompt intervention to alleviate health problems
___ 5. directed toward assessing an individual's risk for injury or disease

Multiple Choice

Circle the correct response for each question.

6. A 32-year-old female client has a family history of heart disease. To decrease her risk of developing heart disease, she regularly participates in a program of aerobic activity, including mountain biking, race walking, and light weight lifting. For this client, aerobic exercise is:
   a. health protection and secondary prevention.
   b. health promotion.
   c. primary prevention.
   d. primary promotion and secondary prevention.

7. Pender's health promotion model is based on the belief that:
   a. if an individual is educated about healthy behaviours, he will modify behaviour to reach a more healthful state.
   b. age, gender, culture, and previous interactions with health-care providers are the key determinants to success with health promotion.
   c. a person's beliefs about health and illness are the key determinants of success with a health promotion program.
   d. primary motivational mechanisms in conjunction with modifying factors and internal/external cues determine the likelihood of engaging in health promotion.

8. Your client has hypertension. The physician has prescribed a low-sodium diet. The client discusses the new diet with you and takes a pamphlet home to share with his wife. What stage of health behaviour change is this client in?
   a. precontemplation stage
   b. contemplation stage
   c. preparation stage
   d. action stage
   e. maintenance stage

9. The primary role the nurse assumes in health promotion is as a:
   a. leader.
   b. manager.
   c. collaborator.
   d. follower.

10. Which of the following is a cue of internal origin?
   a. increased feeling of well-being
   b. easy access to resources
   c. conversations with others about health issues
   d. family's perspectives on aging

True or False

Read the following statements to determine if they are true or false. If a statement is false, alter the statement to make it true.

11. For a behaviour change plan to be constructive, it needs to be based on client ownership of the behaviour to be changed.
    True False
    ____
    ____
    ____

12. After the collection of data about health beliefs, practices, and life events, the nurse reviews and summarizes the information to formulate a plan.
True False

____

____

____

13. Empowerment is the process that describes the way to transform internal feelings of powerlessness, and group actions are initiated to change physical and social living conditions that create inequalities of power.
True False

____

____

____

Completion

14. Provide at least one example of each of the following types of health promotion programs in your community.
    a. information dissemination program

    ____

    b. health appraisal and wellness assessment program

    ____

    c. lifestyle and behaviour change program

    ____

    d. environmental control program

    ____

15. Evaluate your own risk for health problems using the Health-Style: A Self-Test seen in Figure 10.3 of the text.
    a. Describe the results of your assessment.

    ____

    ____

    ____

    ____

    b. On the basis of your self-evaluation, determine how you might improve your health. Follow the nursing process as outlined in the text, and identify at least one health promotion activity to improve your health status.

    ____

    ____

    ____

    ____

c. Identify at least one support service to help you achieve your goal.

Case Study

16. Jack Cooke is 62 years old and physically very fit. He reports to your clinic for a yearly checkup. Jack states that on average, he runs 35 miles per week and does a light weight-training workout three times per week. His vital signs are: BP 98/56, P 52, RR 12, T 36.8C. He is currently taking no medications, does not smoke, and has a low serum cholesterol level. Jack states that he occasionally has a glass of wine with dinner. He estimates that this occurs approximately one to two times per week.

    a. What is your assessment of Jack's health?

    b. Write a nursing diagnosis for Jack.

    c. Identify at least two ways that you can work with Jack to enhance or promote his health.

CHAPTER 11

Holistic Healing Modalities

This chapter introduces you to the important trends of holistic health care and alternative or complementary medical therapies. It offers a concise overview of many holistic healing modalities that will assist you in your care of clients and yourself.

KEY TOPICS

This study guide chapter reinforces the following topics discussed in the textbook chapter:

- alternative medical therapies
- bodymind healing
- holistic nursing care
- role of the nurse as healer

Matching

Match each term with the appropriate description.

a. acupressure
b. acupuncture
c. aromatherapy
d. biofeedback
e. chiropractic
f. herbal medicine
g. homeopathy
h. hypnosis
i. imagery
j. massage
k. music therapy
l. prayer
m. reflexology
n. therapeutic touch
o. yoga

___ 1. a treatment based on foot massage to relieve symptoms in other parts of the body

___ 2. a method to relax muscles and release buildup of lactic acid

___ 3. an altered state of consciousness in which an individual's concentration is focused and distraction is minimized

___ 4. manipulation of the spinal column to produce positive effects on the body

___ 5. the use of plants for medicinal properties

___ 6. a technique that brings under conscious control bodily processes normally thought to be beyond voluntary control

___ 7. a whole person assessment in which the practitioner looks at every aspect of physical and emotional life

___ 8. an approach to balanced life based on ancient Hindu teachings

___ 9. communication with God, a saint, or some other being

___ 10. the internal experience of memories, dreams, fantasies, and visions

___ 11. a process by which energy is transmitted or transferred from one person to another with the intent of potentiating the healing process

___ 12. can be used to alter ordinary levels of consciousness to achieve the fullest potential through use of listening, rhythm, body movement, and singing

___ 13. the insertion of needles into body meridians to balance energy

___ 14. the use of scents to improve mood and promote good health

___ 15. a form of healing in which the therapist exerts finger pressure on specific sites

Multiple Choice

Circle the correct response for each question.

16. Many alternative therapies are based on the concept of holism. Which one of the following statements represents a holistic health belief view on the origin of illness?
    a. Illness results when people are not in touch with their wholeness.
    b. Illness results when there is an imbalance in the forces of nature.
    c. Illness results when inadequate health promotion has been accessed.
    d. Illness results when the person is not treated as a whole.

17. Mainstream medicine is now broadening its view of holistic or nontraditional health-care practices. According to the Office on Alternative Medicine, what era are we currently in?
    a. Era of Awakening – the beginning of understanding about nontraditional care
    b. Era I – the era of the physical
    c. Era II – the era of mind-body medicine
    d. Era Ill – the era of nonlocal or transpersonal medicine

18. *Bodymind* refers to a state of integration that includes body, mind, and spirit. According to this belief system, where is the mind located?
    a. in the brain
    b. in the heart
    c. in the bloodstream
    d. throughout the body

19. Which of the following beliefs underlie holistic practice?
    a. Health encompasses the biopsychosocial aspects of the individual.
    b. The holistic practitioner is the expert in healing the client.
    c. There are two domains of the person that are affected by stress: the body and the mind.
    d. Health involves a transformational change that encompasses the whole person.

20. Which of the following best describes mindfulness meditation?
    a. The person visualizes and focuses on an object.
    b. The individual attempts to remain open to all stimuli.
    c. The person restrains activities of the body as well as the mind.
    d. The individual focuses on a meaningful word or phrase.

True or False

Read the following statements to determine if they are true or false. If a statement is false, alter the statement to make it true.

21. Reduced electromyogram (EMG) activity reflects muscle relaxation.
    True False

    ____

    ____

    ____

22. Novel information, that is, ideas or events that are challenging and intriguing, evokes changes in the body and mind.
    True False

    ____

    ____

    ____

23. Use of humour helps the nurse establish rapport with clients.
    True False

    ____

    ____

    ____

Completion

24. What are two responsibilities that the nurse has as a healer?

    ____

    ____

25. Review the holistic health modalities in the chapter. Identify any modalities with which you have personal experience. What is your opinion of the usefulness of these modalities?

    ____

    ____

    ____

    ____

26. Review the self-healing methods for nurses described in the text. Identify the areas in which you must continue to improve.

Case Study

27. Your manager asks the staff to consider using humour and laughter as part of the nursing care for surgical clients. Identify your feelings about the use of humour in different situations.

CHAPTER 12

Sexuality and Sexual Health Practices

This chapter examines your nursing role in caring for clients with sexual health needs. The focus is on the identification of sexual health issues and health promotion in order to support sexual health practices.

KEY TOPICS

This study guide chapter reinforces the following topics discussed in the textbook chapter:

- sexuality
- sexual attitudes and behaviour
- sexual function
- sexual health practices
- contraception
- breast self-examination
- testicular self-examination

Matching

Match the following terms with their definitions:

a. biological sex
b. gender
c. sexual desire
d. sexual health
e. sexuality

___ 1. a capacity to enjoy and control sexual and reproductive behaviour based on personal and social ethics

___ 2. genetically determined anatomy and physiology

___ 3. an integral characteristic of every human being; all those aspects that relate specifically to being a sexual being

___ 4. a period that precedes sexual response, also known as libido

___ 5. ways in which a person lives life that reflects masculinity or femininity

Match the following contraceptive methods with their descriptions:

a.	chemical barriers	d.	hormonal contraceptives
b.	coitus interruptus	e.	mechanical barriers
c.	fertility awareness	f.	surgical contraceptive methods

___ 6. the insertion of foams, jellies, creams, or suppositories into the vagina prior to intercourse

___ 7. abstinence on days when conception could occur

___ 8. withdrawal of the penis from the vagina prior to ejaculation

___ 9. tubal ligation for women and vasectomy for men

___ 10. a form of chemical contraception that blocks ovulation

___ 11. use of a condom, diaphragm, sponge or cervical cap

Multiple Choice

Circle the correct response for each question.

12. Research on sexual health indicates that certain methods of handling sexual concerns are preferable. Which of the following statements about sexual concerns is true?
    a. The health-care professional should wait for the client to introduce the topic.
    b. Only health-care professionals who are comfortable with sexual topics should engage in their discussion.
    c. Clients prefer health-care professionals to initiate discussions about sexual concerns.
    d. Only specialists in sexuality should assess and assist clients with sexual concerns.

13. Which of the following statements about erectile dysfunction is true?
    a. Psychological factors associated with erectile dysfunction gradually accumulate causing the person to take drugs.
    b. It is manifested by the inability to have an erection that is satisfactory to oneself and to the partner.
    c. It is attributed to both partners' inability to sexually arouse one another.
    d. This type of male dysfunction develops because of the chronic need for rapid orgasm.

14. Which one of the following outcomes denotes that the goal related to sexual health was met?
    a. participates in screening for sexually transmitted infections
    b. describes the effectiveness of alcohol as a sexual stimulant
    c. refuses to use a condom because relationships are fleeting
    d. relates knowledge of sexual autonomy in a superficial manner

15. Sexual issues are of major importance to adolescents. You are designing a teaching project for a group of high-school students. Key topics that should be addressed are:
    a. sexual identity, orientation, and abilities.
    b. sex, sexual actions and consequences, decision making, and STIs.
    c. sexual response and birth control.
    d. treatment of sexually transmitted diseases.

16. Which of the following is a myth about sexuality in older adults?
    a. Interest in sexual activity is not lost among the elderly.
    b. Phases of the sexual response cycle may take longer to occur in older adults.
    c. Women experience a decline in sexual function with menopause, but men do not experience sexual changes as they age.
    d. Lack of privacy and widowhood affect sexual activity among elders.

17. Numerous factors may influence a person's sexuality. These factors include:
    a. developmental level.
    b. onset of menarche.
    c. race.
    d. access to birth control.

18. Sexually transmitted infections (STIs) may affect sexuality and comfort. Which of the following statements about STIs is accurate?
    a. STIs always produce readily detectable signs and symptoms.
    b. Candidiasis only produces clinical symptoms in women.
    c. Clinical symptoms of AIDS appear within 6 to 12 months after exposure.
    d. Men and women may have an STI but be asymptomatic.

19. Which of the following statements accurately portrays an aspect of sexuality?
    a. Gay men do not need to use condoms for anal intercourse since pregnancy is not possible.
    b. Aging results in a decrease in sexual interest in men and women.
    c. Antihypertensive medications may affect sexual desire in both men and women and erectile and ejaculatory functions in men.
    d. Interest in masturbation and sex play declines after adolescence.

20. The sexual response cycle is a four-phase response. The correct order of the cycle is:
    a. plateau phase, excitement phase, orgasmic phase, resolution phase.
    b. excitement phase, vasocongestion phase, myotonia phase, resolution phase.
    c. arousal phase, excitement phase, orgasmic phase, vasodilation phase.
    d. excitement phase, plateau phase, orgasmic phase, resolution phase.

21. Which of the following statements about sexual dysfunction is true?
    a. It is always related to psychological problems.
    b. It occurs only in men and manifests as impotence.
    c. It may be related to physiologic or psychologic factors.
    d. It may be primary in nature (acute) or secondary (chronic).

22. Assessment is an integral part of the nurse's role; however, due to the sensitive nature of sexual health information, its assessment differs from other assessment areas in that:
    a. the nurse's professional preparation and comfort strongly influence his/her ability to assess sexual health concerns, whereas all nurses are expected to perform assessments for physical health concerns.
    b. sexual data must be kept confidential but not other information.
    c. a thorough sexual history and assessment are required for all clients who are sexually active, but other physical health problems may only require a focused assessment.
    d. sexual health should only be assessed if the current complaint is of a sexual nature, and physical health should be addressed with each health-related visit.

True or False

Read the following statements to determine if they are true or false. If a statement is false, alter the statement to make it true.

23. Clients with heart disease, diabetes mellitus, joint disease, and chronic pain have physiological reasons to avoid sex.
    True False

    ____

    ____

24. Breast self-examination for women and testicular self-examination for men should be conducted quarterly.
    True False

    ____

25. Sexual stimulation may occur through physical stimulation, such as masturbation or oral-genital stimulation, and/or through psychological stimulation, such as reading erotic novels.
    True False

    ____

    ____

    ____

Completion

26. Identify the five nursing skills required to help clients in the area of sexuality.

____

____

____

____

____

27. Nurses must help identify clients at risk for altered sexual patterns. Once the problem has been identified and diagnosed, the overall goals are:

____

____

____

28. The PLISSIT model of intervention is often used to help clients with sexual problems. Identify the four progressive levels of this model, and give an example of each type of intervention.

Levels	***Example of Intervention***
P	_______________
	_______________
LI	_______________
	_______________
SS	_______________
	_______________
IT	_______________
	_______________

Case Study

29. Michael Leonard is a 26-year-old man admitted to the hospital after being struck by a truck while riding his bicycle. Michael is being evaluated for a neurological deficit. He has impaired motor and sensory function below the level of the umbilicus. While you are caring for Michael, he makes sexual advances toward you.

    a. How would you handle this situation?

    b. Why might this behaviour be occurring?

CHAPTER 13

Spirituality

This chapter distinguishes between spirituality and religion. You are introduced to the beliefs of selected religions. The chapter emphasizes your role in assessing, diagnosing, and intervening for clients with spiritual distress.

KEY TOPICS

This study guide chapter reinforces the following topics discussed in the textbook chapter:

- spirituality
- faith
- religion
- spiritual needs
- assisting with spiritual needs
- nursing interventions to support spiritual beliefs and religious practices

Matching

Match the following terms with the appropriate definition:

a.	agnostic	e.	meditation
b.	atheist	f.	religion
c.	faith	g.	spirituality
d.	hope	h.	spiritual distress

___ 1. a person who doubts the existence of God or a higher power

___ 2. the act of focusing one's thought in self-reflection

___ 3. the belief that things will get better

___ 4. an organized system of worship that contains central beliefs, rituals, practices, and rules of conduct

___ 5. a belief in, or relationship with, a higher power or creative force

___ 6. a person who denies the existence of God

___ 7. a disturbance in the belief or value system that provides strength, hope, and meaning to life

___ 8. the unquestioning acceptance of a belief that cannot be demonstrated or proved

Multiple Choice

Circle the correct response for each question.

9. Which of the following characteristics applies to preschoolers?
   a. They expect that their prayers will be answered and that their bad behaviour will be punished.
   b. They imitate their parents' rituals, such as bedtime prayers.
   c. They believe that their parents are omnipotent.
   d. They have no spiritual beliefs or sense of right or wrong.

10. All religions share some common spiritual needs, yet spirituality and religion are distinct entities. Which aspects of spirituality extend beyond the common needs of religion?
    a. Spirituality also deals with the unknown or uncertainties in life and the awareness and ability to draw upon inner resources and strength.
    b. Spirituality also deals with the feeling of connectedness with oneself and with God or a higher being and finding meaning and purpose in life.
    c. Spirituality also deals with having belief in more than one God and being able to worship individually.
    d. Spirituality also deals with faith, hope, and meditation.

11. Spiritual beliefs and practices may be quite pervasive. They:
    a. influence lifestyle, attitudes, and feelings about illness and death.
    b. assume the greatest importance at times of death.
    c. should never come in conflict with accepted medical practices.
    d. dictate how a person responds to illness.

12. Meeting the spiritual needs of clients and their support persons is part of the function of nurses. This may be accomplished by:
    a. acknowledging and appreciating the spiritual aspect of the client's life.
    b. giving client health status information to the representatives of the client's religion.
    c. determining how well the client has lived in order to determine the threat of afterlife.
    d. praying for the client.

13. Which of the following statements about older adults and spirituality is most accurate?
    a. Older adults who have developed religious values often endeavour to broaden them and attempt to appreciate the younger generations' values.
    b. Older adults may experience a feeling of deprivation when they retire if they do not have a well-developed faith.
    c. Older adults are generally unable to change spiritual perspectives because they have difficulty with their cognition.
    d. Older adults have positive attitudes toward losses only if they have experienced multiple losses.

True or False

Read the following statements to determine if they are true or false. If a statement is false, alter the statement to make it true.

14. The expressions of a person's spiritual energy can be manifested by acts of compassion, empathy, forgiveness, and hope.
    True False

    ____
    ____
    ____

15. Parish nurses work independently and need to have nursing, health, and theological expertise.
    True False

    ____
    ____
    ____

16. A holy day is any holiday that is dedicated to religious beliefs.
    True False

    ____
    ____
    ____

Completion

17. Identify at least three ways in which the nurse can assess a client's spiritual health and beliefs.

    ____
    ____
    ____

18. Jennifer Parcel has just been told she has breast cancer. She is quite distraught. She asks you, "How long until I die?" Identify at least three actions you could take to alleviate Jennifer's spiritual distress.

    ____
    ____
    ____

Case Study

19. Joseph Stallings is 35 years old and has AIDS. His condition is rapidly deteriorating. Joseph has been living at home with his partner during his illness. He now expresses fear and anger about his condition and states that he does not believe he will live much longer.

    a. As a nurse working for a home health agency describe your process for assessing Joseph's spiritual health and practices.

    ____

    ____

    b. Identify four nursing interventions that might help meet Joseph's spiritual needs, and give examples of each.

    ____

    ____

    ____

    ____

    c. Joseph asks you to pray with him. How would you handle this situation if you are uncomfortable with the request?

    ____

    ____

CHAPTER 14

Culture and Ethnicity

This chapter discusses the role of culture in health-care beliefs and the use of health services. You learn how to perform a cultural assessment and plan culturally competent care. Important tips on communicating with clients from other cultures are offered.

KEY TOPICS

This study guide chapter reinforces the following topics discussed in the textbook chapter:

- culture
- characteristics of culture
- magico-religious, biomedical, and holistic views of health
- culture of the health-care system
- culturally competent care

Matching

Match the term with the appropriate definition.

a. cultural awareness
b. cultural competence
c. culture shock
d. culture
e. diversity
f. ethnic group
g. ethnic identity
h. race

___ 1. a subjective perspective of a person's heritage

___ 2. the state of being disoriented or unable to respond to a different cultural environment because of its sudden strangeness, unfamiliarity, and incompatibility with perceptions and expectations

___ 3. the act of knowing, utilizing, and appreciating another culture while assisting with the resolution of a problem

___ 4. individuals who share a common social and cultural heritage that is passed on to successive generations

___ 5. the learned, shared, and transmitted values, beliefs, norms, and lifeway practices of a particular group that guide thinking, decisions, and actions

___ 6. the state of being different

___ 7. the classification of people according to shared biological characteristics, genetic markers, or features

___ 8. the conscious and informed recognition of the differences and similarities among different cultural or ethnic groups

Multiple Choice

Circle the correct response for each question.

9. Nurses must be aware of how individuals and cultures view the use of space. Which one of the following statements about space is true?
   a. Nurses move through all three zones of space: personal, social, and public.
   b. All North Americans use more personal space than members of other cultures.
   c. The nurse should always explain the procedure and await permission before entering the client's public space.
   d. A hospitalized client gives up the right to declare personal space.

10. The magico-religious health belief view is associated with the belief that:
   a. life and life processes can be manipulated by humans.
   b. illness may result from an evil spirit or from being bad or opposing God.
   c. forces of nature must be kept in harmony.
   d. illness is caused by germs, viruses, bacteria, or the breakdown of the body.

11. The scientific or biomedical health belief view is associated with the belief that illness:
   a. is caused by germs, viruses, bacteria, or the breakdown of the body.
   b. may result from an evil spirit, being bad, or opposing God.
   c. results when harmony or natural balance is disturbed.
   d. in developing nations can be curtailed by adoption of Western health practices.

12. Which of the following statements about culture is *not* correct?
   a. Culture is learned from family, groups, and communities. It originates and develops through interactions.
   b. Minority subcultures have difficulty assimilating into the mainstream culture.
   c. Culture is not synonymous with ethnic beliefs and values.
   d. Culture is embedded in food, language, art, music, philosophy, family patterns and interactions, and holiday traditions.

True or False

Read the following statements to determine if they are true or false. If a statement is false, alter the statement to make it true.

13. Information about the client's culture should be obtained with the general assessment of the client.
    True False

    ____

    ____

14. Cultural practices that significantly affect nursing care include family patterns, verbal and nonverbal communication style, space orientation, time orientation, nutritional patterns, pain responses, death and dying practices, and childbirth and perinatal care.
True False

15. Ito Nakashuri is a 20-year-old Japanese student attending college in Canada. Ito has embraced the Canadian lifestyle and shuns his native food, clothing, and behaviour in favour of this new lifestyle. This is an example of *biculturalism*.
True False

16. Amy Gonzales believes that all people who live in Canada should speak and write English only. She does not support allowing people to speak their native tongue. She frequently says that if you want to live in this country, you should become part of this country or go home. This is an example of *ethnocentrism*.
True False

17. *Racism* occurs when there is differential treatment of an individual or group based on race. *Discrimination* is a hostile feeling toward an individual who is a member of a group that is perceived to have objectionable qualities.
True False

18. *Transcultural nursing* is the study of different cultures and subcultures with respect to nursing and health-illness caring practices, beliefs, and values.
True False

19. When caring for a client who speaks a different language, it is best to utilize a family member or support person for translation services.
True False

20. To provide safe and effective care, all nurses should familiarize themselves with as many cultural behaviour patterns as possible.
True False

21. The value and privileges of family, children, elders, and authority are culturally derived.
True False

Completion

22. What are the six characteristics of culture?

23. Identify your orientation to time. Are you oriented toward the past, present, or future?

24. Identify a classmate, neighbour, friend, family member, or acquaintance from a different culture. Utilize the sample questions and discussion areas presented in the chapter to conduct a cultural assessment. Now imagine that this person is a client undergoing surgery in your facility. How would this knowledge affect your nursing care?

25. Evaluate your knowledge of cultural sensitivity (see the chapter discussion entitled "Conveying Cultural Sensitivity"). Evaluate your current cultural sensitivity. Which suggestions do you currently follow? Which items will require behaviour changes on your part?

Case Study

26. You are working with the nurse manager of an Emergency Department. He asks you about your experiences with different cultures and how you have reconciled your beliefs with individuals from these cultures. You have a basic understanding of the three views of health beliefs. Explain these views by giving specific examples.

CHAPTER 15

Health-Care Delivery Systems

This chapter provides you with an orientation to the health-care system. It explains the roles and responsibilities of other health-care professionals and gives an overview of various levels of care.

KEY TOPICS

This study guide chapter reinforces the following topics discussed in the textbook chapter:

- health-care facilities
- health-care professionals
- Consumer Rights to Health Care
- forces affecting health-care delivery
- models of nursing practice
- models of care delivery

Matching

Match the provider to the description of the provider's role.

a. alternative provider	i. pharmacist
b. case manager	j. physician (MD)
c. chaplain	k. nutritionist
d. dentist	l. registered nurse (RN)
e. dietitian	m. respiratory technologist (RT)
f. licensed practical nurse (LPN)	n. social worker
g. occupational therapist (OT)	o. unlicensed assistive personnel
h. paramedical technologist	p. physical therapist (PT)

___ 1. assists clients with impaired function to gain skills to perform activities of daily living

___ 2. recommends and advises about balanced diets for growing children and pregnant women and assists restaurants to develop heart-healthy menus

___ 3. assesses client status, identifies health problems, develops and coordinates care

___ 4. used by clients in conjunction with, or in lieu of, traditional health providers; includes chiropractor, herbalist, and acupuncturist

___ 5. treats the client's body by means of heat, water, exercise, massage, and electric current

___ 6. may be any member of the health-care team; responsible for ensuring fiscally sound, appropriate care in the best setting

27. Home care services are appropriate only for individuals who need custodial care.
True False

28. Crisis centres help people cope with an immediate crisis and then provide guidance and support for long-term therapy.
True False

Completion

29. Health-care services can be grouped by the type of service they provide. Give two examples of each type of service.
    a. Health promotion and illness prevention
    b. Diagnosis and treatment
    c. Rehabilitation and health restoration

30. Identify the model(s) of nursing in place at the health facilities used for your clinical rotations.

Case Study

Gertrude is a community health nurse working with the homeless individuals in the metro area. When caring for these individuals, Gertrude needs to be aware of the factors that contribute to their health problems.

31. What contributory factors for the health issues of these individuals should Gertrude be aware of?

CHAPTER 16

Community-Based Nursing

This chapter introduces you to the ideas, policies, and forces that are moving health care into the community. A variety of recommendations and competencies that facilitate community-based nursing care are discussed.

KEY TOPICS

This study guide chapter reinforces the following topics discussed in the textbook chapter:

- health-care reform
- Nursing's Agenda for Health Care Reform
- community-based health care
- community-based settings
- community-based nursing
- collaborative health care
- continuity of care

Matching

Match the following terms with the appropriate description below:

a. case management
b. community-based health care
c. community-based nursing
d. community initiatives
e. continuity of care
f. discharge planning
g. integrated health-care systems

___ 1. the process of preparing a client to leave one level of care for the next

___ 2. this process tracks clients through the health-care system to ensure care continuity

___ 3. a system of health care that directs care toward a specific group within the community

___ 4. the coordination of services for clients moving within the health-care system and among health professionals

___ 5. a program that provides seamless care by facilitating continuity of care, recovery, positive health outcomes, and lifestyle modification

___ 6. this involves a network of nursing services directed toward a population within the community

___ 7. this involves members of the community to establish health priorities, set measurable goals, and determine actions to reach these goals

Multiple Choice

Circle the correct response for each question.

8. Primary care and primary health care are two distinct aspects of health-care delivery. How do they differ?
   a. Primary care offers affordable health services in the community, whereas primary health care is institution based.
   b. Primary care is offered by physicians, whereas primary health care is practised by nurses and other health-care team members.
   c. Primary care focuses on personal health services, whereas primary health care focuses on population-based public health services.
   d. Primary care is practised in North America, whereas primary health care is a worldwide practice.

9. Essential elements of a community-based health-care system are:
   a. community nursing centres, wellness programs, parish nursing, and integrated health systems.
   b. physicians, professional health workers, and lay outreach workers.
   c. primary care, secondary care, and tertiary care.
   d. easy access, flexibility, continuity of care, and support for family caregivers.

10. Numerous organizations have made predictions for the future of health care. In general, they all predict:
    a. increased concentration of services in the community and increased emphasis on health, health promotion, and disease prevention.
    b. increased concentration of care in institutions with a simultaneous shift toward health promotion.
    c. decreased concentration of care in institutions and increased illness-oriented care.
    d. increased use of licensed health-care providers in institutions and unlicensed providers in the community.

11. Skills necessary for collaboration include:
    a. advanced education, clinical experience, public speaking training, and poise.
    b. excellent communication skills, mutual respect and trust among participants, and decision-making skills.
    c. excellent verbal communication skills and the ability to read nonverbal communication.
    d. increased accountability and decision-making skills.

CHAPTER 17

Home Care

This chapter introduces you to the important trend of delivering health care in the home. As a nursing student, you will find the discussion of the home visit and safety and infection control in the home setting very helpful for planning care.

KEY TOPICS

This study guide chapter reinforces the following topics discussed in the textbook chapter:

- home health-care system
- home visits
- caregiver role strain
- roles of the home health nurse
- safety and infection control in the home

Matching

Match the term with the appropriate description.

a. caregiver role strain
b. homebound
c. hospice nursing
d. Life Line program

___ 1. an individual who is confined to the home, requires use of supportive devices, and has intermittent nursing care needs

___ 2. evidenced by decreasing ability to perform routine tasks for the client; decline in energy; feelings of anger, depression, and conflict with other roles

___ 3. a subspecialty of home health nursing that involves delivering care to terminally ill clients

___ 4. places all of the client's vital medical information in one place that is available to emergency personnel

Multiple Choice

Circle the correct response for each question.

5. How do home health nursing and community nursing differ?
   a. Home health nursing focuses on health restoration and hospice care, whereas community nursing focuses on disease prevention.
   b. Home health nursing occurs after discharge from the hospital, whereas community nursing may occur at anytime across the health–illness continuum.

c. Home health nursing focuses on the individual and family, whereas community nursing focuses on the aggregate or community.

d. Home health nursing is an extension of hospital-based nursing, whereas community nursing is an extension of public health.

6. Although there are numerous advantages to home health care, there are also disadvantages. What is the chief disadvantage to home health care?

a. increased caregiver burden

b. lack of controlled environment

c. lack of guaranteed entry into the home

d. inadequate living conditions

7. Home care agencies provide a number of services to meet the needs of clients in the home. The scope of services offered includes:

a. RN, LPN, or PT services.

b. housekeeping, chore worker, and food services.

c. physician care in the home.

d. professional and paraprofessional staff, medical equipment, and pharmaceuticals.

8. Which of the following clients would be eligible for home services reimbursed by the provincial or territorial insurance plan?

a. 22-year-old married female with a healthy newborn infant

b. 44-year-old new-onset quadriplegic with a family who desires to learn about his care

c. 66-year-old female with diabetes who has a foot ulcer but is able to drive herself to doctor appointments

d. 88-year-old client with ongoing round-the-clock nursing needs

9. Which one of the following direct care activities is not appropriate for the home health nurse to delegate to a family member or an unlicensed assistive personnel?

a. bathing

b. feedings

c. ostomy care

d. changing linens

True or False

Read the following statements to determine if they are true or false. If a statement is false, alter the statement to make it true.

10. Documentation of care is not necessary in home health nursing.

True False

____

____

____

11. Several trends influencing home care are the increased number of older adults, earlier hospital discharges, and improved technology.
True False

____

____

____

12. Evidence shows that in Canada, home care services are cost effective.
True False

____

____

____

Completion

13. Identify at least three advantages to delivering care in the home.

____

____

____

14. Identify the major nursing roles the home health nurse may practise.

____

____

____

Case Study

15. Diane Hanford is a 30-year-old client recently referred to your home health agency. She has a two-year-old at home and triplets who were born 10 weeks premature. Due to their health-care needs, the triplets remained in the nursery for one month. They are scheduled for discharge from the hospital tomorrow. Her physician has ordered home care follow-up of the infants.

    a. Describe your process for initiating home care.

    ____

    ____

    ____

    b. Describe your main tasks while in Diane's home.

    ____

    ____

    ____

c. Diane lives in a neighbourhood in which you feel unsafe. Identify several ways in which you may protect yourself on this visit.

____

____

____

d. Once in the home, you realize that Diane is overwhelmed by the addition of the triplets and is simultaneously caring for an immunocompromised parent receiving chemotherapy and radiation. Identify your role in infection control and in providing support for Diane.

____

____

____

CHAPTER 18

Rural Health Care

This chapter introduces rural health-care delivery. It focuses on the scope of practice in rural and remote areas.

KEY TOPICS

This study guide chapter reinforces the following topics discussed in the textbook chapter:

- health of rural residents
- special concerns in First Nations communities
- health-care delivery issues
- nursing practice issues

Matching

Match the following terms with the appropriate descriptions:

a. brucellosis
b. socioacusis
c. farm stress

___ 1. various socioeconomic factors in the agricultural industry that cause physical or emotional responses in those who are involved with farming or ranching.

___ 2. hearing loss that results from recreational activities

___ 3. disease communicated from animals, such as cattle and goats, to humans

Multiple Choice

Circle the correct response for each question.

4. According to Statistics Canada, which of the following phrases does not apply to the term "rural"?
   a. communities of less than 1000 persons
   b. a region with a population density of less than 400 persons per square kilometre
   c. communities outside metropolitan areas
   d. farming communities outside of the cities

5. Why is water safety a health concern in rural areas?
   a. Bodies of water, such as lakes, rivers, and irrigation ditches, are common sites of drowning.
   b. Drought is a common occurrence, so the wells for drinking water become substandard.

c. The water in rural areas is exposed to paint fumes, grain dust, and engine exhausts.

d. Water skiing accidents are the most common type of accident among adults.

6. Which of the following conditions affects the mortality rate in the northern and rural regions?

   a. limited emergency personnel and greater distances to medical services
   b. ignorance of the residents and apathetic attitude of the government
   c. lack of safety programs and low interest and participation in these programs
   d. few culture-specific programs related to safety and substance abuse

7. One of the possible reasons that rural residents may not seek help for mental health difficulties is:

   a. attitude of procrastination.
   b. lack of anonymity in rural communities.
   c. perception of treatment failures.
   d. lack of qualified personnel.

8. Which of the following statements about cancer in rural areas is true?

   a. There is epidemiological evidence that cancer is less prevalent among rural residents.
   b. There is no proof that cancer occurs more frequently in rural residents.
   c. Among farmers, the most common types of cancer are Hodgkin's disease, skin cancers, multiple myeloma, and stomach cancer.
   d. There is controversy about the impact of different chemicals in the development of cancer.

True or False

Read the following statements to determine if they are true or false. If a statement is false, alter the statement to make it true.

9. The elderly comprise a much smaller percentage of the population in rural areas than in urban settings.

   True False

   ____

   ____

   ____

10. The poverty rate is higher and the annual salary that determines the poverty level is set lower for rural residents.

   True False

   ____

   ____

   ____

11. Distance and lack of resources affect the emergency care for persons injured in farming or rural areas.
True False

____

____

____

Completion

12. Factors that are believed to contribute to a high incidence of suicide in rural areas are: ____________, ____________, ____________ and ____________.

13. Name four characteristics of rural nursing practice.

____

____

____

____

Case Study

14. As the nurse in a rural community health centre, you are responsible for providing health education in schools and at community meetings that are attended by most of the population (including children and adolescents). The community council has asked you to present a talk on hearing loss next month. Propose your agenda for the community forum.

____

____

____

____

CHAPTER 19

Concepts of Growth and Development

This chapter presents the major concepts of growth and development and their application to nursing. You will read about the ideas and beliefs of the top theorists who have helped shape modern-day tenets of growth and development.

KEY TOPICS

This study guide chapter reinforces the following topics discussed in the textbook chapter:

- growth
- development
- theories of growth and development

Matching

Match the following growth and development terms with their descriptions:

a. cephalocaudal
b. development
c. developmental task
d. differentiated development
e. growth
f. personality

___ 1. An example of this phenomenon is the total body response of an infant to a toy placed within reaching distance as opposed to the grabbing motion of a three-year-old to a similar stimulus.

___ 2. This process is a physical change and increase in size that can be measured quantitatively.

___ 3. This is a task that arises at a period in life which must be achieved to ensure happiness and success at later tasks.

___ 4. This method of growth and development starts at the head and moves to the trunk, the legs, and the feet.

___ 5. This process results in an increase in the complexity of function and skill progression.

___ 6. This is the outward expression of the inner self.

Match the following growth and development theorists with their ideas:

a.	Erikson	f.	Havighurst
b.	Fowler	g.	Kohlberg
c.	Freud	h.	Peck
d.	Gilligan	i.	Piaget
e.	Gould	j.	Westerhoff

___ 7. This theorist adapted and expanded Freud's theory. He believes that development continues to occur throughout life, and he describes eight stages of development, each marked by a task that must be achieved.

___ 8. This theorist describes seven stages of adult development and believes that transformation is a central theme during adulthood.

___ 9. This theorist believes that learning is a lifelong process. As a person grows and develops, developmental tasks are accomplished, which foster further growth.

___ 10. This theorist believes that faith is a force that gives meaning to life. Faith is developed by the person interacting with the environment.

___ 11. This theorist focuses on the reason an individual makes a decision. Three levels of moral development are outlined. All individuals do not necessarily reach the third stage.

___ 12. This theorist believes that the personality develops in five overlapping stages from birth to adulthood. The libido's location of emphasis changes as the person progresses through the various stages of development.

___ 13. This theorist developed a theory of faith development. He describes faith as a way of behaving.

___ 14. This theorist believes that cognitive development and its associated new experiences must exist before intellectual abilities can develop. In each phase of development, the person uses assimilation, accommodation, and adaptation.

___ 15. This theorist focuses on the process of developing an ethic of caring. She believes that women and men see morality differently.

___ 16. This theorist believes that although physical capabilities and function may decline with age, mental and social capacities tend to expand in the latter part of life.

Multiple Choice

Circle the correct response for each question.

17. Freud's developmental theory focuses on psychosexual development. While maturing, a person passes through five stages of development. According to Freud, failure to satisfactorily resolve each stage results in:
    a. negative resolution of the critical life period.
    b. a lower level of moral development.
    c. fixation at the unresolved stage.
    d. a search for faith in adulthood.

18. Your client is a 12-year-old boy attending the seventh grade. He does not interact with peers in school and has missed 40 percent of his classes. According to Erikson, this behaviour is consistent with:
   a. entrance into the Identity versus Role Confusion stage of development.
   b. negative resolution of Industry versus Inferiority stage of development.
   c. negative resolution of Initiative versus Guilt stage of development.
   d. positive resolution of Intimacy versus Isolation stage of development.

19. Which theorist concentrated on the developmental tasks of old age?
   a. Erikson
   b. Gilligan
   c. Gould
   d. Peck

20. The mother of a 16-month-old boy tells you that her child has become inflexible. She says, "He used to be so easy to care for, but now he has a temper tantrum anytime I try to introduce something new." On the basis of Piaget's phases of cognitive development, the nurse realizes that:
   a. this behaviour is consistent with the child's age and stage of development.
   b. this behaviour is consistent with the egocentric behaviour of the preconceptual phase of development.
   c. the child is in the concrete operations phase of development.
   d. the child is in the anal phase of development.

21. The nurse is caring for a client with severe developmental delays. While planning care for this client, the nurse realizes that:
   a. developmental theories cannot be applied to a client who is severely delayed.
   b. developmental theories can be used to assess current level of function and to plan strategies to promote development.
   c. developmental theories can be used to explain how and why the client is severely delayed.
   d. several developmental theories should be applied to this client in order to identify the most appropriate plan to improve function.

True or False

Read the following statements to determine if they are true or false. If a statement is false, alter the statement to make it true.

22. Nurses need to assist an individual who is in the old old stage to maintain as much independence as possible.
   True False

   ____

   ____

   ____

23. Morality refers to the principles of right and wrong, while moral behaviour refers to doing what is right.
True False

24. According to Kohlberg, the reasoning of an adolescent is deductive and futuristic.
True False

Completion

25. What is the nurse's major role in relation to growth and development?

26. You are assigned to care for four clients in a pediatric unit. The ages of the clients are 6 months, 30 months, 5 years, and 12 years. Identify at least one key characteristic of each client and a related nursing implication.

27. Review the numerous growth and development theorists. Which theorist most accurately depicts your personal experience? Identify your current stage of growth and development in this theory.

Case Study

28. Using Gilligan's theory, describe the stage that applies to this client.
A 45-year-old woman's husband has died suddenly after a motor vehicle accident. In the Emergency Department, she starts to weep while you are escorting her to check up on their 12-year-old son, who is waiting in the lobby. She confides in you that she feels guilty about having sent her husband on an errand which resulted in his vehicle being rammed by a big trailer. Upon further exploration, you find that she is scared of telling her son how she feels, as "he might not understand" and she wants him to "feel loved and not feel alone." She asks you if you think she is "selfish for thinking of her son and herself instead of her dead husband."

CHAPTER 20

Development from Conception through Adolescence

This chapter discusses growth and development from conception through adolescence. It emphasizes health assessment, promotion, and teaching throughout these age groups.

KEY TOPICS

This study guide chapter reinforces the following topics discussed in the textbook chapter:

- physical development
- psychosocial development
- cognitive development
- moral development
- spiritual development
- assessment from birth to adolescence
- health promotion from birth to adolescence

Matching

Match each of the following age groups with the appropriate toy or play activity:

a. neonate
b. infant
c. toddler
d. preschooler
e. school-age child

___ 1. tricycle
___ 2. hanging mobile
___ 3. video games or team sports
___ 4. rattles, stuffed animals, plastic blocks
___ 5. simple board games and role-play toys

Match the terms associated with puberty and adolescence with their appropriate descriptions.

a. apocrine glands
b. eccrine glands
c. ejaculation
d. menarche
e. primary sexual characteristics
f. sebaceous glands
g. secondary sexual characteristics

___ 6. characteristics that differentiate male from female but do not directly relate to reproduction

___ 7. glands that produce sweat; found over most of the body

___ 8. glands that are most active on the face, neck, shoulder, back, chest, and genitals; involved in development of acne

___ 9. the onset of menstruation

___ 10. the testes, penis, vagina, and uterus

___ 11. glands that develop in the axillae, genital areas, external auditory canals, and around the umbilicus and areola of the breasts; release sweat in response to emotional stimuli

___ 12. expulsion of semen

Multiple Choice

Circle the correct response for each question.

13. Intrauterine life is divided into two phases: embryonic and fetal. What development occurs during the embryonic phase?
    a. development of the vernix caseosa
    b. maternal perception of fetal movement
    c. tissue differentiation into three layers
    d. development of fetal subcutaneous fat

14. Which of the following activities is important for health promotion in pregnant women during the intrauterine stage of development?
    a. increasing respiratory rate to meet fetal oxygen demands
    b. avoiding alcohol and addictive drugs
    c. watching caloric consumption to reduce unnecessary weight gain
    d. increasing fluid intake during the last trimester

15. Head circumference of an infant should be measured:
    a. at each visit until two years old.
    b. on a quarterly basis until school age.
    c. on an as-needed basis.
    d. at the annual physical exam.

16. According to Erikson, the central crisis for an infant is:
    a. autonomy versus shame and doubt.
    b. industry versus inferiority.
    c. initiative versus guilt.
    d. trust versus mistrust.

17. During which developmental phase does a child acquire the ability to recognize and distinguish sounds?
    a. embryonic phase
    b. fetal phase

c. neonatal phase
d. infancy

18. Numerous health problems in infants require intervention from health-care providers. One such problem is failure to thrive, which is a:
    a. form of colic characterized by abdominal pain and failure to gain weight.
    b. form of child abuse that results from severe shaking of an infant.
    c. syndrome that increases risk of sudden infant death syndrome among infants three to four months of age.
    d. condition characterized by developmental delays and minimal weight gain due to a disturbed parent–child relationship.

19. According to Erikson, the central crisis for the toddler is:
    a. autonomy versus shame and doubt.
    b. industry versus inferiority.
    c. initiative versus guilt.
    d. trust versus mistrust.

20. What physical development change occurs when a child is a toddler?
    a. minimal height increase
    b. improved visual acuity
    c. improved fine and gross motor development
    d. weight increase at a slower rate than during infancy

21. Physical change in a preschooler is characterized by:
    a. continued rapid physical growth and spiritual development.
    b. a slowing of physical growth and an expansion of social contacts.
    c. major changes in weight, height, and head circumference.
    d. a slow improvement in motor ability.

22. According to Erikson, the central crisis for the preschooler is:
    a. autonomy versus shame and doubt.
    b. industry versus inferiority.
    c. initiative versus guilt.
    d. trust versus mistrust.

23. Developmental changes associated with the school-age phase of development include:
    a. continued improvement of muscular skills and coordination.
    b. continued inability to reason by logic.
    c. rejection of religion, briefly for some, permanently for others.
    d. regression in self-care responsibilities.

24. The parents of a 10-year-old boy report that he is struggling in school, has few friends, and is often sullen. This behaviour is indicative of which psychosocial crisis?
   a. development of shame and doubt versus autonomy
   b. struggle between industry versus inferiority
   c. negotiation of the crisis between initiative versus guilt
   d. trust versus mistrust conflict

25. According to Erikson, the central crisis for the adolescent is:
   a. identity versus role confusion.
   b. industry versus inferiority.
   c. intimacy versus isolation.
   d. initiative versus guilt.

26. Some of the key tasks for an adolescent are:
   a. development of psychomotor skills and psychological growth.
   b. loss of fantasy world of school-age period.
   c. sexual identification and peer group development.
   d. personal identification and decisions about use of drugs.

True or False

Read the statements below to determine if they are true or false. If the statement is false, alter the statement to make it true.

27. An infant's basic task is development of voluntary control.
    True False

    ____

28. In infancy, the rate of increase in height is largely related to nutrition and birth size.
    True False

    ____

29. An infant develops depth perception prior to learning to creep and crawl.
    True False

    ____

30. Starting school is significant because it allows a child to play with other children.
    True False

    ____

31. The school-age child experiences substantial changes in weight, height, muscular skills, and coordination.
    True False

    ____

    ____

Completion

32. By 12 months of age, infants usually weigh (a) ______________ their birth weight. By two years of age, a child can be expected to weigh (b) ______________ their birth weight.

33. Moulding of the head occurs during vaginal deliveries because of the fontanelles and (a) ________________________________. The anterior fontanelle usually closes by (b) ____________________. However, the posterior fontanelle closes (c) ________________________________.

34. Identify at least six nursing activities to assess and promote the health of the infant.

____

____

____

____

____

____

35. Identify the four adaptive mechanisms that are learned in the preschool period.

____

____

____

____

36. Preschoolers do not have fully formed consciences, although they do develop some internal controls. For this group, how is moral behaviour learned?

____

____

37. How does health promotion for the preschooler differ from health promotion for the toddler?

____

____

____

38. Describe the nurse's role in promoting cognitive development in children.

____

____

____

39. Identify at least five health promotion areas for adolescents that may be addressed by nurses working with this age group.

____

____

____

Case Study

40. During your pediatric rotation you have the opportunity to work in a pediatric ambulatory care clinic. Children from birth through adolescence are treated in this clinic by a team of nurse practitioners, pediatricians, and registered nurses.

    a. Your first client, Marianna Roberts, is a 14-year-old who is seeking gynecological care. During your interview, Marianna expresses much concern about her sexuality. How can you help Marianna deal with her concerns?

    ____

    ____

    b. The next client is Martin Randall, a three-week-old infant. Martin's mother is concerned that he may have colic. She reports that he cries periodically throughout the day, but each evening, he has crying periods of two hours. How would you proceed?

    ____

    ____

    c. At mid-day, 18-month-old Sherrie Bacon is scheduled to be seen. Sherrie's biological mother has recently died of breast cancer. She has just been adopted by a loving family. They have scheduled Sherrie for a complete physical. The nurse practitioner has asked you to provide teaching on health promotion to the family. What advice would you offer to the new parents?

    ____

    ____

    d. In the afternoon, you work with two additional clients: four-year-old Scott Parker and nine-year-old Sarah Burch. Scott's mother is concerned about school readiness. Scott will be five in September and is scheduled to begin kindergarten. His mother reports that he is extremely shy, has had difficulty with preschool due to his fear of leaving his mother, and does not play with other children. She is concerned about his ability to function in school. Evaluate Scott's level of development.

    ____

    ____

    e. In contrast, Sarah's parents tell you that their daughter is very gregarious and always playing with friends. They ask if their daughter is showing signs of adolescence. What is your assessment?

    ____

    ____

CHAPTER 21

Development from Young through Older Adulthood

This chapter discusses the expected changes that occur in adulthood. It emphasizes the diversity within this age group and distinguishes the needs of young, middle, and older adult clients. It identifies common health concerns and hazards affecting adults and presents nursing interventions for promoting health in this group.

KEY TOPICS

This study guide chapter reinforces the following topics discussed in the textbook chapter:

- growth and development during adulthood
- health assessment guidelines
- common health concerns during adulthood

Matching

Match the following key terms with the appropriate definitions:

a.	frail elder	e.	post-formal operations
b.	maturity	f.	principled reasoning
c.	middle adult	g.	young adult
d.	older adult		

___ 1. refers to development of an understanding of the temporary or relative nature of knowledge

___ 2. an elderly individual with significant physiological and functional impairment

___ 3. a state characterized by full development

___ 4. this group consists of individuals 40 to 65 years of age

___ 5. the central task of this age group is intimacy versus isolation

___ 6. the central task of this group is ego integrity versus despair

___ 7. the central task of this age group is generativity versus stagnation

___ 8. this is a time when people are often considering career choices

___ 9. men and women in this age group experience decreasing hormonal production

___ 10. this process involves defining morality based on personal principles

___ 11. retirement, maintenance of independence, and numerous physical changes are challenges affecting this age group

Multiple Choice

Circle the correct response for each question.

12. Physical development is affected at each developmental stage. In young adulthood:
    a. physical development continues at a brisk pace.
    b. physical change is minimal; the emphasis is on psychosocial development.
    c. the musculoskeletal system continues to increase in coordination.
    d. physical functioning declines.

13. A common health problem that is seen most often in the young adult is:
    a. accidents.
    b. dementia.
    c. hypertension.
    d. sexually transmitted disease.

14. Appropriate health promotion activities for the young adult include:
    a. annual physical examinations.
    b. workplace safety measures.
    c. providing time to review previous interests.
    d. promoting awareness of impending midlife crisis.

15. Both men and women experience changes in hormonal production in the middle adult years. Which of the following statements about these changes is true?
    a. Men frequently experience irritability and a tendency to gain weight as they experience their climacteric.
    b. Menopause and andropause result in inability to reproduce.
    c. Men experience minimal decreases in androgens, whereas women experience significant drops in estrogen during midlife.
    d. Hormonal changes in midlife produce minimal physical changes in men and women.

16. Older adults experience major psychosocial adjustments. Which adjustment is not commonly seen in this age group?
    a. retirement
    b. economic concerns associated with increased health-care costs
    c. economic concerns related to career choice
    d. potential relocation due to declining abilities

17. Which of the following statements about elder abuse is true?
    a. Nurses must be familiar with provincial or territorial laws regarding reported or suspected elder abuse.
    b. To prevent elder abuse, the nurse should recommend that all elderly clients be placed in the care of trained staff at nursing homes.

c. To prevent elder abuse, all family caregivers should be screened for a history of psychological problems or convictions on prior abuse charges.

d. Legal guardianship should be established for all elderly clients being cared for at home.

True or False

Read the following statements to determine if they are true or false. If a statement is false, alter the statement to make it true.

18. Lifestyle, family history, and stressors of a developmental and/or situational nature affect development of health problems in the middle adult years.
True False

____

____

19. Older adults have diminished capacity to tolerate high and low environmental temperatures.
True False

____

____

20. Elderly persons are more susceptible to respiratory infections due to increased ciliary activity and decreased capacity to cough effectively.
True False

____

____

Completion

21. How do you define adulthood? What criteria do you use to determine this state?

____

____

____

22. Complete the table of normal sensory and perceptual changes associated with aging.

Sensory/Perceptual Function	*Changes Associated with Aging*
Vision	
Hearing	
Taste	
Smell	
Touch	

Case Study

Matilda Maigret is an active 70-year-old woman. On the insistence of her employer, she has just retired from work as a real estate agent. She is considering working independently as a real estate agent so that she can set her own schedule and will not be forced out of work. Matilda reports to the Community Health Centre for an annual physical. She is examined by Gerry Berman, Nurse Practitioner. Matilda tells Gerry that she is disappointed that she was forced to retire because she loved her job. She also tells Gerry, "I don't feel old. I'm active. I'm alert. I don't like being treated like a little old lady. What can I do to stay healthy and well as I age?"

23. How should the nurse practitioner respond to Matilda?

____

____

____

____

____

____

24. Examine your own feelings about older adults. How do you feel about Matilda and other older persons? Do you enjoy caring for them, or do you prefer not to care for the elderly?

____

____

____

____

____

____

25. Examine the resources in your community for elderly clients. Look at support services that help clients remain at home: nursing home care, adult day care, and community groups. Evaluate the adequacy of these services.

____

____

____

____

____

____

CHAPTER 22

Critical Thinking

This chapter introduces you to the important role of critical thinking, problem solving, and decision making in nursing practice. It defines and differentiates each of these areas. You are presented with an opportunity to evaluate your own strengths and limitations as a critical thinker.

KEY TOPICS

This study guide chapter reinforces the following topics discussed in the textbook chapter:

- critical thinking
- problem solving
- decision making
- characteristics, skills, and attitudes of critical thinkers

Matching

Match the following terms with their definitions and attributes:

a.	context	e.	deductive reasoning
b.	creative thinking	f.	inductive reasoning
c.	critical thinking	g.	problem solving
d.	decision making	h.	Socratic questioning

___ 1. reasoning that goes from the general to the specific and that requires the ability to see the whole of something

___ 2. used to recognize and examine assumptions, search for inconsistencies, examine multiple points of view, and differentiate the known from the believed

___ 3. process of establishing criteria by which alternative courses of action are developed and selected

___ 4. unique experiences individuals bring with them to their specific situations

___ 5. purposeful thinking in which the thinker systematically and habitually imposes criteria and intellectual standards on the thinking

___ 6. an activity to obtain information to clarify the situation and suggest possible solutions and to make the best choice from these possible solutions

___ 7. process that results in new ideas and products

___ 8. the ability to generalize from a set of facts or observations

Multiple Choice

Circle the correct response for each question.

9. Critical thinking in nursing practice is demonstrated when the nurse:
   a. closely monitors the blood sugar of a client with diabetes every six hours as ordered.
   b. administers an antihypertensive medication at the regularly scheduled time to a client with a BP of 88/60.
   c. modifies a procedure because the optimal equipment is not available.
   d. defers the client's bed bath.

10. Creativity is a major element of critical thinking. The four stages of creative thinking are:
   a. preparation, incubation, insight, and verification.
   b. brainstorming, considering, choosing, and acting.
   c. information gathering, autonomous thought, group discussion, and validation with others.
   d. independent thought, fair-mindedness, curiosity, and intuition.

11. The conditions that must prevail in decision making are:
   a. creativity, rational thinking, and courage.
   b. problem solving, critical thinking, and creativity.
   c. inductive thinking, deductive thinking, and rationality.
   d. rationality, freedom, and voluntarity.

12. Decision making involves:
   a. identifying the problem and choosing the most cost-efficient solution.
   b. logically considering alternatives and making choices.
   c. trying multiple options until the most appropriate one is found.
   d. knowledge base and clinical skill.

13. Which of the following is not an example of Socratic questioning?
   a. What are the alternatives?
   b. What would change your mind?
   c. What would someone who disagrees with your perspective say?
   d. What do you like?

True or False

Read the following statements to determine if they are true or false. If a statement is false, alter the statement to make it true.

14. Critical thinkers may reject an idea held by a peer if they see no rationale in that viewpoint.
    True False

    ____

15. Critical thinkers are very dependent people.
True False

16. Critical thinkers recognize the limitations of their knowledge base and are willing to continue to learn.
True False

17. Critical thinkers are easily thwarted if the first solution does not work.
True False

18. Trial and error implies that a number of approaches are tried until a solution is found.
True False

19. The intuitive method of problem solving may be used by nurses at all levels of skill acquisition.
True False

20. Creative thinkers are rigid and slow to generate ideas.
True False

Completion

21. List at least five attributes of critical thinking.

22. Name five commonly used problem-solving methods.

23. What are the differences between the scientific method and the modified scientific method?

24. Utilize the information contained in the text and "Standards for Critical Thinkers" to evaluate your own critical thinking skills. Are you a critical thinker? What are your strengths in this area? In what areas are you less adept?

Case Study

Elie Alban, a nurse in the psychiatric mental health unit, is the preceptor of new graduates. While the new nurses are shadowing her for a day, she asks them to identify their learning needs related to the psychoeducation of the clients in the unit. The three new nurses identify their need to "learn how to motivate clients to stay on their medications and comply with their group treatment and homework."

25. New nurses can use critical thinking to assess their own learning needs. Use the table to apply and provide a specific example of how to use attitudes of critical thinking.

Attitude That Fosters Critical Thinking	Example of Strategy
Independence of Thought	
Fair-mindedness	
Insight into Egocentricity and Sociocentricity	
Intellectual Humility and Suspension of Judgment	
Intellectual Courage	
Integrity	
Perseverance	
Confidence in Reason	
Interest in Exploring Both Thoughts and Feelings	
Curiosity	
Contextual Awareness	

CHAPTER 23

The Nursing Process

This chapter introduces you to the nursing process and discusses the components and characteristics of the process. You will find the chapter helpful in understanding data collection, interviewing, and decision making. It stresses the importance of formulating nursing diagnoses, setting priorities, generating nursing strategies, and evaluating.

KEY TOPICS

This study guide chapter reinforces the following topics discussed in the textbook chapter:

- nursing process
- assessment
- subjective data
- objective data
- interviewing
- nursing diagnosis
- nursing diagnostic statements
- medical diagnosis
- collaborative problems
- planning process
- nursing care plans
- client goals and desired outcomes
- nursing orders
- Nursing Outcomes Classification (NOC)
- Nursing Interventions Classification (NIC)
- evaluating
- implementing
- quality assurance
- quality improvement

Matching

Match the step of the nursing process with the appropriate description.

a. assessing
b. diagnosing
c. planning
d. implementing
e. evaluating

___ 1. This is the action phase; the care plan is put into action by the RN or the designated person. This phase ends when the care is complete and the client's responses to care are documented.

___ 2. This is the data collection phase; information is gained through a variety of sources.

___ 3. In this phase, the nurse makes a determination of whether the outcome/goals have been met.

___ 4. In this phase, the nurse sorts, clusters, and analyzes data to determine actual and potential health problems.

___ 5. This is a collaborative phase between the nurse and the client; together they set priorities and goals.

___ 6. This phase includes a nursing history, physical examination, review of the record, consultation with other team members, and review of the pertinent literature.

Match the nursing diagnosis term with all of the appropriate definitions.

a. problem statement
b. etiology
c. defining characteristic(s)

___ 7. identifies the probable cause of the health problem

___ 8. directs the formation of client goals and outcome criteria

___ 9. must be specific to be useful

___ 10. is a cluster of signs and symptoms

___ 11. identifies related factors and risk factors

___ 12. is present only with actual nursing diagnosis

Identify the following as a nursing diagnosis, a medical diagnosis, or a collaborative problem.

N = Nursing diagnosis
M = Medical diagnosis
C = Collaborative problem

___ 13. pneumonia

___ 14. ineffective airway clearance related to C-5 paralysis as evidenced by crackles and rales or gurgles on auscultation

___ 15. diabetes mellitus

___ 16. potential complication of diabetes mellitus: altered wound healing

___ 17. health-seeking behaviours

___ 18. potential complication of mastectomy: lymphedema

Match the term with its definition.

a. analysis
b. critical thinking
c. critical pathways
d. desired outcome
e. discharge planning
f. evaluating
g. formal care plan
h. initial planning
i. ongoing planning
j. nursing intervention
k. nursing order
l. protocols
m. implementing
n. interpersonal skills

o. nursing audit
p. quality assurance
q. quality improvement
r. synthesis
s. technical skills

___ 19. the cognitive process of reviewing data and considering possible explanations before forming an opinion
___ 20. separation into components
___ 21. putting together the parts into a whole
___ 22. instructions for specific nursing actions to help the client achieve desired outcomes
___ 23. multi-disciplinary guidelines for client care based on specific medical diagnosis
___ 24. written, approved, preplanned instructions to indicate the actions commonly required for a defined group of clients
___ 25. involves comprehensive and ongoing assessment of physical needs; availability of caregivers, the home environment; and client, family, and community services
___ 26. specific observable criteria used to evaluate whether a goal has been met
___ 27. done by all nurses who work with the client
___ 28. a written plan of action to address client health problems
___ 29. a treatment that a nurse performs to enhance client outcomes
___ 30. the responsibility of the nurse who performs an admission assessment
___ 31. require knowledge and manual dexterity
___ 32. a review of the client charts to evaluate nursing care
___ 33. appraising the client's progress toward goal achievement and the effectiveness of the nursing care plan
___ 34. doing, delegating, and recording nursing care
___ 35. include communication techniques, knowledge of self, and ability to respect and value others
___ 36. designed to evaluate and promote excellence in health care
___ 37. follow client care with the intent of improving the quality of care

Multiple Choice

Circle the correct response for each question.

38. The nursing process is:
    a. a linear process with discrete phases.
    b. a model for nurses focused on disease processes.
    c. based solely on nursing knowledge and nursing action.
    d. applicable to all clients.

39. How do nursing assessments differ from medical assessments?
   a. They do not differ.
   b. Nursing assessments are performed by nurses; medical assessments are performed by physicians.
   c. Nursing assessments focus on the client's response to health problems; medical assessments focus on disease.
   d. Nursing assessments are only performed at the initial meeting with the client; medical assessments are performed with each client interaction.

40. The purpose of assessment is to:
   a. document client progress.
   b. establish a database about the client's response to health and illness.
   c. have access to the client for interview.
   d. establish rapport with the client.

41. You observe a reddened area on the client's coccyx. This is an example of:
   a. objective data.
   b. subjective data.
   c. primary data.
   d. secondary data.

42. Observation involves:
   a. notice of stimuli only.
   b. notice, selection, organization, and interpretation of data.
   c. casual inspection of the client and his surroundings.
   d. inspection, palpation, percussion, and auscultation.

43. Physical examination of the client is a systematic data collection tool. When performing a physical examination, the nurse should:
   a. always compare findings on each side of the body.
   b. always perform assessment in a head-to-toe manner.
   c. always utilize a body system approach.
   d. never limit data collection to a brief screening examination.

44. When planning an interview, the nurse should:
   a. arrange a time for the interview based on her schedule.
   b. arrange a time for the interview based on the client's condition and comfort level.
   c. always create a formal seating arrangement when conducting an intake interview.
   d. sit right next to the client in order to prevent others from overhearing.

45. At the beginning of each shift, the nurse performs an assessment on each of her clients. This type of assessment is known as a(n):
  a. emergency assessment.
  b. initial assessment.
  c. problem-focused assessment.
  d. time-lapse reassessment.

46. The client is coughing frequently but unable to expectorate his pulmonary secretion. The nurse charts the nursing diagnosis as Ineffective Airway Clearance. What type of nursing diagnosis is this?
  a. actual diagnosis
  b. possible nursing diagnosis
  c. risk nursing diagnosis
  d. wellness diagnosis

47. A correctly written diagnosis contains which of the following components?
  a. problem statement, causative agent, and other risk factors
  b. problem statement, problem label, and defining characteristics
  c. problem statement, etiology, and defining characteristics
  d. diagnostic label, risk factors, and qualifiers

48. Which one of the following nursing diagnostic statements is correctly written?
  a. impaired circulation to lower left extremity related to peripheral vascular disease as evidenced by cool extremity
  b. risk for rape-trauma syndrome
  c. risk for impaired skin integrity related to bed rest as evidenced by reddened coccyx
  d. ineffective breast-feeding related to poor sucking reflex as evidenced by breast engorgement in the mother and weight loss in the infant

49. During the planning phase, the nurse determines which of the client's problems may be addressed by individualized plans, standardized plans, and routine care. The nurse must also:
  a. write a nursing diagnosis to address the client problems.
  b. carry out nursing interventions.
  c. evaluate the client's response to the treatment plan.
  d. write individualized desired outcomes and nursing orders.

50. Prioritization of client care is a nursing function in the planning phase. Identify the priority nursing diagnosis for a client with all of the following nursing diagnoses:
  a. risk for skin impairment related to required bed rest.
  b. impaired physical mobility related to multiple trauma and coma.
  c. impaired gas exchange related to fluid volume overload.
  d. ineffective parenting related to inability to communicate with children.

51. Nursing interventions for potential health problems:
  a. emphasize demonstrations of caring.
  b. focus on discharge planning activities.
  c. focus on measures to reduce the client's risk factors.
  d. concentrate on eliminating health problems.

52. While implementing nursing orders, the nurse must constantly:
  a. keep track of the time required to implement nursing orders.
  b. modify the care plan on the basis of staffing and resources.
  c. reassess the client and his response to the nursing actions.
  d. examine the use of unlicensed assistive personnel in the unit.

53. What is the key distinction between delegation and assignment?
  a. Delegation is always a downward or lateral transfer of responsibility and accountability; assignment retains accountability.
  b. Delegation is the transfer of responsibility while retaining accountability; assignment is the transfer of accountability and responsibility.
  c. There is no functional difference between these activities, although physicians assign, while nurses and ancillary personnel delegate.
  d. Delegation is the transfer of responsibility for completion of a task; assignment is the transfer of responsibility while retaining accountability.

54. If a nurse determined that the client's goals have not been met, what may she conclude?
  a. The client's behaviour must change in order for the goals to be achieved.
  b. The physician must be notified of the client's failure to meet the goals of the nursing care plan.
  c. The care plan needs modification, or the client needs more time to achieve the goals.
  d. The client's condition has changed.

55. What type of quality assurance program answers the question, "What is the average time a client waits for lab results in the emergency department?"
  a. outcome evaluation
  b. process evaluation
  c. quality improvement
  d. structure evaluation

True or False

Read the following statements to determine if they are true or false. If a statement is false, alter the statement to make it true.

56. The primary methods used to assess a client are observing, interviewing, and examining.
True False

___

57. "When did you last eat?" is an example of an open-ended question.
True False

____

58. "What can I do to help you?" is an example of an open-ended question.
True False

____

59. "Who are the people you can count on for support?" is an example of a leading question.
True False

____

60. Objectively evaluating subjective complaints of the client, such as when the nurse listens to breath sounds of a client complaining of congestion, is a form of data validation.
True False

____

61. Goals and desired outcomes provide direction for planning nursing diagnoses and enable the physician to determine when and if a problem has been resolved.
True False

____

62. Nursing interventions are focused on accomplishing client goals.
True False

____

63. A nurse may need assistance with a nursing intervention if it is unsafe to carry out the intervention independently.
True False

____

Completion

64. An interview is a (a) ____________________________ with a purpose. Two approaches that may be used are directive and nondirective. These two strategies differ significantly. A directive interview is designed to elicit (b) ____________________________. The pace of the interview and the questions are controlled by the (c) ____________________. This type of interview may be used to (d) ____________________________ when there is limited time for interaction.

A nondirective interview is designed to (e) ____________________________.
The pace of the interview and the questions are controlled by the (f) ____________.
This type of interview may be used to (g) ____________________________, or ____________________________.

65. The two purposes of the opening phase of an interview are to:

____

____

66. What is the purpose of the body of an interview?

____

____

67. What are the main goals in the closing phase of an interview?

____

____

68. Examine the data collection tool used in your clinical unit. What conceptual model(s) does this tool follow?

____

____

69. (a) ______________________ are responsible for making nursing diagnoses, whereas (b) ______________________ may contribute to the care planning and delivery of care.

70. Identify at least three methods to avoid diagnostic errors.

____

____

____

71. List five factors that the nurse must consider when setting priorities for nursing care.

____

____

____

____

____

72. Provide two examples of independent nursing interventions.

____

____

73. Provide two examples of dependent nursing interventions.

____

____

74. Provide two examples of collaborative interventions.

____

____

75. Define a standing order.

______

______

______

Identify which of the following goals or expected outcomes are well stated by placing a checkmark in front of them. Rewrite those that are incorrectly written.

___ 76. Client will be able to successfully draw up and administer her own insulin by Thursday, 6/16.

______

___ 77. Client will ambulate.

______

___ 78. By the end of the week, Mr. Teak will lose 10 kg.

______

___ 79. The client will increase the amount of fluids ingested and participate in unit social activities.

______

___ 80. Fluid volume status will improve as evidenced by a minimum of 1500 mL intake every 24 hours beginning today, 2/22/04.

______

___ 81. What are the three types of nursing audit?

______

______

______

Case Study

82. Abah Singh is a 47-year-old South Asian male being admitted to the hospital for management of Congestive Heart Failure (CHF). On arrival at the floor, he is short of breath and appears fatigued. Admission vital signs are: BP 158/98, P 104 irregular, RR 26, T 36.5C oral. While you are taking his vital signs, Mr. Singh tells his wife, "I am dying. Let me rest. I will sleep and die." Mrs. Singh is teary-eyed and asks if she can speak with you. Outside the room she tells you, "My husband had a heart attack four months ago. Over the last month, it has been harder and harder for him to breathe. He is so short of breath he sleeps sitting up in a chair."

a. What are the objective data?

______

b. What are the subjective data?

______

c. What factors will you need to consider when planning your admission interview and physical assessment?

____

____

d. Identify potential sources of data for your assessment.

____

____

83. Natalie Egan is a 47-year-old woman who reports to your outpatient surgery department at 0630. She is scheduled for an 0830 surgery. Natalie detected a lump in her breast approximately three weeks ago. She underwent a mammogram and, on the advice of a surgeon, is here today for a right breast biopsy and possible radical mastectomy. Natalie informs you that she and her husband are certain that the lump is benign and "this whole silly business will be over shortly." She giggles nervously after making the statement.

During your interview, you assess the following:

BP 162/94 (elevated)

P 112 (elevated)

RR 22 (elevated)

T 36.7C

Skin, cool and dry

Height 150 cm

Weight 51 kg

a. Write at least two nursing diagnoses for Natalie.

____

____

____

____

____

____

Natalie is admitted to the hospital after undergoing a radical mastectomy for carcinoma. As the nurse caring for her in the surgical unit, you assess her upon arrival to the unit. Natalie reports that she is in "tremendous pain." She requests that her family be allowed to see her right away. She also tells you she wants to "get on top of this right away. I want to know everything I can do to get back up to speed and beat this cancer." Natalie's dressing is dry and intact. Her vital signs are:

BP 138/94

P 110 (elevated)

RR 20

T 37C

b. Generate additional nursing diagnoses on the basis of this information.

84. Ginger Harod is a 26-year-old woman with severe seasonal allergies. She is seen today in the outpatient clinic complaining of wheezing and shortness of breath. The nurse practitioner has outlined a rigorous treatment plan that includes an inhaled bronchodilator and an inhaled steroid. Ginger tells you, "I'm sick of being sick. I wheeze so much it affects everything about my life. I've got to get this under control, but I don't know anything about these medications." As the nurse, you recognize that the client has a knowledge deficit about these new medications.

a. Write an expected outcome/goal for this nursing diagnosis.

b. Write two nursing orders designed to accomplish this goal.

CHAPTER 24

Documenting and Reporting

This chapter introduces the purpose and method of charting and communicating client information. Different types of charting, intraprofessional and interprofessional communication, and guidelines for charting are presented.

KEY TOPICS

This study guide chapter reinforces the following topics discussed in the textbook chapter:

- client records
- documentation methods
- legal and ethical standards for documentation
- abbreviations and symbols
- confidentiality of client records

Matching

Match the type of documentation system with the appropriate description.

a.	case management	g.	narrative charting
b.	charting by exception	h.	outcome documentation
c.	computerized record	i.	PIE charting
d.	CORE documentation	j.	problem-oriented medical record
e.	FACT system	k.	SOAP format charting
f.	focus charting	l.	source-oriented clinical record

___ 1. This chronological charting record includes a description of client assessments and care rendered.

___ 2. This documentation system consists of four components: database, problem list, plan of care, and progress notes.

___ 3. This documentation outlines the nursing care the client is receiving. Entries are organized by data, action, and response (DAR).

___ 4. This system consists of a database, plans of care, flow sheets, progress notes, and a discharge summary.

___ 5. In this type of record, each person or department records notes in a separate section.

___ 6. In this documentation system, only significant findings or exceptions to norms are recorded.

___ 7. This charting format is organized by subjective data, objective data, assessment, and plan.

___ 8. This system emphasizes quality, cost-effective care within an established length of stay and utilizes critical pathways.

___ 9. This documentation originated from the nursing process: assessment data are organized into a list of client problems; interventions are organized to address the problems, and charting reflects the nurse's evaluation of the client's progress toward resolving the problem.

___ 10. This type of record uses assessment flow sheets with integrated progress notes to document the client's condition and response to treatment in a timely manner.

___ 11. This documentation evaluates the client's condition in relation to predetermined outcomes.

___ 12. This documentation system links various sources of information, such as bedside terminals and hospital departments, to allow health-care providers to retrieve information in a variety of formats.

Multiple Choice

Circle the correct response for each question.

13. Because the client's record is a legal document, health-care personnel must meet legal standards in the process of recording. It should be:
    a. regular, that is, at least every two hours for inpatients and every day for outpatients.
    b. timely, accurate, confidential, and client specific.
    c. multi-disciplinary, legible, standardized, and according to agency policy.
    d. confidential, private, descriptive, and without use of abbreviations.

14. As part of your clinical education, you are working on 6 East, a surgical floor. A client's spouse asks to read her husband's chart. What must you do?
    a. Inform the wife that the record is confidential and you are unable to grant permission for her to read the chart.
    b. Inform her that she may read the chart as long as the record remains at the nursing station.
    c. Inform her that she must request permission from the physician and medical records department.
    d. Inform her that under no circumstances may any persons other than direct health-care providers read the chart.

15. The Kardex is a widely used client data system. Which of the following statements is true about the Kardex?
    a. The Kardex is always part of the client's permanent medical record.
    b. The Kardex is used to document nursing care that has been delivered.
    c. The Kardex is the same thing as the problem-oriented medical record.
    d. The Kardex is a concise data system, which usually contains a summary of client information and data.

16. Which of the following elements of care is *not* an aspect of long-term care documentation?
    a. complete assessment
    b. record of visits and calls from family, friends, or others
    c. monthly progress note to the reimburser
    d. nursing summaries and progress notes

17. A change-of-shift report is:
    a. always an oral report.
    b. designed to provide continuity of care.
    c. an exchange of feelings about clients and their families.
    d. a lengthy process that occurs once per day.

18. If you make an error while charting, you should:
    a. use white-out to cover the error and record over it when the solution has dried.
    b. recopy the whole page.
    c. use a thick black marker to cover the error.
    d. draw a line through the error and write "error" above it with your initials.

19. Your client refuses to allow you to perform a prescribed wound care treatment. How should you chart this?
    a. You must only chart care that has already been given; since the client refused the care, there is nothing to chart.
    b. You must document that the client refused wound care and any reason offered for refusal as well as who was notified of this refusal.
    c. You must convince the client to undergo the prescribed wound treatment.
    d. The client's refusal of wound care should be documented on the Kardex but never on the client chart.

True or False

Read the following statements to determine if they are true or false. If a statement is false, alter the statement to make it true.

20. Information contained in the health-care record is confidential.
    True False

    ____

21. The client may not read his or her own chart.
    True False

    ____

22. All charting must be timed, dated, and signed. Entries may be made in #2 pencil or ink.
    True False

    ____

23. The frequency of charting is based on agency policy alone.
True False

____

24. The nurse must question the physician about any order that is ambiguous, unusual, or contraindicated by the client condition.
True False

____

25. A telephone order must be countersigned by the physician after the client has been discharged.
True False

____

Completion

Complete the following paragraph about client records.

26. Client records are used for many purposes. The record assists with planning client care by (a) ______________________. As a form of communication, the chart helps avoid (b) ______________, ______________, and ______________. The chart also serves as a legal document. As a student, you may also use the client record for (c) ______________ ______________. Other health-care professionals may use the chart to gather data for research purposes. Peer review groups may use the record for (d) ______________________. The hospital or health-care agency uses client charts to compile statistics. Statistical information is used to (e) ______________________. Accrediting agencies review charts to (f) ______________________. Health planners review records for (g) ______________________.

27. Which form of care planning does your institution use?

____

____

28. Name one advantage and one disadvantage for each of the following types of care planning.

a. traditional care plans

____

b. standardized care plans

____

c. critical pathways

____

29. What are four types of clinical flowsheets you may use in providing client care?

____

____

____

____

30. What is the purpose of discharge summaries or referral summaries?

____

31. What is the difference between a nursing conference and nursing rounds?

____

____

32. Complete the following list of common abbreviations and terms

Abbreviation		**Term**
a.	NPO	______________
b.	______________	out of bed
c.	hs	______________
d.	______________	immediately
e.	bid	______________
f.	q6h	______________
g.	______________	bathroom privileges
h.	ADL	______________
i.	______________	diet as tolerated
j.	po	______________

Case Study

33. You are doing a chart audit. Review the following charting entries and correct any inaccuracies.

a. Date: 9/8/00 Time: 0900
On 1800 calorie ADA diet. Appetite good. R. Shay, RN

b.

9/16/00 1000	C/o chest pain. BP 98/56 P 180 RR 30. Mucous membranes pale and dusky. Oxygen at 2 lpm begun via nasal cannula. NTG 0.4 mg SL given. MD notified.
9/16/00	Client reports return of chest pain. BP 78/40 P 140 RR 28.
1010	Additional NTG 0.4 mg tab given.
1020	Client transported to CCU for ongoing cardiac monitoring.
9/16/00	Received in CCU from 4 North. BP 68/40 P 200 RR 30.
1035	ECG monitor shows atrial fibrillation. MD notified. Digoxin 0.5 mg IV given. ______________ N. North, RN

____

____

____

c.

2/18/00 1400	Mr. Smith is a nice man with a kind face and smile who was admitted to the hospital for problems with urination. He is anxious to undergo his surgery so that he can get home to his daily walks and poker nights with his friends at the VFW. He is a sharp dresser and quick witted, though I suspect that he drinks alcohol more than he admits. He smokes cigars at times. ______________ S. Lo, RN

____

____

____

CHAPTER 25

Nursing Informatics

This chapter discusses the growing use of computers in nursing education, practice, and research. The discussion on the expanding use of computers by nurses and other health-care providers offers insight into the expanding world of informatics.

KEY TOPICS

This study guide chapter reinforces the following topics discussed in the textbook chapter:

- uses of computers in practice
- uses of computers in nursing education
- uses of computers in nursing administration
- uses of computers in research

Matching

Match the term with the appropriate description.

a.	distance learning	e.	software
b.	personal digital assistant	f.	telemedicine
c.	nursing informatics	g.	telenursing
d.	interactivity		

___ 1. a criterion to evaluate health information that includes a feedback mechanism and a means of information exchange among users

___ 2. handheld device used for scheduling

___ 3. the sharing of nursing information using electronic means to answer consumer questions

___ 4. the science of using computer information systems in the practice of nursing

___ 5. computer programs or applications

___ 6. teachers and learners connected by technology from distant locations

___ 7. the use of technology to transmit electronic information about clients to persons at distant locations

Multiple Choice

Circle the correct response for each question.

8. Which of the following statements about the use of computers in education is most accurate?
   a. All examinations can be marked with ease.
   b. All students can access an exam online.
   c. Potential test items can be written and stored into a computer bank, and students can write different tests, depending on the faculty-selected criterion.
   d. Potential candidates to a nursing school can access pre-registration exams online.

9. Computer-assisted instruction (CAI) and computerized distance learning are tools used by nurses to further their education. They differ in that:
   a. CAI may be purchased and used individually, but computerized distance learning usually involves interaction with fellow students and faculty.
   b. CAI is used in formal degree programs, but computerized distance learning is predominantly used for continuing education.
   c. CAI is less costly than computerized distance learning.
   d. CAI requires proximity to an instructor, and computerized distance learning does not.

10. Novice and experienced nurse researchers use computers in their work. In which phase of the research process are computers most widely used?
    a. grant-writing phase
    b. all phases
    c. literature review phase
    d. quantitative analysis phase

11. What does data integrity mean?
    a. collection, storage, and transmission of data in a manner that preserves its accuracy and completeness
    b. a third-party obligation to ensure that all personal data entrusted to it are kept in privacy
    c. retrieval of data in a manner that is safe and accessible
    d. a set of principles that preserves data for a maximum of 20 years

12. The criterion of credibility as it applies to the evaluation of health information on the Internet refers to the inclusion of:
    a. the source, currency, relevance, utility, and editorial review process.
    b. information for the user about the purpose of the site as well as any collection of information associated with the use of the site.
    c. clarification of whether the site functions to market products or to provide information.
    d. links that are appropriate for the content.

True or False

Read the following statements to determine if they are true or false. If a statement is false, alter the statement to make it true.

13. A consumer's copy of the health data, which might be paper or electronic, is called a personal health record.
    True False

14. With electronic health records, data are automatically verified as they are entered to ensure accuracy.
    True False

15. Computers are used for administration purposes to communicate with employees, create budget projections, and examine staffing trends.
    True False

Completion

16. Identify a client situation or clinical issue of interest to you and/or your class. How would you research this topic using computerized literature access and retrieval systems?

17. Investigate the variety of clinical facilities used as educational sites by your nursing program. Do any of them use bedside data entry or computer-based client records? If so, what advantages and disadvantages of these systems have been identified by other students, faculty, and staff?

18. Visit a ward/unit at your local hospital. Identify at least 10 ways in which computers are used to assist client care.

Case Study

19. A panel of guest speakers has come to talk about the use of informatics in nursing and health care. They were entertaining questions from a group of enthusiastic graduating students. One student asked the panel to envision what computers can do for nurses in the future. If you were one of the guest speakers, what would be your response?

CHAPTER 26

Nurse-Patient Relationship

This chapter presents a concise discussion of the role of therapeutic relationships in the delivery of client care. It introduces techniques that facilitate communication and the helping relationship and alerts you to potential barriers to these goals. Through extensive examples, you examine the relationship of verbal and nonverbal communication and distinguish the skills necessary for interpersonal and group communication.

KEY TOPICS

This study guide chapter reinforces the following topics discussed in the textbook chapter:

- caring
- helping relationships
- communication process
- comforting process
- verbal communication
- nonverbal communication
- communication problems
- group communication

Matching

Match the following phases of the helping relationship with the tasks and skills that are associated with the phase. Some tasks and skills may have more than one correct answer.

a. introductory phase
b. preinteraction phase
c. termination phase
d. working phase

___ 1. clarifying the problem
___ 2. making decisions and setting goals
___ 3. summarizing
___ 4. planning for the initial visit
___ 5. listening and attending
___ 6. resisting and testing by the client
___ 7. empathizing and comforting
___ 8. developing trust

Match the following type of personal space with the associated distances:

a.	intimate	c.	public
b.	personal	d.	social

___ 9. 3.5 metres and beyond

___ 10. physical contact to 45 cm

___ 11. 1 metre to 3.5 metres

___ 12. 45 cm to 1 metre

Place an F in front of those factors that facilitate communication and an I in front of those factors that inhibit communication.

___ 13. showing a lack of interest

___ 14. showing acceptance

___ 15. demonstrating respect for the client

___ 16. patting a client on the head and calling her "dear"

___ 17. responding to a client's request by saying, "What do you want now?"

Multiple Choice

Circle the correct response for each question.

18. Which of the following statements about caring is true?
    a. Caring is always associated with verbal interaction.
    b. Caring evokes tangible outcomes that may be evaluated.
    c. Caring is a skill that may be enhanced through practice.
    d. Physical cure of disease may occur without the presence of caring.

19. Comforting a client is a complex task that involves meeting human needs for ease, relief, or transcendence. Which of the following is true of comfort needs?
    a. They are predominantly physical, but occasionally include psychological distress.
    b. They may be physical, psychospiritual, social, and environmental in nature.
    c. They can usually be met through communication skills.
    d. They must always be met in a therapeutic relationship.

20. A helping relationship is characterized by:
    a. trust between the client and the family.
    b. the belief that the client cares and wants to help his/her self.
    c. a dynamic state in which the welfare of the client is central to the interaction.
    d. the nurse doing as much as possible for the client.

21. Which of the following statement(s) reflects appropriate verbal communication by a nurse?
    a. "Mr. Senna, I'm going to take you to 3 for an MRI."
    b. "I'd like you to take deep breaths and cough frequently."
    c. "I will be getting a blood sample from your arm in order to check the amount of sugar in your blood."
    d. "I'm going to take you to 4 North for PT. You're scheduled for touch-down weight-bearing instruction."

22. Which of the following is true of *nonverbal communication?*
    a. It is all that is observed and heard.
    b. It should be accepted as the true message from the person.
    c. It should be measured against the person's words.
    d. It includes posture, gait, and dress, but not facial expressions.

23. Intimate distance between a nurse and a new client should be preceded by the nurse:
    a. letting the client know what she is going to do.
    b. signalling the intent to approach by a clearing of the throat.
    c. telling the client to relax.
    d. extending conversation in the social space.

24. Attentive listening requires:
    a. hearing but does not require sight.
    b. absorbing the content and feeling that is being conveyed.
    c. an innate talent.
    d. selectivity on the part of the listener.

25. Which of the following is a barrier to communication?
    a. caring
    b. open-ended questions
    c. knowing your role and limitations
    d. inability to speak the native language

26. Which of the following statements is true of group communication?
    a. In any given group, there will always be members who are at varying stages in the group process.
    b. Effective groups maintain a degree of unity as they move through the phases of the relationship.
    c. Self-help groups run most efficiently when the nurse serves as the leader.
    d. Therapy groups are important adjuncts to the treatment plan for people who share a similar health, social, or daily living problem.

True or False

Read the following statements to determine if they are true or false. If a statement is false, alter the statement to make it true.

27. A person's ability to speak, hear, see, and comprehend stimuli influences the communication process.
    True False

    ____

    ____

28. Attentive listening is passive and requires little energy.
    True False

    ____

29. When assessing nonverbal behaviours, the nurse needs to consider cultural influences.
    True False

    ____

    ____

30. Process recordings are frequently made by nurses to evaluate their own communication. Process recordings allow the nurse to analyze the content and the process of the communication.
    True False

    ____

    ____

    ____

Completion

31. Identify at least five factors that may influence the nurse–client helping relationship.

    ____

    ____

    ____

    ____

    ____

32. Jackson Brandy is an 11-year-old boy admitted to the pediatric unit from the emergency department. Jackson has asthma that has been poorly controlled. His mother tells you that he is not consistent in taking his medications. You have planned an interview and teaching session with Jackson. Identify at least five actions you can take to facilitate a helping relationship.

____

____

____

____

____

33. Complete the communication process diagram.

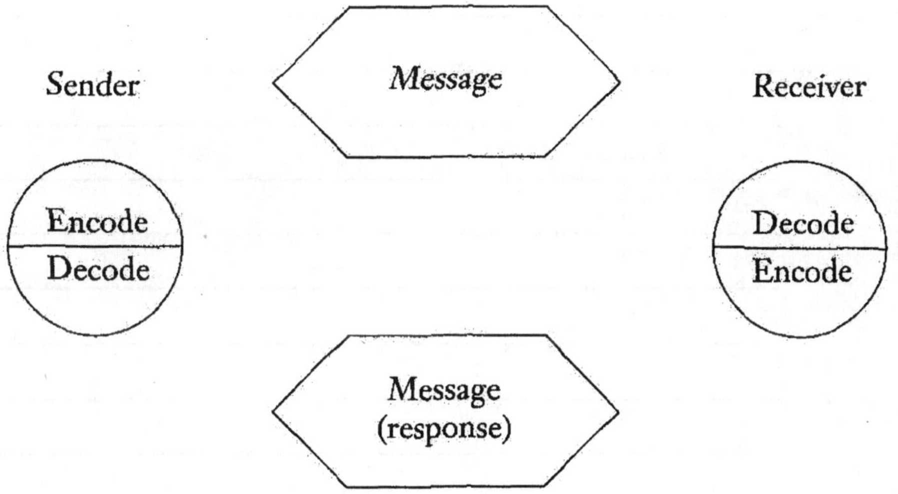

34. Give an example of a nursing activity that might be conducted in each of the four space distances.

Space Distance	*Nursing Activity*
Intimate	
Personal	
Social	
Public	

35. List the three main functions of a group.

____

____

____

____

____

____

____

____

____

Case Study

Bob Change, a 28-year-old nursing student, has been assigned his first admission interview. He will be interviewing Jean LaGuardia, a 24-year-old second-year university student. Jean was brought to the emergency department by her roommate because she complained of severe abdominal pain. Jean was examined and scheduled for surgery this afternoon for surgical excision of an ectopic pregnancy (pregnancy outside of the uterus, usually in the fallopian tube). She has been brought to the surgical unit for preoperative care. Jean is teary-eyed and complaining of pain.

36. In an effort to create a positive environment for the interview, Bob might want to:
    a. sit next to Jean, facing her.
    b. stand facing Jean.
    c. sit across the room from Jean.
    d. unplug the phone.

37. Bob should keep in mind that interpersonal space between him and Jean is affected by:
    a. the cultural heritage of the client.
    b. the client's anxiety level.
    c. the nature of the communication.
    d. all of the above.

38. During the interview, Jean tells Bob that she is very frightened. She has never had surgery, and she is concerned about future ability to conceive. Bob considers sharing with Jean his personal experience with surgery. What is the primary consideration in using self-disclosure?

   a. Self-disclosure is never appropriate in a therapeutic relationship.
   b. Self-disclosure should only be used in the termination phase of the interview.
   c. Self-disclosure is inappropriate because Bob has never experienced a tubal pregnancy.
   d. Self-disclosure must primarily meet the client's needs.

39. Bob asks Jean about her understanding of the planned surgery. Jean starts to sob and stops talking. Bob recognizes that her silence:

   a. is not appropriate in an interview.
   b. provides her with time to control her emotions.
   c. impedes his ability to gather information.
   d. indicates he is a poor interviewer.

40. Bob recognizes Jean's obvious emotional distress. What are at least three therapeutic responses he could employ?

____

____

____

____

____

____

41. Jean is very tearful. She is unable to make eye contact with Bob. She says, "I can't believe this is happening." Which of the following would be Bob's most appropriate verbal response?

   a. "I know how you must feel. My wife had a tubal pregnancy, too. We were both very upset. She had a really hard time with it for about two weeks. But everything turned out OK. We have three children now: two boys and one girl. They are ages eight, five, and two."
   b. "You are scheduled for an exploratory laparotomy at 5 PM this afternoon. Do you have any questions about the surgery?"
   c. "This is really hard for you."
   d. "Do you have fears about the surgery? Are you worried about your future ability to conceive? Would you like me to call someone for you?"

CHAPTER 27

Health Assessment

This chapter discusses health assessment through the use of physical examination techniques. The ample information in this chapter will help you get started in learning how to become an excellent examiner.

KEY TOPICS

This study guide chapter reinforces the following topics discussed in the textbook chapter:

- health assessment
- inspection
- percussion
- physical examination
- palpation
- auscultation

Matching

Match the following integumentary terms with their definitions:

a.	bromhidrosis	f.	jaundice
b.	cyanosis	g.	melanin
c.	edema	h.	pallor
d.	erythema	i.	vitiligo
e.	hyperhidrosis		

___ 1. excessive perspiration
___ 2. patches of hypopigmented skin
___ 3. bluish tinge that is most evident in nail beds, lips, and buccal mucosa
___ 4. absence of underlying red tones in the skin
___ 5. foul-smelling perspiration
___ 6. presence of excess interstitial fluid
___ 7. dark pigment of the skin
___ 8. redness associated with a variety of rashes
___ 9. yellowish tinge best seen in the sclera

Match the following visual terms with the correct descriptions:

a. anisocoria
b. astigmatism
c. cataracts
d. conjunctivitis
e. glaucoma
f. hyperopia
g. miosis
h. mydriasis
i. myopia
j. presbyopia
k. visual acuity
l. visual field

___ 10. an opacity of the lens or its capsule that tends to occur in people over 65 years old

___ 11. the degree of detail an eye can discern in an image

___ 12. an uneven curvature of the cornea that prevents rays from focusing on the retina; often associated with myopia and hyperopia

___ 13. farsightedness; difficulty seeing near objects

___ 14. unequal pupils

___ 15. enlarged or dilated pupils

___ 16. constricted pupils

___ 17. the area an individual can see when looking straight ahead

___ 18. the most common cause of blindness in people over 40 years of age; causes an increase in intraocular pressure

___ 19. loss of elasticity of the lens resulting in difficulty seeing close objects

___ 20. nearsightedness; difficulty seeing objects at a distance

___ 21. inflammation of the conjunctiva; may be related to a foreign object, viral or bacterial infection, or allergies

Multiple Choice

Circle the correct response for each question.

22. What is the purpose of a physical examination?
    a. to establish the nurse–client relationship
    b. to obtain information about the client's place of work
    c. to obtain information about the client's health
    d. to identify inconsistencies in the client's presentation

23. The physical examination of the client:
    a. should always be conducted in a head-to-toe fashion.
    b. should be condensed to save time for nursing interventions.
    c. should be systematic and efficient in order to conserve the client's energy and time.
    d. must be ordered by the physician.

24. What are the environmental issues that you should consider when preparing to physically examine a client?
   a. equipment and draping
   b. equipment, lighting, privacy, timing, and temperature of the room
   c. the client's physical condition and age
   d. instruments and personnel

25. Physical examination begins with a general survey. Which of the following choices contains all aspects of the general survey?
   a. appearance, behaviour, vital signs, height, and weight
   b. body build, posture, hygiene, and mental status
   c. history, review of the systems, and vital signs
   d. age, gender, ethnicity, religion, and cultural values

26. You read the following notation on a chart: Normocephalic male with alopecia. You recognize that this notation means the client has a(n):
   a. enlarged head with excessive hair growth.
   b. normal size head with normal hair pattern.
   c. unusually small head with an unusual hair pattern.
   d. normal size head with hair loss.

27. You are using an otoscope to examine the middle ear of a client. Which structures can be visualized with this assessment technique?
   a. pinna, tympanic membrane, mastoid, and helix
   b. malleus, incus, and stapes
   c. tympanic membrane, eustachian tube, and cochlea
   d. lobule, helix, and antihelix

28. Hearing loss that is the result of interrupted transmission of sound waves through the outer and middle ear structures is known as:
   a. conduction hearing loss.
   b. high-frequency hearing loss.
   c. mixed hearing loss.
   d. sensorineural hearing loss.

29. Your client complains of irritation and pain in the roof of the mouth. You assemble the following equipment to examine the mouth: tongue blade, gauze square, and penlight. What else must you add to your equipment list to be complete?
   a. cotton swab
   b. gloves
   c. otoscope with nasal speculum attachment
   d. toothbrush

30. You are auscultating the breath sounds of a client. You hear high-pitched harsh sounds. In a healthy client, what type of breath sound is this, and where is your stethoscope placed?
    a. bronchial breath sound; your stethoscope is on the anterior chest over the trachea
    b. bronchovesicular breath sound; your stethoscope is on the anterior chest over the bronchi
    c. crackle breath sound; your stethoscope is on the anterior chest over an area consolidated by mucus
    d. vesicular breath sound; your stethoscope is on the anterior chest over the peripheral lung fields

31. Which type of adventitious breath sound may be cleared by coughing?
    a. crackles
    b. friction rub
    c. gurgles
    d. wheeze

32. The correct order of examination techniques for the abdomen is:
    a. inspection, auscultation, palpation, and percussion.
    b. auscultation, palpation, inspection, and percussion.
    c. inspection, palpation, percussion, and auscultation.
    d. palpation, percussion, auscultation, and inspection.

33. Examination of the neurological system includes:
    a. joint movement.
    b. emotional condition.
    c. history of psychological counselling.
    d. level of consciousness.

34. Examination of the prostate is usually conducted with the client in which position? a. lithotomy
    b. right lateral Sims position
    c. standing position bent over the exam table
    d. supine

True or False

Read the following statements to determine if they are true or false. If a statement is false, alter the statement to make it true.

35. The nail beds may be used to conduct a blanch test for capillary refill.
    True False

    ____

36. The assessment techniques used in breast examination are inspection and palpation. Inspection should be followed by palpation of the breast. Palpation is conducted in a systematic fashion in order to ensure completeness.
True False

____

____

____

____

37. When assessing the vascular system, it is important to palpate all pulses on both sides of the body simultaneously to determine symmetry of the pulse volume.
True False

____

____

____

38. Assessment of a client's mental status includes evaluating the client's ability to express herself verbally, level of orientation, memory, attention span, and calculation ability.
True False

____

Completion

39. Complete the table of techniques for physical examination.

Technique	**Description**	**Example of Use**
Inspection		refers to inspection of skin, fundoscopic examination of eyes, inspection of a wound
	examination of the body using the sense of touch, light or deep; examiner primarily uses pads of fingers	
		used to determine the size and shape of internal organs; may be used to delineate a liver margin or fluid in the lungs
Ausculation		

40. When describing a skin lesion you should always include the following points:

____

____

____

41. Describe the five sounds elicited by percussion. Give an example of where these sounds may be heard.

a. Flatness: ______________________________

b. Dullness: ______________________________

c. Resonance: ______________________________

d. Hyper-resonance: ______________________________

e. Tympany: ______________________________

42. In the diagrams below, label the following chest landmarks: midsternal line, midclavicular line, anterior axillary line, midaxillary line, and posterior axillary line.

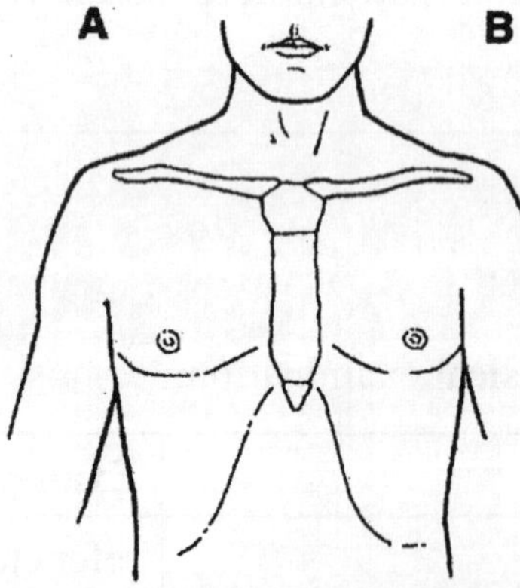

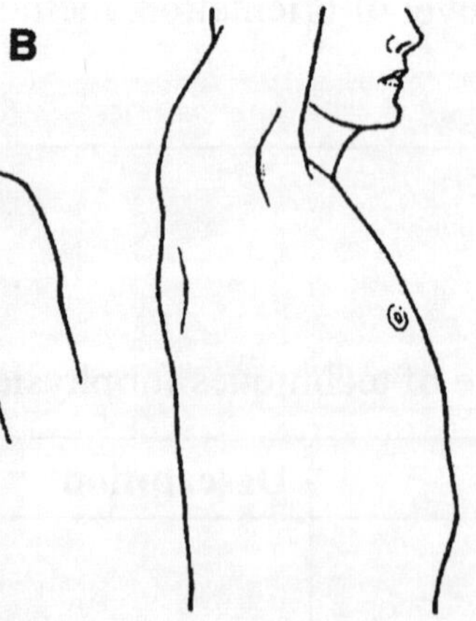

43. Label the key areas for auscultation of the heart.

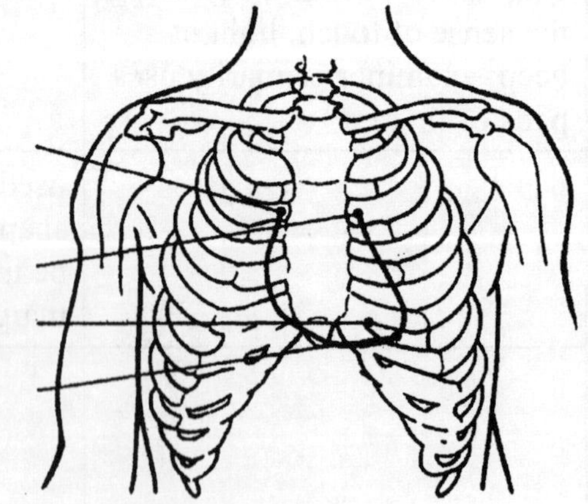

44. What are two questions you should ask the client when assessing the musculoskeletal system?

____

____

45. Evaluate your own comfort with assessment of male and female genitalia. Can you successfully conduct a matter-of-fact examination?

____

____

46. Complete the following table by supplying information on the cranial nerve, classification (S = sensory M = motor, B = both), or how each cranial nerve is assessed.

Name of Nerve	***Type***	***Assessment***
I: Olfactory	_____	ask client to close eyes and identify common smells
II: ____________________	S	______________________________ ______________________________
III: ____________________	M	______________________________ ______________________________
IV: ____________________	M	assess six ocular movements
V: Trigeminal	_____	______________________________ ______________________________
VI: ____________________	_____	assess directions of gaze
VII: Facial	_____	______________________________ ______________________________
VIII: ____________________	_____	______________________________ ______________________________
IX: ____________________	B	______________________________ ______________________________
X: Vagus	B	assess with cranial nerve IX; check speech for hoarseness
XI: ____________________	_____	______________________________ ______________________________
XII: Hypoglossal	M	ask client to protrude tongue and move from side to side

Case Study

47. As part of your clinical rotation, you have been assigned to an outpatient clinic. At the clinic, you are asked to conduct a head-to-toe physical assessment on several clients.

    a. The first client is an 82-year-old woman with severe rheumatoid arthritis. What considerations should you keep in mind while conducting this examination?

    ____

    ____

    ____

    ____

    ____

    ____

    ____

    b. The second client you have been asked to examine is a three-year-old boy with complaints of sore throat, earache, and fever. How should you alter the examination with this client?

    ____

    ____

    ____

    ____

    ____

    ____

    ____

CHAPTER 28

Medications

This chapter introduces you to the safe administration of medications. You will learn the variety of routes for drug administration as well as the skills required to administer drugs through these routes. Client safety and bloodborne pathogen precautions are emphasized.

KEY TOPICS

This study guide chapter reinforces the following topics discussed in the textbook chapter:

- medication administration
- legal aspects of administering drugs
- routes of drug administration
- injection sites
- safety

Matching

Match the following pharmacology terms to their definitions:

a.	anaphylactic reaction	e.	drug toxicity
b.	drug allergy	f.	idiosyncratic effect
c.	drug interaction	g.	side effect
d.	drug tolerance	h.	therapeutic effect

___ 1. a state of requiring increased dosage of a drug to maintain a given therapeutic effect

___ 2. a situation in which a drug given with another drug alters the effect of one or both drugs

___ 3. the desired effect of the drug or the reason the drug is prescribed

___ 4. an immunological reaction to a drug

___ 5. a severe allergic reaction that usually occurs immediately after the administration of the drug

___ 6. a secondary effect or one that is unintended

___ 7. an unexpected and individual response

___ 8. a condition that may result from an overdose, ingestion of a drug intended for external use, or a cumulative effect

Match the following pharmacology terms with their descriptions:

a. absorption
b. agonist
c. biotransformation
d. excretion
e. half-life
f. metabolites
g. peak plasma level

___ 9. a process by which a drug is converted to a less active form

___ 10. the point at which elimination rate equals the rate of absorption

___ 11. the process by which metabolites and drugs are eliminated from the body

___ 12. a drug that interacts with a receptor to produce a response

___ 13. the end-product of biotransformation; may be active or inactive

___ 14. the time required to reduce the concentration of a drug in the body by one-half

___ 15. the process by which a drug passes into the bloodstream

Multiple Choice

Circle the correct response for each question.

16. One drug can have many different names. The brand name of a drug is the name:
    a. listed in official publications, such as the British Pharmacopeia.
    b. used before a drug becomes official.
    c. by which the chemist knows it.
    d. given by the drug manufacturer.

17. A nurse is caring for a 61-year-old client. The client returned from surgery six hours ago after undergoing a bowel resection and removal of a tumour. The physician has ordered morphine 100 mg q1h IV. The nurse recognizes that this order is potentially lethal as written. If the nurse administers this medication as prescribed, who would be responsible for the error?
    a. the physician
    b. the nurse manager
    c. the nurse
    d. the hospital pharmacist

18. Which of the following statements about controlled substances is true?
    a. Controlled substances are kept in a location monitored by surveillance cameras.
    b. Any discrepancy in the controlled substance count must be reported immediately.
    c. Use of controlled substances and any waste must be recorded at the conclusion of each shift.
    d. Computer-controlled dispensing systems have completely eliminated the need to count and document controlled substances.

19. Your client drinks 12 beers per day. His wife is concerned about his daily beer intake and fears he is becoming an alcoholic. She suggests that he stop drinking. After 24 hours without a beer, he says he is "craving" a beer. He elaborately describes the way an imagined glass of beer looks and tastes. To get his mind off beer, he takes a long walk. His cravings demonstrate:
    a. drug misuse.
    b. physiological dependence.
    c. psychological dependence.
    d. alcohol withdrawal.

20. Which route of medication administration is the most common, least expensive, and most convenient?
    a. buccal
    b. oral
    c. parenteral
    d. sublingual

21. You have received an order to administer a drug via the sublingual route. To correctly give this medication you would:
    a. place the drug under the client's tongue and allow it to dissolve.
    b. instill the drug into the client's urinary bladder via a Foley catheter.
    c. apply the drug directly on the client's skin in the affected area.
    d. infuse the drug via a catheter into the client's bone.

22. The physician orders Ancef (cephalosporin) 1 g q12h IV This is an example of a:
    a. prn order.
    b. single order.
    c. stat order.
    d. standing order.

23. The physician orders Valium (diazepam) 2 mg IV stat. The medication should be given:
    a. immediately and only once.
    b. once and at a specified time.
    c. on an indefinite basis.
    d. when the nurse determines the medication is needed.

24. Your client is a young male, 160 cm tall, and 70 kg in weight. You will be administering a subcutaneous injection. Which of the following is the appropriate needle for his body size?
    a. #18 gauge, 5/8 in length
    b. #25 gauge, 5/8 in length
    c. #22 gauge, 1.5 in length
    d. #22 gauge, 3/8 inch length

25. Your client has insulin-dependent diabetes. He states that he uses a #28 gauge needle and only uses his abdomen for insulin administration. He shows you how he pinches a skinfold in his abdomen and administers the injection at a 45° angle. What health teaching does this client need relative to insulin administration?
   a. Instruct the client to use a smaller gauge needle and inject at 90°.
   b. Instruct the client on the necessity of rotating injection sites. He needs to use the lateral upper arms and anterior and lateral thighs for injection sites, too.
   c. Praise the excellent technique currently used by the client. Assess whether he has other teaching needs.
   d. Instruct the client to avoid creating a skinfold prior to injection.

26. You are preparing to give your client an intramuscular injection and have selected the right dorsogluteal site. As you turn the client over to expose the site, you note that multiple injections have been previously given in this site and that a portion of the area is erythematous. What should you do?
   a. Give the medication at this site.
   b. Give the medication at this site but avoid the erythematous area.
   c. Hold the medication.
   d. Select another site for administration.

27. You will be administering an immunization via intramuscular route to a five-month-old infant. Which of the following is the most appropriate injection site?
   a. deltoid
   b. dorsogluteal
   c. rectus femoris
   d. vastus lateralis

28. You are administering an immunization via intramuscular route to a 35-year-old adult. Which of the following is the most appropriate injection site?
   a. deltoid
   b. dorsogluteal
   c. rectus femoris
   d. ventrogluteal

29. Oxycodone, a controlled substance, is ordered for your client. You will find this medication in the:
   a. client's medication drawer.
   b. locked cabinet.
   c. ward stock cupboard.
   d. refrigerator.

30. Intravenous administration of medication is most appropriate in which of the following circumstances?

  a. for standard administration of cardiac medications
  b. when a rapid effect is desired
  c. for pain relief
  d. when the client has multiple skin lesions

31. Sterile technique is indicated for administration of medications in which of the following routes?

  a. ophthalmic and otic, if the tympanic membrane is damaged
  b. otic
  c. nasal
  d. vaginal

True or False

Read the following statements to determine if they are true or false. If a statement is false, alter the statement to make it true.

32. In an intradermal injection, the syringe is held at a 60° angle to the skin with the bevel of the needle upward.
True False

____

____

33. The speed of absorption of a drug given by intramuscular injection is slower than injection via the subcutaneous route.
True False

____

____

34. Usually, a larger volume of medication can safely be injected into muscle tissue than into subcutaneous tissue.
True False

____

____

35. An IV lock may be used for clients who require IV medications but not the fluid volume of an intravenous infusion.
True False

____

____

36. Percutaneous absorption of a medication is not altered by lacerations, burns, or other skin irritations.
True False

____

____

37. A metered dose inhaler is often used to administer medications to clients with respiratory disorders.
True False

____

____

Completion

38. Identify the factors that influence medication action.

____

____

____

39. Identify the seven essential aspects of a drug order.

____

____

____

____

____

____

____

40. Complete the following equivalency problems.

a.	3 g	= ___________	mg
b.	198 lbs	= ___________	kg
c.	500 mcg	= ___________	mg
d.	1.5 L	= ___________	mL
e.	30 minims	= ___________	mL

41. The physician has ordered tetracycline 500 mg po q6h x 10 days. You have tetracycline 250 mg tablets on hand. How many would you give?

42. Demerol 35 mg IM stat is ordered. You have on hand prefilled syringes that contain 50 mg of Demerol in 1 mL. You would give:

43. List at least three nursing actions to avoid puncture injuries.

____

____

____

44. Mark the appropriate area for subcutaneous parenteral administration on the diagram.

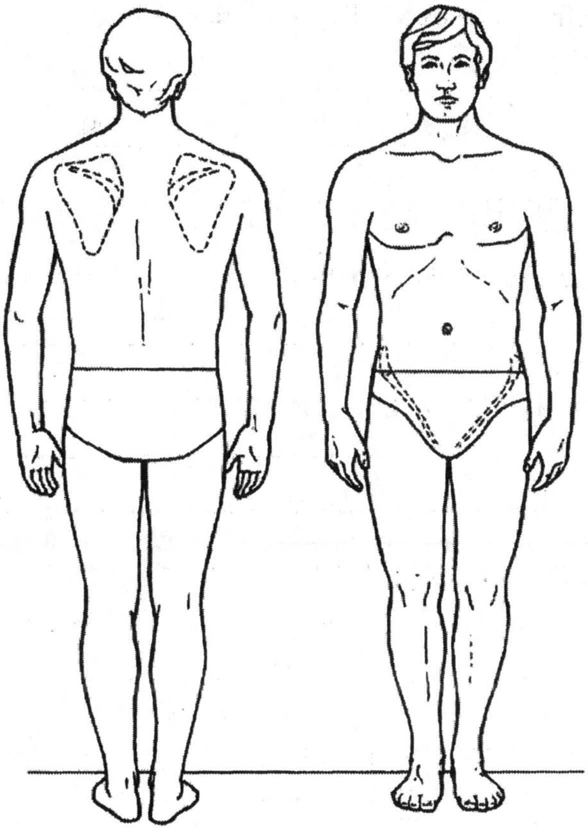

Case Study

You will be administering digoxin 0.5 mg po to Rose Banda, an awake and alert client.

45. To safely administer the medication, you must follow the five rights. The five rights are:

____

____

____

____

____

____

46. Describe your process for administering the medication.

____

____

____

____

____

Rose is complaining of severe nausea. The physician has ordered Gravol (dimenhydrinate) 50 mg IM q4h PRN. In the ward stock drawer there is an ampule marked "Gravol (dimenhydrinate) 50 mg/mL, 2 mL."

47. Calculate the volume of medication you will administer.

____

48. How will you draw up the medication from the ampule?

____

____

____

49. What are the potential sites for administration?

____

____

After her nausea subsides, Rose is examined by the nurse practitioner. Additional medications are ordered as follows:

Pilocarpine 1% i gtt OS q6h

D-5-W @ 75 mL/hr

Strict NPO

50. Describe how you will instill the pilocarpine as ordered.

____

____

51. After the IV infusion has been established, how can additional medications be given through the IV route?

____

____

CHAPTER 29

Teaching

This chapter discusses the importance of teaching and learning in the delivery of health care. You will begin by assessing learning needs. Practical tips are offered on how to facilitate learning and avoid barriers to the teaching/learning process. You will also learn to develop a teaching plan and evaluate the effectiveness of your teaching.

KEY TOPICS

This study guide chapter reinforces the following topics discussed in the textbook chapter:

- learning theories
- factors that facilitate learning
- factors that interfere with learning
- effective teaching
- teaching plans
- teaching strategies

Matching

Match the following terms with the appropriate definitions:

a. andragogy
b. compliance
c. learning
d. pedagogy
e. teaching

___ 1. the art and science of helping children learn

___ 2. a change in human disposition or capability that persists over a period of time and that cannot be solely accounted for by growth

___ 3. a system of activities intended to produce learning

___ 4. the art and science of teaching adults

___ 5. an individual's desire to learn and to act on the learning

Evaluate whether the following teaching strategies are effective. Place an E in front of those items that are effective teaching techniques. Place an I in front of those items that are ineffective teaching strategies.

___ 6. Nancy Gonzales, senior nursing student, decides that her client would benefit from information on weight loss.

___ 7. Jim Richards, clinical nurse specialist, introduces himself to the client and his family and gets to know them prior to commencing cardiac rehabilitation teaching.

___ 8. Christine Gann, RN, allocates a minimum of 15 minutes at the end of her teaching session for questions on low-sodium foods.

___ 9. Nadia Bige, RN, conducts a sibling preparation class. She begins her class by determining the age range of the participants and their experiences with other children. She modifies the class each time she teaches it in order to be responsive to her audience.

Multiple Choice

Circle the correct response for each question.

10. Nurses use tenets from behaviourism, cognitivism, and humanism in nursing and client education. Identify the theoretical construct that is best exemplified in the following example: On her first clinical day in the nursing program, a student nurse is assigned to accompany and observe an experienced nurse on a medical unit.
    a. andragogy
    b. behaviourism
    c. cognitivism
    d. humanism

11. The nurse is caring for a client who will be discharged from the hospital with a wound that requires dressing changes. The nurse plans a teaching session with the client. She will teach the client how, why, and when to change the dressing and what signs to report to the physician. What aspect of learning has the nurse omitted?
    a. affective domain
    b. cognitive domain
    c. humanist domain
    d. psychomotor domain

12. Your six-year-old client was recently diagnosed with asthma. He tells you he wants to breathe better so he can play with his friends. He lives in a supportive family environment. His parents have requested a conference to discuss his medications, treatment plan, and coordination with the child's school. They state they are willing and able to provide any care to facilitate their son's treatment. Which element in the nursing history provides the greatest clues to the client's learning needs?
    a. age and developmental level
    b. client's understanding of current health status
    c. culture and lifestyle data
    d. learning style

13. Your client has been newly diagnosed with hypertension. He speaks limited English, but a professional interpreter is available with advance notice. You attempt to communicate with him independently through nonverbal communication and the use of a teenage family member who is bilingual. Select an appropriate nursing diagnosis.
    a. health-seeking behaviour: hypertension

b. noncompliance related to language barrier as evidenced by limited verbal interchange between nurse and client
c. knowledge deficit: hypertension management related to new diagnosis
d. risk for knowledge deficit

14. Which of the following learning objectives is correctly written?
    a. By the end of the cardiac rehab teaching class, the client will understand the importance of taking his prescribed medications.
    b. The client will increase physical activity after the exercise training class.
    c. By the end of the week, the client will recognize which foods to avoid on a low-fat diet.
    d. Before discharge, the client will be able to demonstrate the correct technique for measuring blood glucose using the Accu-check monitor.

15. The optimum time for a nurse to schedule a teaching session is:
    a. in the morning after the client has had a full night of sleep.
    b. in the evening when the client is resting.
    c. when the client indicates interest in learning.
    d. when other family members are present.

16. Learning may be enhanced by allowing the client to manipulate equipment she or he will be asked to use at home. Which of the following represents the best approach for facilitating a learning environment?
    a. Allow the client to remain in bed. Whenever possible, use videos to demonstrate skills prior to direct hands-on manipulation.
    b. Provide an overview of the entire teaching plan. After the overview, ask the client to identify the key points.
    c. If possible, get the client out of bed. Utilize teaching aids or equipment that the client will actually use.
    d. Assist the client out of bed before all teaching sessions. Encourage the client to take notes during the teaching session.

17. The use of special teaching strategies, such as computer-assisted instruction or group teaching, is always:
    a. based on the nurse's assessment of the client.
    b. appropriate.
    c. an economical way to provide client instruction.
    d. superior to one-on-one teaching.

18. When teaching a client of a different culture or ethnic background, the nurse should:
    a. avoid using slang or colloquialisms.
    b. use humour frequently to get through the awkwardness of the situation.
    c. recognize that the client understands when she is nodding.
    d. speak loudly and clearly so the client can lip read.

True or False

Read the following statements to determine if they are true or false. If a statement is false, alter the statement to make it true.

19. Motivation may be enhanced by offering positive reinforcement for what the client has already learned.
True False

____

____

20. Motivation can be enhanced by letting the client see the end product. The whole skill or task should be taught at once, rather than breaking it down into small parts.
True False

____

____

____

21. When implementing client teaching, you should always address any areas that are causing anxiety at the end of the teaching session.
True False

____

____

22. Before you begin teaching a client with diabetes about his revised insulin schedule, you should assess his existing knowledge.
True False

____

____

23. Cognitive learning may be evaluated by observing the client carrying out a procedure or skill.
True False

____

____

24. It is more difficult to evaluate affective learning than cognitive or psychomotor learning.
True False

____

____

Completion

25. Obtain a pamphlet or client handout on a health topic by visiting your library or a health agency. What is the readability of the material? Which population is this material best suited for?

____
____
____
____
____
____
____

26. You are planning a teaching session with your client on safer sex. What five characteristics should the information you present have?

____
____
____
____
____
____
____

27. Documentation of the teaching process is essential. The elements that must be documented are:

____
____
____
____
____
____
____

28. Sarah Scott will be caring for her elderly mother upon her mothers' discharge from the hospital. Her mother has had a cerebrovascular accident (stroke). Physical therapy and occupational therapy will be provided in the home. Sarah will need to learn how to bathe her mother in bed. Devise a teaching plan for providing a bed bath. Include sample documentation of your teaching.

____
____
____
____

Case Study

29. Elsa Kolinas is a client newly diagnosed with diabetes. As part of her orientation to diabetes management you will be teaching Elsa how to administer her own insulin.

    a. Identify at least five ways in which you can facilitate Elsa's learning.

    b. Identify three factors that could inhibit Elsa's learning.

    c. Readiness is essential for learning. Identify what you must assess to determine Elsa's readiness to learn.

CHAPTER 30

Leading, Managing, and Influencing Change

This chapter focuses on leadership, management, change, and power. It explains the difference between leadership and management and exposes you to various styles of leadership. Creating change is the central theme of the chapter. While managers create a positive work environment using formal power, leaders may be vested with power or be informal leaders from the group. The chapter examines several change theories that leaders or managers may utilize. It discusses the importance of power and political influence as well as opportunities for political involvement.

KEY TOPICS

This study guide chapter reinforces the following topics discussed in the textbook chapter:

- leadership theory
- levels of management
- change theories
- effective leadership
- management skills and functions
- examples of change

Matching

Match the roles to the appropriate descriptions.

a. manager

b. leader

___ 1. appointed to a position in an organization that grants the individual the power to guide and direct the work of others

___ 2. interested in risk taking and exploring new ideas

___ 3. relates to people personally in an intuitive and empathetic manner

___ 4. relates to people according to their roles

___ 5. carries out policies, rules, and regulations

Match the following management terms with the appropriate definitions:

a. accountability
b. authority
c. delegation
d. effectiveness
e. efficiency
f. productivity

___ 6. a performance measure of effectiveness and efficiency

___ 7. the ability and willingness to assume responsibility for one's actions and accept the consequences of one's behaviour

___ 8. a measure of the quality or quantity of services provided

___ 9. the assigning of responsibility and authority to another person or group of people

___ 10. official power given by an organization to an individual to direct the work of others

___ 11. a measure of the resources used in the provision of services

Multiple Choice

Circle the correct response for each question.

12. A staff nurse on the labour and delivery unit is extremely interested in reorganizing the unit to improve client and nurse satisfaction. The nurse has attended numerous conferences and has several possible solutions for improving client care. She is very excited about the possibilities for positive change and has shared her excitement with her peers. She has approached the nurse manager and the informal leader on the unit with her ideas. What aspect of effective leadership does the staff nurse possess?

    a. expert power
    b. influence
    c. legitimate power
    d. vision

13. The charge nurse on Unit 2 is responsible for making nursing assignments for the shift, assisting with the delivery of client care on the shift, and requesting adequate staffing for the next shift. What is the charge nurse's level of management responsibility?

    a. first-level manager
    b. middle-level manager
    c. upper-level manager
    d. nurse executive

14. A nurse working in a newly established outpatient wound centre has been designated as the liaison between the centre's clients and their private physicians. No prior work has been done in this area. What management functions will she need to utilize?

    a. planning and organizing
    b. vision, power, and influence
    c. controlling, directing, organizing, and planning
    d. assignment and delegation

15. Which of the following statements most accurately depicts the differences between leaders and managers?
    a. Managers lead through charisma and influence. They provide vision for an organization. Leaders may exist within nonmanagerial positions and usually encourage the group to follow.
    b. Leaders often possess vision, power, and influence but may not have authority, accountability, or responsibility. Managers, by virtue of their appointed positions, have authority, accountability, and responsibility.
    c. Leaders are never managers, but managers may be leaders.
    d. Managers utilize authority to accomplish the work of an institution. Leaders utilize influence to accomplish the work of an institution.

16. Managing resources is an important aspect of the management role. Which of the following choices most accurately reflects resource management?
    a. Nurse managers are responsible for human resource management as well as financial and material management of their designated areas.
    b. Nurse managers must develop and administer a budget that is principally focused on personnel.
    c. Nurse managers must work in conjunction with financial officers to develop and administer financial resources. Education for the management role is insufficient to conduct these tasks independently.
    d. Nurse managers are responsible for networking and delegating resource management to the appropriate personnel.

17. Change, an integral part of nursing, is often spearheaded by change agents. A change agent:
    a. is a manager.
    b. initiates, motivates, and implements change.
    c. is always formally designated.
    d. is always an informal leader.

18. Nurse A believes that all of her staff should participate in unit management. She encourages her staff to speak up and be part of the decision-making process that will make the unit superb. What is Nurse A's leadership style?
    a. autocratic
    b. charismatic
    c. democratic
    d. laissez faire

19. Nurse B runs a "tight ship." She writes the rules and ensures that they are enforced. Nurse B believes that she must be part of every aspect of the unit in order to make the unit work. What is Nurse B's leadership style?
    a. autocratic
    b. democratic
    c. laissez faire
    d. situational

20. Nurse C believes that all her staff nurses are intelligent and mature professionals. She believes her role on the unit is to function as a resource. She trusts that her staff will consult her when they need her. What is Nurse C's leadership style?
    a. democratic
    b. laissez faire
    c. situational
    d. transformational

21. Nurse D is the President of the Canadian Nurses Association. Using her position, she encourages legislators to see the value of expanding the nursing role. She meets with the Minister of Health to present a clear plan for delivery of primary care to all citizens of Canada by expanding the role of the RN. She encourages the membership of the CNA to write letters to the Members of Parliament and the Prime Minister in support of this legislation. She actively involves the provincial and territorial nursing associations in the change process. What is Nurse D's leadership style?
    a. democratic
    b. laissez faire
    c. situational
    d. transformational

22. Nurse E believes a leader should be flexible and adaptive depending on the personnel involved, the situation, and the importance of the outcome. At staff meetings he encourages the staff to speak up and participate, but at management meetings he is very directive about the needs of his staff and unit. What is Nurse E's leadership style?
    a. democratic
    b. laissez faire
    c. situational
    d. transformational

True or False

Read the following statements to determine if they are true or false. If a statement is false, alter the statement to make it true.

23. Scott Fortier is an informal leader on his nursing unit. He acquired the role through appointment.
    True False

    ____

    ____

24. Change associated with significant personal cost may be resisted.
    True False

    ____

25. Unplanned change requires problem-solving, decision-making, and interpersonal skills. Drift and natural change are examples of this type of change.
True False

Completion

26. Former American president John F. Kennedy inspired strong feelings of loyalty and enthusiasm. His presence triggered a reaction in most people he encountered. What type of leader was he?

27. What is your leadership style?

28. Identify your own mentor. How has this person been instrumental in your professional development?

29. Discuss the similarities and differences in the planned change theories of Lewin, Lippitt, Havelock, and Rogers.

30. As the nurse manager of a surgical unit, you would like to introduce a new wound-care protocol. Your staff say they are too busy to attend an inservice, and the physicians question why change is necessary. List at least three strategies that will improve your chances of success with this change.

Case Study

31. In Unit A of a long-term care hospital, client care is currently provided by RNs, LPNs, and Nurse's Aides. Due to decreased provincial funding, the Manager has been directed to cut personnel costs. She is considering increased use of Nurse's Aides to deliver client care. Her proposal is to decrease RN positions by 10 percent and LPN positions by 25 percent and to increase Nurse's Aide use by 25 percent. The RNs and LPNs on the unit are extremely unhappy about the recent changes; however, the Nurse's Aides are happy with the changes and believe they are adequately prepared to take on more client-care activities.

    a. As the manager of the unit, how would you handle this conflict?

    ____

    ____

    ____

    ____

    ____

    b. Identify the motivating and restraining forces for RNs, LPNs, Nurse's Aides, and the Manager.

    ____

    ____

    ____

    ____

    ____

CHAPTER 31

Vital Signs

This chapter explores the importance of vital signs and the techniques for evaluating these cardinal signs. In this chapter, you examine the factors that affect all of the vital signs and examine common errors in their measurement.

KEY TOPICS

This study guide chapter reinforces the following topics discussed in the textbook chapter:

- temperature
- respirations
- factors that affect the vital signs
- pulse
- blood pressure

Matching

Match the following vital sign terms to their definitions:

a.	basal metabolic rate	h.	pulse pressure
b.	cardiac output	i.	pyrexia
c.	core temperature	j.	systolic pressure
d.	diastolic pressure	k.	surface temperature
e.	external respiration	l.	ventilation
f.	internal respiration	m.	viscosity
g.	pulse deficit		

___ 1. body temperature above the usual range

___ 2. the movement of air in and out of the lungs

___ 3. the physical property that results from friction of molecules in a fluid

___ 4. the difference between the diastolic and systolic pressures

___ 5. the temperature of deep tissues of the body, such as the abdominal or pelvic cavity

___ 6. any difference between the apical and radial pulses

___ 7. the interchange of carbon dioxide and oxygen between the circulating blood and the cells of the body

___ 8. the temperature of the skin, the subcutaneous tissue, and fat

___ 9. the pressure within the ventricles at rest

___ 10. an equivalent to stroke volume multiplied by heart rate (SV X HR)

___ 11. the interchange of oxygen and carbon dioxide between the alveoli and pulmonary blood

___ 12. the pressure generated within the circulatory system by the contraction of the ventricles

___ 13. the rate of energy utilization in the body required to maintain essential activities

Multiple Choice

Circle the correct response for each question.

14. When a client is inadequately covered, heat is lost through:
    a. conduction.
    b. convection.
    c. radiation.
    d. vaporization.

15. If a febrile client is placed in a cool bath in order to decrease body temperature, the heat loss is a result of:
    a. conduction.
    b. convection.
    c. radiation.
    d. vaporization.

16. Insensible heat loss accounts for about 10 percent of basal heat loss. Insensible heat loss is accompanied by insensible water loss. This water loss is a result of
    a. conduction.
    b. convection.
    c. radiation.
    d. vaporization.

17. In everyday circumstances, a small amount of heat is always lost through:
    a. conduction.
    b. convection.
    c. radiation.
    d. vaporization.

18. Which of the following key factors that affects body temperature may be manipulated by the nurse?
    a. age
    b. circadian rhythms
    c. environmental conditions
    d. hormones and gender

19. Your client's temperature is 38.5 C. What is her temperature on the Fahrenheit scale?

    a. 98.7F
    b. 101.3F
    c. 102.5F
    d. 126.9F

20. Which of the following temperature readings is considered to be most accurate?

    a. axillary
    b. oral
    c. rectal
    d. tympanic

21. Pulse rate is affected by:

    a. amount of time since the last meal.
    b. degree of involvement in health care.
    c. developmental level.
    d. stress.

22. Pulse is measured by applying moderate pressure with the three middle fingers of the hand over the pulse point. How long must the pulse be counted if the client has an irregular pulse?

    a. 15 seconds and multiply by 4
    b. 30 seconds and multiply by 2
    c. one full minute
    d. two full minutes and divide by 2

23. When assessing respirations, the nurse should evaluate:

    a. respiratory rate, rhythmic character, and depth.
    b. respiratory rate and volume.
    c. respiratory effort, rate, and sound.
    d. respiratory rate.

24. To properly evaluate blood pressure, the cuff must be the correct size for the client. The correct size cuff is __________ the width of the arm circumference.

    a. 30 percent
    b. 40 percent
    c. 50 percent
    d. 75 percent

25. When taking a blood pressure, the nurse identifies five phases in the Korotkoff's sounds. Systolic blood pressure is measured at:
    a. the beginning of Phase 1.
    b. the end of Phase 1.
    c. the beginning of Phase 2.
    d. the end of Phase 4.

26. Your client's vital signs are BP 80/50, P 112, RR 26, T 39.6C oral. Your client is:
    a. hypotensive, bradycardic, tachypneic, and hypothermic.
    b. hypertensive, tachycardic, eupneic, and febrile.
    c. hypotensive, tachycardic, tachypneic, and febrile.
    d. hypotensive, bradycardic, bradypneic, and afebrile.

27. Your client's vital signs are BP 130/78, P 84, RR 18, T 36.8C oral. Your client is:
    a. hypertensive, tachycardic, eupneic, and afebrile.
    b. hypotensive, bradycardic, tachypneic, and hypothermic.
    c. hypotensive, tachycardic, tachypneic, and febrile.
    d. within normal range for all vital signs.

True or False

Read the following statements to determine if they are true or false. If a statement is false, alter the statement to make it true.

28. The young and the old are most sensitive to environmental temperature fluctuations.
    True False

    ____

    ____

29. Nursing goals for the client with a fever are designed to determine the etiology of the fever.
    True False

    ____

    ____

30. For an accurate oral temperature measurement, the thermometer should be left in place for 10 minutes.
    True False

    ____

    ____

31. For an accurate rectal temperature measurement, the thermometer should be left in place for 10 minutes.
True False

32. The apical pulse should be used to evaluate the pulse in newborns, infants, and children up to two to three years old; any time it is difficult to evaluate a peripheral pulse; and when the peripheral pulse is irregular.
True False

33. Normally, the apical pulse rate is greater than the radial pulse rate.
True False

34. Arterial blood pressure is a result of interaction between the pumping action of the heart, peripheral vascular resistance, blood volume, and viscosity.
True False

Completion

35. Identify the five most important factors that affect heat production.

36. At 8 AM, you note that your client's temperature is 35.0C. What questions should you consider to determine if this reading is accurate?

37. On the figure below, label the sites where a pulse is commonly taken.

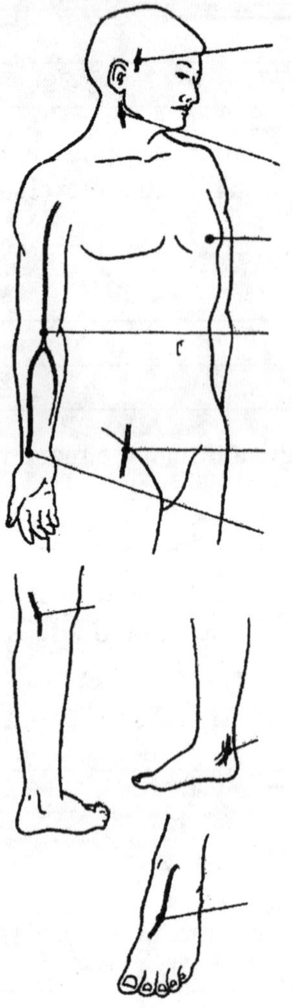

38. Identify the nine factors that significantly affect blood pressure.

Case Study

39. Susan Santos, a 15-year-old high-school student, reports to the Urgent Care Clinic with complaints of fever, chills, and fatigue. Her vital signs upon admission are: BP 120/70, P 116, RR 20, T (oral) 39.0C. She is examined by the nurse practitioner (NP). The NP orders blood and urine lab work.

    a. Evaluate Susan's vital signs.

    b. During her stay at the Urgent Care Clinic, how often should Susan's vital signs be assessed?

    c. Identify at least three independent nursing interventions for Susan's fever.

    d. Identify the data that should be evaluated when assessing Susan's pulse.

CHAPTER 32

Asepsis

This chapter discusses your role in the control of infection. It highlights natural defences that protect the body against infection and presents potential risk factors for development of infection. It emphasizes nursing interventions to protect clients and staff from transmission of microorganisms.

KEY TOPICS

This study guide chapter reinforces the following topics discussed in the textbook chapter:

- anatomical and physiological barriers to microorganisms
- active immunity
- passive immunity
- chain of infection
- measures that break each link in the chain of infection
- infection risk
- nosocomial infections
- medical and surgical asepsis
- infection risk reduction
- isolation precaution systems
- bloodborne pathogens
- evaluation of protective measures

Matching

Match the following key terms to the appropriate definitions:

a.	asepsis	e.	infection
b.	communicable disease	f.	normal flora
c.	disease	g.	opportunistic pathogen
d.	etiological agent	h.	virulence

___ 1. This is the microorganism responsible for producing a disease.

___ 2. This is the ability of a microorganism to produce disease.

___ 3. This type of microorganism causes disease only in a susceptible individual.

___ 4. This term describes an invasion and proliferation of microorganisms in body tissue.

___ 5. This infectious agent can be transmitted to an individual by direct or indirect contact, through a vector or vehicle, or as an airborne infection.

___ 6. This is a detectable alteration in normal tissue function.

___ 7. This term describes the collective vegetation in a given area of the body that can cause infection in another part of the body.

___ 8. This term refers to freedom from disease-causing materials.

Match the following immune system terms with their descriptions:

a active immunity
b. antibody
c. antigen
d. cellular immunity
e. humoral immunity
f. immunity
g. passive immunity
h. primary immune response
i. secondary immune response

___ 9. This first interaction between an antigen and an antibody is characterized by a latent period before the appearance of the antibody and development of memory cells capable of responding to the antigen in the future.

___ 10. This is also known as immunoglobulin; it is part of the body's plasma proteins.

___ 11. The host produces its own antibodies in response to antigens.

___ 12. This term refers to resistance of the body to infection.

___ 13. This occurs after an initial immune response. B cells proliferate and rapidly differentiate into plasma cells to produce large quantities of antibody.

___ 14. This antibody-mediated defence resides in antibodies produced by B cells.

___ 15. The host receives natural or artificial antibodies produced by another source.

___ 16. These are foreign proteins in the body.

___ 17. This is mediated through the T-cell system and lost with HIV infection.

Multiple Choice

Circle the correct response for each question.

18. Which of the following statements about surgical asepsis is true?
    a. In surgical asepsis, the goal is to reduce the number of potentially infective agents.
    b. In surgical asepsis, items are sterile, clean, or dirty.
    c. Surgical asepsis keeps an area free of all microorganisms.
    d. Surgical asepsis is the state of infection that requires surgery for eradication of microbes.

19. Infection is a serious health hazard. Microorganisms responsible for infections include:
    a. bacteria, fungi, parasites, and viruses.
    b. bacteria, flora, and opportunistic pathogens.
    c. communicable diseases.
    d. bacteria and viruses.

20. Your client has a small wound on his left hand. A culture of this wound is positive for skin flora and one pathogen. He has no fever. You would be correct to describe this wound as:
    a. colonized.
    b. locally infected.
    c. systemically infected.
    d. free of infection.

21. Your client has a fever, localized pain, and purulent drainage from a wound. Your client is in which stage of the infectious process?
    a. incubation period
    b. prodromal period
    c. illness period
    d. convalescent period

22. Your client has been exposed to chickenpox but does not display any signs or symptoms. Your client is in which stage of the infectious process?
    a. incubation period
    b. prodromal period
    c. illness period
    d. convalescent period

23. The body has several anatomical and physiological defences against infection. All of the following items are nonspecific body defences, except:
    a. acid pH in GI tract and vagina.
    b. antibodies.
    c. cilia in the nasal passages.
    d. intact skin and mucous membranes.

24. You are asked to examine a leg wound. The client is unable to provide information about the wound. You note that it is reddened with clearly defined margins. A serosanguineous exudate is oozing from the site. On the basis of this information, you conclude that the:
    a. injury occurred only moments ago.
    b. injury is relatively new as evidenced by the hyperemia.
    c. wound is in the reparative phase of healing.
    d. exudate contains fluid from blood vessels and dead phagocytic and tissue cells.

25. Numerous factors have been identified that affect a person's resistance to infection. Which of these factors may be altered by the nurse?
    a. All of the factors may be manipulated through independent or collaborative nursing functions.
    b. None of the factors may be altered.

c. Stress levels, nutritional and immunization status, and some medical therapies may be adjusted by the nurse in collaboration with the physician.

d. Medical therapy and pre-existing disease processes may only be affected by the physician.

26. Your client is a preschool teacher. She complains that since she started working with small children she has had numerous colds and infections. She reports that she showers twice daily and washes her hands frequently while at work. She eats a balanced diet, drinks plenty of water, and gets seven to eight hours of sleep per night. What other strategies might you recommend to your client to decrease her risk for infections?

   a. She is adequately supporting her own defences. There are no other recommendations.

   b. Encourage her to maintain her current healthy habits. You may also wish to discuss her level of stress and strategies to reduce stress.

   c. Since she is still experiencing frequent colds and infections, you might recommend additional vitamins and sleep to decrease her risk.

   d. You might suggest additional immunizations for her.

27. Antiseptics break the chain of infection by:

   a. destroying all pathogens.

   b. destroying all pathogens except spores.

   c. inhibiting the growth of some microorganisms.

   d. cleaning visible stores of microorganisms.

28. Disinfectants break the chain of infection by:

   a. destroying all pathogens.

   b. destroying all pathogens except spores.

   c. inhibiting the growth of some microorganisms.

   d. cleaning visible stores of microorganisms.

29. Common sterilization methods are:

   a. moist heat, antibiotics, radiation, and high-dose disinfectants.

   b. boiling water, antiseptics, gas, and dry heat.

   c. antibiotics, antiseptics, antifungals, and antivirals.

   d. steam heat, gas, boiling water, and radiation.

30. Which of the following clients is at highest risk for infection?

   a. a 14-year-old girl

   b. an 86-year-old nursing home resident

   c. a 35-year-old runner

   d. a 40-year-old client undergoing dental care

31. You are caring for a toddler who is not toilet trained. The child is experiencing frequent episodes of vomiting and diarrhea. Identify the appropriate precautions you should utilize when changing the diaper of this child.
   a. No protective gear is required, as there is no documentation of infection by culture.
   b. Gloves only should be worn.
   c. Gloves and gown should be worn.
   d. Gloves should be worn and a gown, too, if it appears that your uniform might be soiled. The diaper should be discarded in a sturdy bag for disposal.
   e. Gloves should be worn and a gown, too, if it appears that your uniform might be soiled. The diaper should be discarded in a sturdy bag for disposal. Any soiled linen should be minimally handled and disposed of in the appropriate container.

32. Which statement accurately reflects surgical asepsis?
   a. Clean gloves are used to change a wound dressing.
   b. A sterile field is created by use of a sterile drape. Clean materials are added to the sterile field.
   c. A sterile item that is out of direct sight of the nurse is considered unsterile.
   d. The nurse sets up the sterile field well in advance of the time it is required.

33. You will be performing a sterile dressing change of a wound. The wound requires irrigation and packing. You do not have a latex allergy. In this circumstance, you should wear:
   a. sterile latex gloves.
   b. sterile vinyl gloves.
   c. clean latex gloves.
   d. clean vinyl gloves.

True or False

Read each statement to determine if it is true or false. If the statement is false, alter the statement to make it true.

34. A nosocomial infection may be acquired through the hospital environment or hospital personnel, from other clients, by being immunocompromised, or through insufficient hand washing.
    True False

    ____

    ____

    ____

35. During the nursing history, the nurse should examine the client for signs of infection.
    True False

    ____

    ____

36. A fever accompanies both a localized infection and a systemic infection.
True False

37. Laboratory data used in the diagnosis of an infection include total WBC count, differential cell count, ESR, and cultures.
True False

38. *Asepsis* is the freedom from infection or infectious material. In medical asepsis, sterile technique is used, but in surgical asepsis, objects are referred to as clean or dirty.
True False

39. Clients who are placed in isolation may experience sensory overload, feelings of inferiority, or decreased self-esteem.
True False

Completion

40. Inflammation is a local and nonspecific defensive response to injury or infection. It destroys or dilutes the agent, prevents its spread, and promotes repair of damaged tissue. What are the five signs of inflammation?

41. Label the chain of infection, and identify at least one way to break the chain at each link.

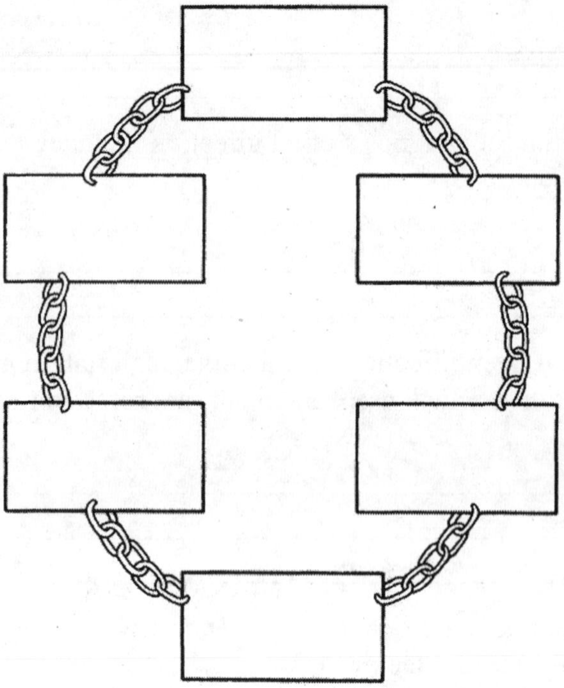

42. Complete the following table of laboratory data by filling in the blanks.

Type of WBC	***Normal Range as a Percentage of Total WBC***
Neutrophils	________
________	20% to 40%
Monocytes	________
Eosinophils	________
________	0.5% to 1%
Total WBC	100% or 4500 to 11,000/cu mm

43. Reggie is admitted to the hospital for initiation of treatment for pulmonary tuberculosis. What type of isolation precaution is appropriate for Reggie?

44. Marsha is admitted to the hospital from the emergency department with a closed head injury as a result of a motor vehicle accident. What type of isolation precaution is appropriate for Marsha?

45. Initiation of precautions to prevent the transmission of microorganisms is generally a nursing responsibility. You must assess the client to determine if any special precautions must be taken. What actions must you take in all client situations?

46. You are asked to speak at a neighbourhood preschool about reducing the risk of infection among the students. The preschool staff will attend along with the parents of the children. What instruction would you offer?

47. After administering an injection to an agitated client, you inadvertently stick yourself with the needle. What should you do?

Case Study

You are a staff nurse on a busy medical-surgical unit at a community hospital. You realize that nosocomial infections are associated with increased risk for morbidity and mortality among clients, higher health-care costs, and increased nursing time.

48. How can you decrease the risk of nosocomial infections when providing routine care?

49. How would you modify your efforts if there are clients with known multi-drug–resistant bacteria on your unit?

You are caring for a client with diarrhea who is incontinent of stool. This client also has a productive cough. On the basis of the client's history, you suspect that he may have pneumonia. You enter the room to bathe the client and change the linen. The client is too weak to get out of bed, and the linen is saturated with stool.

50. What protective garb should you wear?

51. What precautions should be taken with the dirty linen?

You receive an order to give Gravol (dimenhydrinate) to this client by intramuscular injection.

52. What precautions must you take when disposing of the needle after giving the injection?

After a seven-day hospital stay, the client is discharged home. He is no longer incontinent of stool, but your suspicion of pneumonia has been confirmed.

53. What process will you use to evaluate the client's ability to successfully manage his pneumonia at home?

CHAPTER 33

Safety

This chapter provides you with working knowledge of common hazards and factors that affect client safety. It highlights your role as a nurse in assessing hazards and developing interventions to promote safety for your clients.

KEY TOPICS

This study guide chapter reinforces the following topics discussed in the textbook chapter:

- safety assessment
- common hazards in the home
- strategies for preventing injury
- prevention of hazards

Matching

Match the following safety restraints to their definitions:

a. Geri chair
b. hand restraint
c. jacket or vest restraint
d. mummy restraint
e. safety strap

___ 1. used to prevent confused clients from using their hands or fingers to scratch themselves
___ 2. used to ensure the safety of confused or sedated clients in beds or wheelchairs
___ 3. used to ensure the safety of all clients who are being transported via stretcher or wheelchair
___ 4. used to restrain a child during a procedure
___ 5. an informal restraint used to confine client activity

Multiple Choice

Circle the correct response for each question.

6. Numerous factors affect peoples' ability to protect themselves. Some of these factors may be affected by the nurse. Which of the following sets of factors is most amenable to nursing intervention?
   a. development, lifestyle, and environmental factors
   b. mobility and heath status, age, and psychosocial state

c. lifestyle, safety awareness, and environmental factors
d. environmental factors, ability to communicate, and sensory state

7. Which of the following statements is true about environmental safety factors?
    a. A safe internal home environment is the most effective way to decrease safety hazards.
    b. When evaluating a client's hazard potential, it is important to evaluate conditions in the home, workplace, and community.
    c. Ensuring access to health care and health-care information are the most important safety-promoting activities.
    d. Hazard reduction can best be accomplished by legislative acts.

8. On the basis of your knowledge of common safety hazards for infants, which of the following is an appropriate intervention to improve infant safety?
    a. Teach parents about appropriate infant care.
    b. Teach parents to keep hot pots on back burners with handles turned inward.
    c. Teach parents about stranger danger.
    d. Teach parents to set a good example for the child to follow.

9. Preschoolers are extremely active and communicative. Their skills also are rapidly expanding; therefore, parents should be cautioned that preschoolers:
    a. need to be allowed to explore but may have more accidents as a result.
    b. are less susceptible to injury than infants and toddlers.
    c. usually think before they act; therefore, they should be given more freedom.
    d. need careful surveillance, and safety measures must keep pace with their new skills.

10. You are a nurse working for a large school district. You have been asked to present a safety program to high-school students. What important topics should be included in this talk?
    a. home safety, workplace safety, and hazards of drugs
    b. driver safety, safety in sports, avoidance of firearms and drugs
    c. safe use of medications, prevention of fires, and safe driving habits
    d. falls prevention and poison information

11. You work in a community clinic that serves a large population of teenagers and young adults. Several clinic clients have committed suicide since you began working at this site. What is your role in suicide prevention?
    a. identification of those at risk and referral to professional or crisis counselling
    b. referral of those at risk to the physician for medication and treatment
    c. direct confrontation with those deemed to be at risk
    d. identification of those at risk and referral back to the family support network

12. A client reports to the urgent care clinic with a burn related to use of a hot pack on his lower back. He has no underlying health problems. He states that the hot pack was in proper working order and that he used the protective cover that came with the pack. He followed the directions completely and propped the pack next to his back while lying on his side. What other questions must you ask to fully evaluate this burn?
    a. Who directed you to use a hot pack? Does your doctor know about your back pain?
    b. Did you place this underneath your back?
    c. How long was the pack in place? Were you also using any ointments or salves that produce heat?
    d. Do you have a history of diabetes or circulatory problems in your family?

13. Which two age groups are at greatest risk for falls?
    a. infants and toddlers
    b. toddlers and preschoolers
    c. adults and older adults
    d. infants and older adults

14. Which of the following are appropriate client teaching topics for poison prevention?
    a. Keep all toxic agents, such as bleach and medications, out of the reach of infants.
    b. Store toxic liquids in plain household containers so they are uninviting to young children.
    c. Thoroughly cook all unknown mushrooms or leaves to destroy potential toxins.
    d. Use syrup of ipecac immediately after a suspected poisoning.

15. Carbon monoxide is a serious health hazard. Why is this chemical so potentially dangerous?
    a. It is colourless, odourless, and pleasant tasting.
    b. There is no accurate way to detect its presence.
    c. It is produced by vehicles and common equipment used in and around the home.
    d. It is the most frequently used agent for committing suicide.

16. You are eating in the cafeteria when one of your classmates begins to choke. What action should you take?
    a. Allow her to clear her own airway. If unable, call for help.
    b. Assess that she is choking. Perform abdominal thrusts to dislodge the foreign object, and re-establish the airway.
    c. Perform rescue breathing once respirations have ceased.
    d. Call 911, and offer comfort.

17. Physiological effects that may be associated with excess noise include:
    a. increased heart rate and decreased respiratory rate.
    b. increased heart and respiratory rate.

c. muscle relaxation.
d. increased appetite.

18. Barry Essa is recovering from a major automobile accident. He is restless and agitated. Which of these nursing interventions should be your first?
    a. Assess the client's body size to determine the appropriate type and size of restraint.
    b. Call the physician to report his condition and ask for appropriate sedation.
    c. Assess the client to determine the etiology of the confusion and agitation.
    d. Apply the most restrictive device in order to provide the greatest protection.

19. Ensuring client safety is an ongoing goal of nursing care. Appropriate nursing interventions to prevent suffocation might include:
    a. educating adults not to leave young children unsupervised near water.
    b. teaching clients to avoid keeping paper bags at home.
    c. encouraging the use of baths instead of showers.
    d. encouraging clients of all ages to wear life jackets when swimming.

20. Which of the following factors must be evaluated when assessing a client's safety risk?
    a. age and developmental level
    b. time of day
    c. sensory enhancements
    d. family willingness to help with care while the client is hospitalized

True or False

Read the following statements to determine if they are true or false. If a statement is false, alter the statement to make it true.

21. Use of physical restraints requires a physician's order.
True False

____

22. The nurse is not relieved of responsibility for client safety if the family offers to watch the client.
True False

____

____

23. Restraints may be used to control noncompliant clients.
True False

____

Completion

24. Conduct an assessment of your own safety awareness and practices. What are your strengths? Which areas need improvement?

____

____

____

____

25. Now that you have completed your own safety awareness assessment, consider how you might use this tool in the clinical setting. Identify at least three ways you could incorporate this assessment into your nursing care.

____

____

____

____

26. Name at least three environmental factors that may be modified to improve client safety.

____

____

____

27. In the event of a fire, what four priorities should guide the nurse's behaviour?

____

____

____

____

28. List four alternatives to restraints.

____

____

____

29. Firearms in the home are a potential health hazard to all family members. Discuss with your family and classmates your experiences with firearms and your feelings about having them in the home.

____

____

____

30. List three approaches to ensure a safe workplace.

31. What are the most significant threats to safety in your home environment?

Case Study

Kylie Fallon is a 73-year-old widowed woman who lives alone. She has been admitted to the hospital for surgical repair of a fractured ankle. As the nurse assigned to her care, you will need to modify her environment to protect her against hazards.

32. List at least three nursing interventions that will help ensure Kylie's safety during her hospitalization.

33. Kylie has recovered well from her surgery but is experiencing pain and swelling on discharge. As the student nurse who has cared for her during her stay, you will continue to monitor her after discharge. You have arranged to make a home visit the next day. What assessments and interventions should you perform in order to ensure Kylie's safety?

34. Identify at least two ways to decrease Kylie's risk for falls.

CHAPTER 34

Hygiene

This chapter discusses the importance of hygiene in the maintenance of health. It provides information on common normal and abnormal findings while providing personal hygiene care. The chapter builds on assessment information presented in previous chapters. Client safety and the control of the transmission of microorganisms as you provide care are emphasized.

KEY TOPICS

This study guide chapter reinforces the following topics discussed in the textbook chapter

- hygienic care
- bathing
- bedmaking procedures
- personal hygiene

Matching

Match the following terms to the definitions:

a. apocrine glands
b. eccrine glands
c. fissures
d. gingivitis
e. hirsutism
f. scabies
g. sebum

___ 1. produce sweat that cools the body through evaporation
___ 2. red, swollen gums
___ 3. an oily substance secreted by the skin that softens hair and skin, lessens heat and water loss, and is bactericidal
___ 4. the growth of excessive body hair
___ 5. deep grooves that may occur in the skin due to drying and cracking
___ 6. a type of sweat gland located in the axillae and anogenital regions
___ 7. a contagious infestation characterized by burrows in the upper layers of the skin

Multiple Choice

Circle the correct response for each question.

8. Skin is considered the body's first line of defence because it:
   a. regulates body temperature.
   b. transmits sensations of pain.
   c. secretes sebum.
   d. protects underlying tissue from injury from many microorganisms.

9. A 27-year-old client who underwent an appendectomy for a ruptured appendix last evening is sweating profusely. Her temperature is 39.5C. She is unable to perform personal hygiene care due to her acute illness. The most appropriate nursing diagnosis for this client is:
   a. Knowledge Deficit related to lack of experience with febrile conditions.
   b. Risk for Impaired Skin Integrity due to inability to perform hygiene care.
   c. Self-Care Deficit: bathing/hygiene related to acute illness.
   d. Self-Esteem Disturbance related to acute illness.

10. What is the most important factor that should be considered when planning to assist a client with personal hygiene?
    a. client's age
    b. client's gender
    c. client's condition and preferences
    d. unit's unwritten policy that all baths should be given on day shift

11. You work in a small hospital in a rural area. It is not unusual for you to have clients of all ages in your unit. What important considerations must you keep in mind when bathing clients of all ages?
    a. Infants lose heat rapidly and must be dried and covered quickly.
    b. You should never use soap when bathing an elderly person.
    c. Clients are not usually embarrassed about personal care until they are in their teens.
    d. Teenagers must be bathed more frequently than children or adults.

12. A major role of the nurse in promoting oral health is to teach clients about oral hygiene. Which of the following statements about oral hygiene is accurate?
    a. Cleaning of temporary teeth is not required. Oral hygiene should be instituted once permanent teeth begin to erupt.
    b. Since deciduous teeth guide the entrance of permanent teeth, care of these teeth and the surrounding gums is essential.
    c. Flossing is essential for oral health once the wisdom teeth have emerged.
    d. To avoid tooth decay, sweet foods should be taken in combination with fibrous foods.

13. The appearance of the hair reflects a person's feelings of well-being and state of health. Which of the following solutions would improve hair care for clients who are debilitated and bedridden?
    a. mandating weekly hair care for each client
    b. employing a hair care professional to provide care two times per week
    c. improving the nurse's ability to cut and shape hair
    d. carefully assessing the client's physical condition prior to instituting care

14. Which of the following statements most accurately reflects appropriate technique for eye care?
    a. Allow secretions to dry before cleaning. This prevents the secretions from entering the eye.
    b. Loosen secretions with the use of baby oil on a cotton swab. Wipe the eye from outer to inner canthus.
    c. Order lubricating eye drops for all clients on bedrest.
    d. Soften secretions by applying cotton balls moistened with sterile saline or water. Wipe the eye from inner to outer canthus.

15. Which of the following statements describes the proper use of common health equipment?
    a. A footboard is needed for a client who will require bedrest for one day.
    b. A bed cradle would be appropriate to use for a client with a painful leg injury that must avoid pressure on the leg.
    c. An IV pole is required on all hospital and long-term care beds.
    d. A special bed is required for any obese client.

16. When making an occupied bed, you should:
    a. continually assess the client's condition and tolerance of the procedure.
    b. move as quickly as possible without concerning yourself with being smooth or gentle; this approach may be rougher on the client, but the discomfort ends more quickly.
    c. make the bed prior to giving the bed bath.
    d. always have two other nurses to help you.

17. Before bathing a client, which of the following must you do?
    a. Assess the type of bath required and the client's ability to get out of bed.
    b. Determine the type of bath the client requires, the equipment and supplies needed, and how you will provide privacy.
    c. Delay the provision of hygiene until after the physician's scheduled visit.
    d. Gather a gown, gloves, and a mask for protective purposes.

18. Gloves should be worn when providing:
    a. mouth care.
    b. a back rub.
    c. routine foot care.
    d. hair care.

True or False

Read the following statements to determine if they are true or false. If a statement is false, alter the statement to make it true.

19. Bed linens should be kept clean and wrinkle-free to reduce friction and abrasion to the client's skin.
True False

____

____

20. Bathing removes accumulated oil, perspiration, dead skin cells, and bacteria. Bathing also produces a sense of well-being and stimulates the circulation. However, because of the need to drape the client and ensure privacy bathing provides limited opportunity to assess the client.
True False

____

____

____

____

21. Cleansing baths are chiefly for hygiene purposes and are ordered by the nursing staff. Therapeutic baths are given for physical effects and may be ordered by the physician.
True False

____

____

____

22. All clients with long or ragged toenails should have their nails clipped as part of routine foot care.
True False

____

____

23. Clients at risk for oral problems include clients with nasogastric tubes, comatose clients, dehydrated clients, critically ill clients, confused clients, clients who have had oral surgery, and clients who are inadequately nourished.
True False

____

____

____

____

24. Brushing and flossing teeth removes gingival pockets and stimulates the gums.
True False

25. Dentures or partial plates may be removed and cleaned with a toothbrush and toothpaste or with a dentrifice.
True False

26. Ongoing use of lemon juice and oil (lemon-glycerin) mouth swabs can lead to dryness of the mucosa and changes in tooth enamel.
True False

27. In the healthy adult, the lacrimal fluid washes the eyes, and the lids and the lashes protect the eye from foreign particles.
True False

28. Ears may be cleaned with cotton-tipped applicators as long as the applicator is not deeply inserted.
True False

29. If side rails are required, the nurse should never leave the bedside when the rails are lowered.
True False

30. As you provide perineal care for a woman, you should wash the labia from pubis to rectum to avoid contamination of the genitals with bacteria from the rectum.
True False

31. When providing perineal care to a man, wash and dry the shaft of the penis only.
True False

Completion

32. Identify three ways you assess your client's skin and hygiene practices.

____

____

____

____

____

33. Josie Keefer is a 97-year-old woman who has just been admitted to your unit at the Rehabilitation Centre. Josie has lived independently until a recent fall that resulted in a severe head laceration. During your intake interview, Josie complains of dry and itchy skin. What nursing actions would you take to correct this problem?

____

____

____

____

____

34. Anna Treffel is incontinent of urine and stool. What nursing actions would you take to protect her skin?

____

____

____

____

____

35. Identify at least three health concerns that may affect a client's ability to maintain foot care independently.

____

____

____

____

____

Case Study

You are assigned to provide care to Bryan White, a 16-year-old boy who recently suffered a C-5 fracture as a result of a diving accident. As a result of this accident, Bryan is a quadriplegic. He is awake, alert, and oriented. Bryan is hospitalized on a neurological unit at a major medical centre.

36. What can you do to provide the most comfortable environment for Bryan?

37. Due to his injury, Bryan is dependent on nursing staff for hygiene care. How can you make this a comfortable experience for him?

CHAPTER 35

Fecal Elimination

This chapter presents normal and common abnormal elimination patterns. It emphasizes your role in assessing and promoting regular fecal elimination patterns. The chapter introduces the skills of enema administration, application of an ostomy appliance, and evaluation of elimination.

KEY TOPICS

This study guide chapter reinforces the following topics discussed in the textbook chapter

- functions of the lower intestinal tract
- fecal elimination patterns
- bowel diversion ostomies
- measures to maintain normal fecal elimination patterns

Matching

Match the following elimination terms with the appropriate definitions below:

a. bowel incontinence
b. constipation
c. diarrhea
d. fecal impaction
e. flatulence

___ 1. a collection of hard stool in the folds of the rectum resulting from prolonged retention and accumulation of fecal material

___ 2. the loss of voluntary ability to control fecal and gaseous discharges through the anal sphincter

___ 3. the passage of small, dry, hard stool or the passage of no stool over a period of time relative to the person's normal elimination pattern

___ 4. excessive flatus in the intestines that leads to intestinal distention

___ 5. the passage of liquid stool or an increased frequency of defecation

Multiple Choice

Circle the correct response for each question.

6. The large intestine plays numerous roles in digestion and defecation. Which function is *not* associated with the large intestine?
   a. absorption of water
   b. absorption of chyme
   c. mucal protection of the intestinal wall
   d. fecal elimination

7. Your client states that he is concerned that his stool is black in colour. As part of your assessment, you should inquire about use of which of the following over-the-counter medications?

   a. antibiotics and aspirin

   b. vitamins and iron

   c. antacids and antibiotics

   d. aspirin and iron

8. Your client complains of nausea. You notice that she has a distended abdomen and a small amount of liquid stool on the bed linens. Which fecal elimination problem would you would want to assess for?

   a. bowel incontinence

   b. constipation

   c. diarrhea

   d. fecal impaction

9. Removal of a fecal impaction is accomplished by:

   a. digital removal of impacted feces or administration of a laxative.

   b. administration of a cleansing enema.

   c. digital removal of impacted feces or administration of an oil-retention enema followed by a cleansing enema.

   d. an increase in fibre and liquid intake and administration of a stool softener.

10. To provide adequate protection against body fluids, what should the nurse wear when offering a bedpan?

   a. gown

   b. gloves

   c. gown and gloves

   d. gown, gloves, and mask

11. Which of the following statements correctly describes the use of medications for bowel function?

   a. Lifestyle and dietary changes should be instituted in conjunction with the use of laxatives for clients with constipation. A purgative should be added if results are not achieved in 24 hours.

   b. Laxative use is appropriate for clients over the age of 70 because of decreased muscular tone in the elderly. In addition, clients with neuromuscular impairment should be given purgatives routinely.

   c. Antidiarrheal medications may be prescribed for all clients with more than one bowel movement per day. Defecation more than one time per day may produce serious fluid and electrolyte problems.

   d. An enema is given to remove feces and/or flatus. The amount of fluid instilled is dependent on the type of enema, the age of the individual, and the client's ability to retain the solution.

12. Your client is scheduled for a proctosigmoidoscopy. You understand that this procedure is used to:

    a. view the rectum and the sigmoid colon.
    b. visualize the large intestine usually through a flexible fibre-optic device.
    c. directly view the anal canal.
    d. examine the large intestine by introduction of a radiopaque substance followed by roentgenography.

13. A guaiac test may be performed by the nurse to detect:

    a. inflammatory disease of the bowel.
    b. cancerous cells in the intestinal tract.
    c. blood in the stool.
    d. fibre content in the diet.

14. What is the correct position for a client receiving an enema?

    a. knee-chest position
    b. left lateral position
    c. prone position
    d. right lateral position

15. Your bedridden, hospitalized client complains of bloating and gas. Of the following measures to decrease flatulence, which could you implement independently?

    a. insert a rectal tube
    b. administer an enema
    c. frequently change the client's position in bed
    d. administer simethicone tablets

16. A fecal incontinence pouch may be used to:

    a. collect stool for a client who is bedridden.
    b. stimulate the urge to defecate.
    c. save nursing time by keeping linens clean.
    d. collect and contain large volumes of feces.

17. Which of the following statements correctly depicts concerns that arise when assisting a client to care for an ostomy?

    a. Ostomy effluent, management, and skin care concerns are largely dictated by the location of the ostomy within the tract.
    b. The consistency of the stool from an ostomy is dependent on the location of the ostomy and does not change over time.
    c. Scrupulous skin care is a concern for ileostomy clients only.
    d. The effluent of a sigmoid colostomy is always liquid and cannot be controlled.

True or False

Read the following statements to determine if they are true or false. If a statement is false, alter the statement to make it true.

18. The normal frequency of defecation is one time per week.
True False

____

19. Control of defecation is usually learned in the toddler stage of development.
True False

____

20. A cleansing enema removes feces and flatus. A retention enema softens stool and lubricates the rectum and anal canal. Both a carminative enema and a return flow enema expel flatus.
True False

____

____

____

21. Establishing a colostomy irrigation schedule will result in regular evacuation of the bowel. However, the client must still wear a pouch or appliance to collect the liquid drainage.
True False

____

____

____

Completion

22. Identify at least 10 potential causes of constipation.

____

____

____

____

____

____

____

23. Identify at least three potential causes of diarrhea.

____

____

____

24. List at least five high-fibre foods.

Case Study

You are assigned to care for Earl Pagano, a teenage client recovering from orthopedic surgery. During his surgery, pins were placed in his left femur and tibia to enable skeletal traction. Due to the traction, he is confined to bed. This is his third postoperative day, and he has not had a bowel movement since admission.

25. What nursing action should you take?

26. Earl is at risk for constipation. Identify at least two risk factors for constipation for him.

By the sixth postoperative day, Earl has still not had a bowel movement. Earl has been eating 100 percent of a regular diet for five days. He complains of feeling bloated. His normal elimination pattern is one time per day.

27. Write a nursing diagnosis for Earl.

28. Develop a plan for Earl to promote regular elimination without the use of medications.

CHAPTER 36

Urinary Elimination

This chapter presents normal and common abnormal urinary elimination patterns. It emphasizes your role in assessing and promoting regular urinary elimination patterns. The chapter introduces the skills of urine specimen collection; insertion, maintenance, and discontinuation of urinary catheters; and catheter irrigation.

KEY TOPICS

This study guide chapter reinforces the following topics discussed in the textbook chapter:

- urinary elimination
- common alterations in urinary elimination
- collection of urine specimens
- urine tests
- interventions to maintain normal urinary elimination

Matching

Match the following terms with their descriptions:

a. dysuria
b. enuresis
c. neurogenic bladder
d. nocturia
e. oliguria
f. polyuria
g. urinary retention

___ 1. involuntary urination beyond the age when control is normally established
___ 2. voiding two or more times at night
___ 3. the production of abnormally large volumes of urine
___ 4. voiding that is either painful or difficult
___ 5. overdistention of the bladder due to impaired emptying
___ 6. alteration of urinary function due to impaired neurological function
___ 7. low urine output

Multiple Choice

Circle the correct response for each question.

8. The kidneys are extremely influential in the maintenance of health. Their primary role is:
   a. elimination of urine from the body.

b. regulation of body fluid and acid-base balance.

c. to serve as a reservoir for urine.

d. to reabsorb filtrate.

9. Urine in the bladder stimulates stretch receptors and triggers the need to void. In the adult the need to void is signalled after how much urine enters the bladder?

a. <50 mL

b. 50–100 mL

c. 150–200 mL

d. 250–450 mL

10. A 30-year-old client complains of urinary frequency. What factors would you want to assess?

a. developmental level, psychosocial concerns, and past history of similar problems

b. muscle tone, surgical procedures, and pathology

c. fluid and food intake, medications, and health history

d. polyuria, oliguria, and dysuria

11. To conduct a routine urinalysis, what type of specimen is needed?

a. a clean-catch midstream sample

b. a clean, freshly voided sample

c. a sample obtained from a catheter

d. a timed specimen

12. To collect a urine sample for a culture and sensitivity exam on an ambulatory client, which of the following supplies is required?

a. disposable or sterile gloves

b. disposable specimen container with label

c. sterile specimen container with label

d. a large refrigerated bottle or carton

13. The physician has written an order for a urine culture from a client with a Foley catheter. What steps should you take to collect the sample?

a. Clamp the drainage tubing to allow fresh urine to collect in the catheter. Aspirate 3 mL from the self-sealing rubber port with a sterile syringe and needle. Place in a sterile container, label, and send to the lab.

b. Open the drainage port of the drainage collection bag, and place 10 mL into a sterile container. Label the sample, and send to the lab.

c. Insert a needle into the plastic tubing of the catheter. Withdraw at least 3 mL with the syringe, and place into a disposable specimen container. Label properly, and send to the lab.

d. Clamp the drainage tube for two hours. Disconnect the catheter from the drainage tubing, and place the catheter end into a sterile container. Unclamp the tubing, and drain all the urine. Label the specimen, and send to the lab.

14. Which of the following urine characteristics is abnormal?
    a. pH 6.0
    b. specific gravity 1.018
    c. ketones: 2+
    d. occult blood: negative
15. Your client is scheduled for a cystoscopy. You realize that this procedure is:
    a. a blood test to evaluate kidney function.
    b. a test that involves injection of dye into the venous system and x-ray examination of the kidneys, bladder, and ureter.
    c. an x-ray procedure that can distinguish minor differences in the radiodensity of soft tissue.
    d. the direct visualization of the bladder, ureteral orifices in the bladder, and the urethra.
16. Use of a condom catheter for an incontinent male client is preferable to insertion of a retention catheter because:
    a. it is less embarrassing for the client.
    b. the risk of urinary tract infection is minimal.
    c. it prevents skin breakdown.
    d. it may be applied by the client independently.
17. Which of the following statements about the nurse's role with clients with urinary diversions is true?
    a. A major nursing responsibility for clients with urinary diversions is the application and maintenance of an external pouch system.
    b. Because the Kock pouch, or ileal bladder conduit, provides some protection from ascending infection, prevention of UTI is not a major nursing focus.
    c. A priority nursing goal is the maintenance of skin integrity around exit sites of urinary diversions.
    d. A priority nursing goal is to improve the body image of clients with urinary diversions.

True or False

Read the following statements to determine if they are true or false. If a statement is false, alter the statement to make it true.

18. In the male and female, the urethra serves as a passageway for reproductive fluid as well as urine.
    True False

    ____

    ____

19. Voluntary control of urination is possible only if the nerves supplying the bladder and urethra, the neural tracts of the cord and brain, and the motor area of the cerebrum are all intact.
True False

____

____

____

20. All timed urine specimens should be refrigerated to prevent bacterial growth and decomposition of the urine components, unless a special preservative has been added.
True False

____

____

____

Completion

21. Identify at least five factors that inhibit voiding.

____

____

____

____

____

22. A complete assessment of urinary function includes:

____

____

____

____

23. Gail Chan is a 15-year-old high school student. She is seen by the nurse practitioner (NP) in the ambulatory clinic for a urinary tract infection. The NP prescribes an antibiotic for the infection. During the physical examination, the NP determines that Gail is an active, normally healthy adolescent. As part of her treatment plan, provide Gail with at least three suggestions to prevent further urinary tract problems.

____

____

____

____

24. Ethel Jackson is a 78-year-old client with urinary incontinence. Ethel lives independently at home. She reports that she has curtailed many of her social activities due to her incontinence. How you would instruct Ethel on managing her urinary incontinence?

____

____

____

____

Case Study

James Saratoga is a 58-year-old client with severe urinary retention. The physician has ordered insertion of a Foley catheter for ongoing urinary drainage.

25. Identify the precautions you must take to protect James while inserting a retention catheter.

____

____

____

____

26. What nursing interventions are required to maintain James's catheter?

____

____

____

____

James's condition has improved and the physician has ordered discontinuation of the Foley catheter.

27. Describe how you would remove the catheter.

____

____

____

____

____

CHAPTER 37

Skin Integrity and Wound Care

This chapter presents your role in caring for clients with wounds and pressure ulcers. It presents assessment guidelines and interventions to promote skin integrity, prevent and treat pressure ulcers, and support wound healing. You are introduced to a variety of wound care procedures as well as dressing and bandage equipment and techniques.

KEY TOPICS

This study guide chapter reinforces the following topics discussed in the textbook chapter:

- skin integrity
- pressure ulcers
- wound care
- wound healing
- skin integrity risk assessment

Matching

Match the following terms to their descriptions:

a.	débridement	g.	keloid
b.	dehiscence	h.	maceration
c.	evisceration	i.	phagocytosis
d.	exudate	j.	pressure ulcer
e.	hemostasis	k.	reactive hyperemia
f.	ischemia	l.	shearing force

___ 1. a combination of friction and pressure resulting in damage to blood vessels and tissues in the area

___ 2. the protrusion of the internal viscera through an incision

___ 3. a lesion caused by unrelieved pressure that results in damage to the underlying tissue

___ 4. a bright red flush caused by vasodilation

___ 5. a deficiency in the blood supply to the tissue

___ 6. tissue softened by prolonged wetting or soaking

___ 7. the cessation of bleeding

___ 8. the partial or total rupturing of a wound

___ 9. material that has escaped from blood vessels during the inflammatory process and is deposited in tissue or on tissue surfaces

___ 10. the process by which macrophages engulf microorganisms and cellular debris

___ 11. removal of infected and necrotic material

___ 12. a hypertrophied scar

Multiple Choice

Circle the correct response for each question.

13. Your client is a six-year-old boy who sustained a fracture of the right humerus when he fell off his bike. The skin of the upper arm is erythematous and tender to the touch. The bone is not protruding through the skin. This wound would be classified as a(n):
    a. unintentional clean-contaminated wound.
    b. intentional trauma
    c. closed wound.
    d. accidental contaminated wound.

14. Your client had abdominal surgery for incision and drainage of an abscess. The wound margins have not been approximated. The wound is being irrigated and packed every four to six hours. The client is receiving IV antibiotics. The surgeon believes that this wound can be surgically closed within two weeks. This wound will heal by:
    a. primary intention.
    b. secondary intention.
    c. tertiary intention.
    d. fibrin deposits.

15. When you remove the old dressing on a surgical wound, you note a large pool of pus on the dressing and in the central portion of the wound. This exudate would most appropriately be called:
    a. serous exudate.
    b. sanguineous exudate.
    c. purosanguineous exudate.
    d. purulent exudate.

16. Which of the following clients is most likely to heal a wound quickly?
    a. a healthy 15-month-old girl
    b. a 40-year-old client with diabetes and peripheral vascular disease
    c. a 51-year-old who smokes three packs of cigarettes per day
    d. a 76-year-old woman with low total protein and albumin levels

17. What is the major advantage of a wet-to-damp dressing over a wet-to-dry dressing?
    a. It is not as messy to apply.
    b. A wet-to-damp dressing causes less maceration than a wet-to-dry dressing.
    c. A wet-to-damp dressing does not disrupt new granulation tissue.
    d. A wet-to-dry dressing allows for greater bacterial growth in the wound.

18. Which of the following accurately depicts the use of heat and cold in wound care?
    a. Use of heat or cold should be monitored to prevent rebound phenomenon.
    b. Application of a warm pack for one hour will produce maximum effect.
    c. Within 10 minutes after heat is applied to an injury, temperature receptors in the skin have adjusted to the rise in temperature. To compensate for this adaptation, the temperature of the heat pack should be increased.
    d. To achieve maximum effect, cold packs should be applied until skin temperature reaches 0°C.

19. Earl Mason has a pressure ulcer on his coccyx that must be irrigated and packed. When you remove the old dressing, you note that there is a long sinus tract extending down the left thigh. Muscle tissue is visible and a yellow exudate is present in the wound. This is evidence of which pressure ulcer stage?
    a. Stage I
    b. Stage II
    c. Stage III
    d. Stage IV

20. On your morning rounds you note that one of your clients has a reddened area on her right hip. When you apply pressure to the erythematous region it does not blanch. This is evidence of which pressure ulcer stage?
    a. Stage I
    b. Stage II
    c. Stage Ill
    d. Stage IV

21. Your client is terminally ill and is being cared for at home by his family. His family is overwhelmed by the amount of care he currently requires. On his admission to the hospice unit, you perform a complete assessment. On both heels you note reddened and abraded areas. This is evidence of which pressure ulcer stage?
    a. Stage I
    b. Stage II
    c. Stage III
    d. Stage IV

22. Your co-worker has an ulcerated area on her left hand. She has cleaned, rinsed, and dried the area and applied a transparent dressing over the site. She asks for your opinion about this choice of dressing, and you reply that:
    a. a wet-to-dry dressing would be more appropriate for this wound.
    b. a hydrocolloid dressing is the most appropriate choice for this wound.
    c. a transparent dressing is appropriate for an ulcerated or burned area.
    d. exudate absorbers are required for ulcerated areas.

23. Your client is febrile and uncomfortable. You are considering giving her a tepid sponge bath. Which of the following techniques would be appropriate?
   a. Sponge all body parts rapidly with cool (18.2C) water.
   b. Sponge the face, arms, legs, back, and buttocks slowly and separately with 32.2C water.
   c. Apply ice packs to the forehead and groin while sponging the body with water that is progressively cooled to 18.2C.
   d. Slowly sponge the body with wash cloths saturated with rubbing alcohol.

True or False

Read the following statements to determine if they are true or false. If a statement is false, after the statement to make it true.

24. To stimulate circulation and avoid development of pressure ulcers, routinely massage bony prominences.
True False

____

____

25. All bedridden clients should be regularly repositioned and assessed for development of pressure ulcers.
True False

____

____

26. The most serious complication of pressure sores is existing and potential infections.
True False

____

____

27. During the inflammatory phase, which initiates at the time of injury and lasts three to four days, hemostasis and phagocytosis are the major processes.
True False

____

____

28. During the proliferative phase of wound healing, the scar becomes thin and less elastic.
True False

____

____

29. Wound cleaning is usually undertaken to provide humidity to the granulating tissue.
True False

30. A hydrocolloid dressing may be used for many purposes, including maintenance of a moist wound surface to promote healing, minimization of bacterial contamination of the wound, minimization of discomfort, and absorption of exudate.
True False

31. Hydrocolloid dressings should not be used for infected wounds or those with deep tracts or fistulas.
True False

32. Clients with neurosensory impairment, impaired mental status, or impaired circulation are at high risk for injury related to application of heat or cold.
True False

Completion

33. What are the risk factors for pressure ulcer formation?

34. Report has just finished for the evening shift on a medical-surgical unit. One of your clients returned from the operating room during the change of shift. You find the client sleepy but arousable. The dressing is saturated with bloody drainage. When you remove the dressing, you see a constant flow of bright red blood from the suture line. What should you do?

35. Aaron Souza is four days post-operative from a colon resection. You are assisting him to get out of bed when he starts coughing. He grimaces in pain and states, “Oh, that hurt. I swear it felt like my insides popped.” You assist Aaron back to bed and place him in a

semi-Fowler's position. The wound dressing appears dishevelled. When you remove the dressing to examine the wound you find a loop of bowel protruding through the suture line. What should you do?

36. Grant Martin reports to the emergency department with a laceration to his left hand. While pruning roses, he accidentally cut his hand. How would you assess this wound?

37. Robert Wayne successfully underwent knee surgery 24 hours ago. When you examine the wound you find dried blood on the old dressing. The wound edges are approximated but the margins are slightly red and inflamed. There is no odour. Robert complains of moderate pain which he describes as "burning" in nature. He reports that the pain medication provides significant relief. What is your assessment?

38. Identify at least five purposes of a wound dressing.

39. What safeguards should be taken when irrigating a wound?

40. Why are heat or cold applications applied to a wound?

____

____

____

____

41. The RYB colour code of wounds can assist you in providing appropriate care to wounds healing by secondary intention. Complete the following table:

Colour	***Goal of Wound Care***	***Intervention Example***
Red		
Yellow		
Black		

Case Study

Martin Rogers is a 19-year-old first-year university student who sustained a C-5 spinal cord injury as a result of a diving accident one week ago today. Martin has no movement or sensation below his shoulders. Martin's vital signs are: BP 100/48, P 124, RR 24, and T 39°C. A chest x-ray reveals bibasilar pneumonia. Martin is receiving IV fluids at 100 mL/hr. You have observed that he is despondent about his recent injury He was placed on a diet as tolerated three days ago, but he has refused food. He is only taking sips of liquid by mouth. He has not had a bowel movement since his hospitalization. A Foley catheter is attached to straight drainage.

42. Identify Martin's risk factors for development of a pressure ulcer.

Martin continues to refuse to eat. By the twelfth day of hospitalization, Martin weighs 4.5 kilograms less than his preinjury weight. As you turn Martin, you note that he has developed a pressure ulcer.

____

____

____

____

____

____

____

____

____

43. Which aspects of your findings should be recorded in the chart?

44. What nursing actions can you take to prevent further pressure ulcers?

45. You determine that Martin's existing pressure sore is at Stage II. What type of dressing might be appropriate for this pressure ulcer?

46. Identify at least two nursing diagnoses appropriate for Martin.

CHAPTER 38

Nutrition

This chapter discusses the importance of nutrition in the maintenance of health. It highlights your role in assessing the adequacy of nutrition, teaching nutritional content, and assisting the client to receive adequate nutrition through oral, enteral, or parenteral routes.

KEY TOPICS

This study guide chapter reinforces the following topics discussed in the textbook chapter:

- nutrition
- metabolism
- nutritional requirements
- nutritional assessment
- interventions to promote optimal nutrition
- enteral and parenteral nutrition

Matching

Match the nutritional terms with their descriptions:

a. basal metabolic rate
b. body mass index
c. caloric value
d. enteral feedings
e. metabolism
f. nutrients
g. parenteral feedings

___ 1. the amount of energy that nutrients or foods supply to the body

___ 2. the rate at which the body metabolizes food to maintain the energy requirements of a person who is awake and at rest

___ 3. a feeding administered through a tube into the gastrointestinal system

___ 4. the organic and inorganic substances found in foods

___ 5. a feeding administered through the intravenous route

___ 6. the biochemical and physiological processes by which the body grows and maintains itself

___ 7. the relationship of weight to height

Multiple Choice

Circle the correct response for each question.

8. Which of the following clients has an increased need for calories?
   a. a sedentary 75-year-old client
   b. a client with a temperature of 38.5C
   c. a client with a temperature of 36.1C
   d. clients in warm climates

9. Which of the following developmental periods are associated with increased caloric needs?
   a. infancy and adolescence
   b. school age and young adulthood
   c. adolescence and older adulthood
   d. young adulthood and older adulthood

10. What is the body's most basic nutrient need?
    a. carbohydrate
    b. fat
    c. protein
    d. water

11. Carbohydrates, fats, and proteins are energy-providing nutrients. Which statement about these nutrients is accurate?
    a. One gram of fat provides more than twice the calories contained in one gram of protein or carbohydrates.
    b. Carbohydrates, fat, and protein liberate four calories with metabolism.
    c. Fats provide the major source of body energy on a day-to-day basis.
    d. Nonessential amino acids are those that the body does not require on regular basis.

12. Which of the following foods is a complex carbohydrate?
    a. yogurt
    b. ice cream
    c. apple
    d. butter

13. Cholesterol is a substance that has been linked to many health hazards. Which of the following represents the major source of cholesterol in the body?
    a. diet
    b. synthesis in the liver
    c. animal protein
    d. excess carbohydrates and protein

14. Which vitamins are water-soluble?

   a. C and B-complex
   b. C, D, and E
   c. A, D, E, and K
   d. A, B-complex, and D

15. Which of the following sets of biochemical data may indicate poor nutritional status?

   a. low hemoglobin level, high albumin level, low total lymphocyte count, and low BUN level
   b. high hematocrit level, high albumin level, high total lymphocyte count, and high BUN level
   c. low hematocrit level, low albumin level, low total lymphocyte count, and low BUN level
   d. low hemoglobin level, low albumin level, low total lymphocyte count, and high BUN level

True or False

Read the following statements to determine if they are true or false. If a statement is false, alter the statement to make it true.

16. The major health concerns for vegetarians include obtaining all the essential amino acids, obtaining adequate vitamin B_{12}, increasing absorption of iron by eating foods in combination with those containing vitamin C, and ensuring adequacy of calcium intake (especially for strict vegetarians).
   True False

   ____
   ____
   ____
   ____

17. In general, metabolic rates, vitamin and mineral requirements, and appetite increase in the elderly.
   True False

   ____
   ____

18. When feeding a client, the nurse should adopt an unhurried manner and be sensitive to the client's feelings of embarrassment, resentment, or loss of autonomy.
   True False

   ____
   ____
   ____

19. Crash diets, gastric surgery, and single food diets are all effective ways to lose weight and maintain weight loss.
True False

20. Bryan Arrendon reports to the clinic complaining of fatigue. His skin is dry and his lips are cracked. His BP is 98/60, and his pulse is 106. He is irritable and underweight. The nurse recognizes that all of these clinical signs are consistent with acute illness, rather than a potential nutritional problem.
True False

Completion

21. What are the three major functions of nutrients?

22. Evaluate your own diet for compliance with Canada's Food Guide to Healthy Living. How well do you comply with these recommendations?

23. What are the factors that influence an individual's eating habits?

Case Study

Thad Denois is recovering from neurosurgery. The neurosurgeon orders placement of *a* nasogastric tube for short-term enteral feedings.

24. Explain how you would insert a nasogastric tube.

____

____

____

25. How would you verify tube placement?

____

____

26. The physician orders a commercially prepared tube feeding to be administered at 50 mL/hr. What nursing actions must you take to ensure safe administration?

____

____

____

____

CHAPTER 39

Oxygenation

This chapter provides an overview of respiration, ventilation, and the importance of adequate oxygenation. It introduces you to vital information and skills that will enable you to maintain a patent airway and to identify actual or potential hazards to optimum oxygenation.

KEY TOPICS

This study guide chapter reinforces the following topics discussed in the textbook chapter:

- breathing and ventilation
- gas exchange and respiration
- manifestations of impaired respiratory function
- therapeutic measures to promote cardiorespiratory function
- cardiopulmonary resuscitation

Matching

Match the following terms with their definitions:

a. cardiac output
b. lung compliance
c. partial pressure
d. respiration
e. surfactant
f. tidal volume
g. ventilation

___ 1. inflow and outflow of air between the atmosphere and the alveoli of the lungs
___ 2. pressure exerted by each individual gas in a mixture
___ 3. amount of blood pumped by the heart per minute
___ 4. process of gaseous exchange between the individual and the environment
___ 5. expansibility of lung tissue
___ 6. normal volume of air inspired and expired with each breath
___ 7. lipoprotein mixture that facilitates lung expansion

Multiple Choice

Circle the correct responses for each question.

8. Ventilation of the lung depends on several factors, such as clear airways. What other factors must be present?
   a. adequate oxygen, hemoglobin, and alveoli
   b. an intact sneeze and cough reflex, as well as ciliary action to keep the airways clear
   c. an intact thoracic cavity, central nervous system and respiratory centre, and adequate pulmonary compliance and recoil
   d. intact accessory muscles, adequate supplies of surfactant, and sufficient stores of oxygen to support life

9. Oxygen must be transported from the lungs to the tissues. Approximately 3 percent of the oxygen dissolves in the plasma and cells, but most is transported by:
   a. passively diffusing from the alveoli.
   b. combining with hemoglobin.
   c. attaching to carbon dioxide in the bloodstream.
   d. dissolving directly into tissue.

10. The four-part process of respiration includes all of the following as well as diffusion and perfusion of gases:
    a. inhalation, exhalation, and rest.
    b. inhalation of oxygen, gas exchange, and exhalation of carbon dioxide.
    c. pulmonary ventilation, diffusion of gases, and transport of oxygen and carbon dioxide.
    d. lung expansion, diffusion, and lung recoil.

11. Under normal conditions, intrapleural pressure is:
    a. equivalent to atmospheric pressure.
    b. negative.
    c. positive.
    d. 700mm Hg.

12. Which of the following statements correctly describes factors that affect oxygenation?
    a. A person at high altitude has increased respiratory rate and depth and increased cardiac rate to compensate for the lower partial pressure of oxygen in the ambient air.
    b. As temperature rises, the need for oxygen decreases. In cold environments, oxygen requirements soar.
    c. Physical exertion is associated with increased rate and depth of respirations but a decrease in oxygen supply to the muscles.
    d. Opioids stimulate the respiratory centres; therefore, the client receiving opioids should be observed for signs and symptoms of hyperventilation.

13. The chart describes the client as "experiencing frequent episodes of hypoxia." You recognize that this means that the client is experiencing a(n):
    a. accumulation of carbon dioxide in the blood.
    b. condition of insufficient oxygen.
    c. excessive amount of air in the lungs.
    d. inability to breathe, except in an upright position.

14. Your client has a decreased cardiac output. A compensatory mechanism you might expect to see on assessment is a(n):
    a. increased respiratory rate.
    b. decreased blood pressure.
    c. decreased temperature.
    d. increased heart rate.

15. Your client has hypertension; therefore, your client has increased:
    a. afterload.
    b. mean arterial pressure.
    c. preload.
    d. increased cardiac output.

16. The history and physical examination state that your client was found at home unresponsive and cyanotic with shallow spontaneous respirations. You recognize that your client experienced:
    a. difficult or laboured breathing.
    b. abnormal breath sounds.
    c. increased movement of air into the lungs.
    d. reduced hemoglobin-oxygen saturation.

17. You evaluate your client's oxygen saturation by pulse oximetry. The saturation is 85 percent. What is your first priority?
    a. This result is normal. No further action is required.
    b. This result is grossly abnormal. This is an emergency. Your client requires resuscitation.
    c. Your client requires immediate suctioning and application of oxygen by mask or cannula.
    d. This result is abnormal. Assess your client for possible causes.

18. Leg exercises for a bedridden client are useful to help maintain muscle strength and prevent venous thrombosis. Leg exercises promote cardiovascular function by:
    a. improving general muscle tone.
    b. promoting venous return to the heart.
    c. increasing oxygen demand.
    d. decreasing oxygen uptake in the periphery.

19. When is it appropriate to suction a client?
   a. when the client will not cooperate with the treatment schedule
   b. when the client is tired
   c. when the client has difficulty handling secretions
   d. when the client has pneumonia

20. A suction attempt of the oropharynx or nasopharynx should last:
   a. less than five seconds.
   b. 10 to 15 seconds.
   c. approximately 30 seconds.
   d. one full minute, followed by a five-minute rest period.

21. Which of the following statements accurately describes chest drainage systems or conditions that may necessitate a chest tube?
   a. A pneumothorax is the collection of air and fluid in the pleural space that results in collapse of the lung.
   b. Chest drainage systems instill positive pressure within the pleural space to facilitate lung re-expansion.
   c. A physician inserts chest tubes. However, the staff nurses monitor, maintain, and remove chest tubes.
   d. A chest tube to remove air is usually inserted superiorly and anteriorly. A tube to drain fluid is usually inserted inferiorly.

22. Which of the following therapeutic measures prevents venous stasis?
   a. artificial airways and anti-embolism stockings
   b. a chest tube and drainage system
   c. anti-embolism stockings and sequential compression devices
   d. leg exercises and postural drainage

23. The three cardinal signs of cardiac arrest are:
   a. apnea, absence of a carotid or femoral pulse, and dilated pupils.
   b. apnea, absence of a pulse, absence of blood pressure.
   c. unresponsiveness, absence of a palpable peripheral pulse, and shallow or absent respirations.
   d. cyanosis, apnea, and absence of blood pressure.

True or False

Read the following statements to determine if they are true or false. If a statement is false, alter the statement to make it true.

24. In the healthy individual, respiration is largely controlled by chemoreceptors in the medulla oblongata, which respond to increases in oxygen concentration. However, in individuals

with a pulmonary disease, such as emphysema, carbon dioxide levels, not oxygen, play a major role in regulating respirations.
True False

25. Increased fluid intake and humidifiers help moisten the respiratory mucous membranes. Such measures diminish irritation of the airways and help loosen secretions for easier expectoration.
True False

26. Expectorants are medications that suppress or stop the cough reflex. Codeine is a common constituent of these medications.
True False

27. Oropharyngeal or nasopharyngeal suctioning removes secretions from the deeper airways, such as the trachea and bronchi. Endotracheal suctioning removes secretions from the upper respiratory tract.
True False

28. Exercise caution when suctioning a client's airway. Use sterile equipment and wear sterile gloves. Monitor suction time. Applying suction for too long may decrease the client's oxygen supply.
True False

29. An oropharyngeal airway does not stimulate the gag reflex, and therefore, may be used in clients who are alert.
True False

30. Nasopharyngeal and endotracheal intubations are routinely conducted by nurses.
True False

Completion

31. Identify the body's five cleaning mechanisms that protect the airways.

32. In the healthy individual, adequate ventilation is maintained by frequent changes of position, ambulation, and exercise. Identify four nursing interventions to maintain normal respiratory function in the ill client.

33. Identify at least two nursing goals when caring for a client with a tracheostomy.

Case Study

Linda Jaia is a 42-year-old woman complaining of shortness of breath. Examination reveals the following findings:

BP	132/85
P	128
RR	32
T	39.8C
SaO_2	91% on room air

Fine crackles audible throughout left lung fields

34. Identify the abnormal findings.

The physician orders the following diagnostic studies:
Sputum C&S (culture & sensitivity)
Chest x-ray
CBC

35. Describe how you would carry out each of these orders.

Chest x-ray confirms a diagnosis of pneumonia. The physician orders:
Deep-breathing exercises q2h
O_2 at 5 litres per minute via nasal cannulae
Chest PT (chest physiotherapy or percussion, vibration, and postural drainage) q4h while awake
Pulse oximetry

36. Describe the deep-breathing exercises that you will teach Linda.

37. What would be an appropriate chest physiotherapy schedule for Linda?

38. Briefly describe how you would utilize pulse oximetry. What is the normal range of values for this monitor?

39. Describe the advantages of supplying oxygen via nasal cannulae.

CHAPTER 40

Fluid, Electrolyte, and Acid-Base Balance

This chapter discusses the complex nature of fluid and electrolyte status in health and disease. It emphasizes your role in assessing actual and potential fluid and electrolyte imbalances. You are introduced to a variety of laboratory findings and to the regulation and maintenance of intravenous fluids, nutrition, and blood products.

KEY TOPICS

This study guide chapter reinforces the following topics discussed in the textbook chapter:

- electrolytes
- fluid and electrolyte balance
- acid-base balance
- fluid, electrolyte, and acid-base imbalances

Matching

Match the following terms with their definitions:

a. electrolyte
b. diffusion
c. filtration
d. osmosis
e. active transport

___ 1. This process involves the movement of pure solvent from the less concentrated solution to the more concentrated solution.

___ 2. This is a charged particle capable of conducting electricity.

___ 3. This process maintains the difference in sodium and potassium ion concentrations of extracellular and intracellular fluid.

___ 4. This is the movement of fluid and solutes across a membrane from one compartment to another; movement is from an area of higher pressure to an area of lower pressure.

___ 5. When molecules enter a compartment, they move from an area of higher concentration to an area of lower concentration. The size of the molecule and ambient temperature affect the speed of molecule movement.

Match the following electrolytes to their description(s). There may be more than one correct response for each statement.

a. calcium
b. chloride
c. magnesium
d. potassium
e. phosphate
f. sodium

___ 6. the most abundant cation in the ECF

___ 7. frequently used in combination with sodium in such foods as ham, bacon, and potato chips

___ 8. functions in bone formation, transmission of nerve impulses, muscle contraction, blood coagulation, and enzyme activation

___ 9. affects most body systems, including the cardiovascular, GI, neuromuscular, and respiratory systems

___ 10. the principal ions of extracellular fluid

___ 11. the principal ions of intracellular fluid

___ 12. affects intracellular metabolism and protein and DNA syntheses within cells

___ 13. functions largely in the control and regulation of body fluids; increases the fluid held in the body when reabsorbed from the kidney

___ 14. maintains a balance with calcium; important in bone and tooth formation

Match the following age groups to their fluid and electrolyte status:

a. infants
b. children
c. adults
d. older adults

___ 15. have greater fluid turnover than adults do

___ 16. experience fluid and electrolyte imbalances often in association with kidney or cardiac problems

___ 17. are less able to concentrate urine compared with adults

Multiple Choice

Circle the correct response for each question.

18. A cation is:
    a. a positively charged particle.
    b. a negatively charged particle.
    c. neutral; it has no charge.
    d. Na^+, Cl^-, and H_2O.

19. An anion is:
    a. a positively charged particle.
    b. a negatively charged particle.
    c. neutral; it has no charge.
    d. a solute dissolved in a solution.

20. Which of the following statements is true of active transport?
    a. It is a passive process much like diffusion.
    b. It is the movement of solvent across cell membranes.
    c. It involves the use of a carrier, an energy source, and enzymes.
    d. It moves substances across the cell membrane from an area of higher concentration to one of lesser concentration.

21. Diffusion involves movement of:
    a. molecules from an area of higher concentration to an area of lesser concentration.
    b. fluid and solutes across a membrane from an area of higher pressure to an area of lesser pressure.
    c. pure solvent from a solution of lesser concentration to one of greater concentration.
    d. water across semipermeable cellular membranes.

22. Which of the following solutions is a hypotonic solution?
    a. 5% dextrose in 0.9% saline
    b. 0.9% saline
    c. 0.45% saline
    d. Lactated Ringers solution

23. Fluid is an essential body requirement. How much fluid does the average adult who is engaged in moderate activity require per day?
    a. 1000 mL
    b. 1500 mL
    c. 2000 mL
    d. 2500 mL

24. Which of the following statements about fluid volume deficit is true?
    a. occurs when the body loses water only from the intravascular compartment
    b. occurs when the body loses water and electrolytes from the ECF
    c. may be caused by increased fluid intake or excessive hydration
    d. is also known as hypervolemia

25. Which of the following statements about dehydration is true?
    a. occurs when the body loses only water from the interstitial and intracellular compartments
    b. occurs when the body loses water and electrolytes from the ECF
    c. is more common in children
    d. is also known as hypovolemia

26. Which of the following statements about fluid volume excess is true?
    a. occurs when the body retains water only
    b. occurs when the body retains water and electrolytes in the ICF
    c. may be related to diabetes insipidus
    d. is also known as hypervolemia

27. Which of the following statements about overhydration is true?
    a. occurs when the body retains water and electrolytes in the ECF
    b. may be related to excessive expenditure of energy resulting in increased thirst
    c. occurs with water gain, but without the proportionate gain of electrolytes
    d. is also known as hypervolemia

28. A note on your client's chart states, "Observe for evidence of third spacing." Which of the following statements accurately depicts this phenomenon?
    a. a shift of fluid from the ECF to the ICF that results in cellular lysis
    b. increased fluid in the intravascular and interstitial spaces
    c. massive fluid loss due to drainage from a wound
    d. fluid is sequestered in an area and unavailable for use

True or False

Read the following statements to determine if they are true or false. If a statement is false, alter the statement to make it true.

29. A crystalloid is a protein or large molecule that does not readily dissolve into true solution; a colloid is a salt that readily dissolves into true solution.
    True False

    ____

    ____

30. Each kilogram of weight gained or lost is equivalent to one quart of fluid gained or lost.
    True False

    ____

31. To assess a client's fluid and electrolyte status, the physical exam focuses on the skin, oral cavity, eyes, jugular veins, veins of the hand, and neurological system.
True False

32. Chvostek's sign is commonly used to assess imbalances of calcium and magnesium. A positive response may occur in clients with hypercalcemia or hypermagnesemia.
True False

33. Compared with plasma, an isotonic solution has the same concentration of solutes, a hypertonic solution has a greater concentration of solutes, and a hypotonic solution has a lesser concentration of solutes.
True False

34. Both an implantable venous access device and a central venous catheter provide access to the central venous system.
True False

Completion

35. What are the four routes of fluid output for a healthy adult?

36. What are the seven major factors that affect fluid and electrolyte balance?

37. How do isotonic imbalances and osmolar imbalances differ?

____

____

38. Describe the difference between dependent edema and pitting edema.

____

____

39. Identify five ways to assess a client who has or is at risk for developing fluid and electrolyte disturbances.

____

____

____

____

____

40. Explain the nurse's responsibilities in IV therapy.

____

____

41. What type of IV therapy equipment is used in your facility?

____

42. Order: Give a bolus of 500 mL of Lactated Ringer's solution over 2 hours followed by 1000 mL over 8 hours.

   a. What is the hourly rate of infusion for the bolus? ____________

   b. What is the hourly rate for the continued infusion? ____________

43. Identify your own blood type. ____________

44. Identify three key safety measures to protect the client receiving TPN.

____

45. Complete the following table:

Electrolyte	**Role/Location**	**Signs/Symptoms of Hypo-**	**Signs/Symptoms of Hyper-**
Sodium (Na^+)			
Chloride (Cl^-)			
Potassium (K^+)			
Calcium (Ca_2^+)			

Electrolyte	Role/Location	Signs/Symptoms of Hypo-	Signs/Symptoms of Hyper-
Magnesium (Mg^{2+})			
Phosphate (PO_4^-)			

46. Create a table of normal values.

Hematocrit ____________________

Serum osmolality ____________________

Urine osmolality ____________________

Urine pH ____________________

Urine specific gravity ____________________

47. Identify the normal range of values.

pH ______________________________

$PaCO_2$ ______________________________

PaO_2 ______________________________

HCO_3^- ______________________________

Base excess ______________________________

Analyze the following ABG results. What is your diagnosis?

48.

pH	7.26	
PaO_2		80
$PaCO_2$		40
HCO_3^-		18.1

Analysis: ______________________________

49.

pH	7.32	
PaO_2		56
$PaCO_2$		64
HCO_3^-		33.5

Analysis: ______________________________

50.

pH	7.48	
PaO_2		60
$PaCO_2$		40
HCO_3^-		30

Analysis: ______________________________

51.

pH	7.5	
PaO_2		88
$PaCO_2$		27
HCO_3^-		22

Analysis: ______________________________

Case Study

Elsa Tan has an IV that has been infusing overnight. On the day shift, you have a student nurse who is on orientation. You are giving the student some practical tips about monitoring a peripheral intravenous infusion.

52. Identify at least four aspects to be assessed or monitored while the client's IV is infusing.

53. You explain to the student that there are certain factors that influence the flow rate. List and briefly explain these factors.

54. You notice that Elsa's arm where the IV is inserted is wet and the bedding underneath is damp. What do you need to do?

55. When should you change the IV bag and tubing?

CHAPTER 41

Sensory Perception

This chapter discusses the importance of sensory and perceptual function in the maintenance of health. The chapter emphasizes the detection of sensory alterations and your role in caring for clients experiencing alterations in sensory reception or perception.

KEY TOPICS

This study guide chapter reinforces the following topics discussed in the textbook chapter:

- sensory function
- sensory deprivation
- sensory overload
- assessment of sensory/perceptual function
- promoting and maintaining sensory stimulation
- preventing sensory overload
- interventions with altered sensory function
- measures to enhance orientation

Matching

Match the sensory terms with their definitions:

a. awareness
b. cognition
c. kinesthetic
d. reticular activating system
e. sensoristasis
f. stereognosis
g. visceral

___ 1. a process synonymous with cerebral functioning that includes conscious thought, reality orientation, problem solving, judgment, and comprehension

___ 2. refers to any large organ within the body

___ 3. this centre, located in the brain stem, is believed to control the arousal mechanism

___ 4. an awareness of an object's size, shape, and texture

___ 5. the state of optimum arousal

___ 6. the ability to perceive internal and external stimuli and to respond appropriately through thought and action

___ 7. awareness of the position and movement of body parts

Match the sensory alterations with their associated signs, descriptions, and risk factors.

a. sensory deprivation

b. sensory overload

___ 8. periodic disorientation

___ 9. decreased or lack of meaningful stimuli

___ 10. increased quantity or quality of internal or external stimuli

___ 11. sleeplessness, restlessness, irritability, and increased muscle tension

___ 12. yawning, decreased attention span, boredom, and apathy

___ 13. a client confined to bed

___ 14. a client in pain, undergoing diagnostic procedures with multiple IV lines

Multiple Choice

Circle the correct response for each question.

15. Sensory reception is the:
    a. process of receiving stimuli or data.
    b. organization and translation of data into meaningful information.
    c. combination of stereognosis and kinesthesia.
    d. ability to speak about stimuli.

16. Sensory reception and sensory perception are two important aspects of the sensory experience. They are distinct in that:
    a. sensory perception can exist without sensory reception.
    b. sensory reception involves external stimuli, but sensory perception involves internal stimuli.
    c. sensory reception involves receiving data, and sensory perception involves organizing and translating the data into meaningful stimuli.
    d. sensory perception involves stereognosis, and sensory reception involves kinesthesia.

17. Your client has experienced a cerebrovascular accident, or stroke, which has resulted in severe damage to the visual centre in the brain. As a consequence, her sensory process is altered. Which aspect of the sensory process has been altered?
    a. impulse conduction
    b. perception
    c. receptor
    d. stimulus

18. Numerous factors affect the quality and quantity of sensory stimulation and function. Of the following factors, which plays an important role in sensory stimulation?
    a. developmental stage
    b. race
    c. use of antihypertensives
    d. use of diuretics

19. Which of the following stimuli in the health-care environment may produce sensory deprivation?
    a. constant bright lights
    b. equipment noise
    c. noise from staff
    d. surgical bandages that limit ability to see

20. You are communicating with an elderly client who has a hearing impairment. You are in a quiet room and directly facing the client. To improve communication, you might also:
    a. announce your presence and show the client your name tag.
    b. speak loudly directly into his ear.
    c. speak clearly and signal change of subject with a keyword.
    d. speak in short phrases.

21. You have admitted a blind client to your unit. What is the most appropriate nursing action for this client?
    a. Reorganize the room after the client has settled in so that there is no clutter.
    b. Orient the client to the room and furnishings.
    c. Place self-care articles in a drawer so that the client will not topple them over.
    d. Speak loudly and clearly as you orient the client.

22. A client with peripheral neuropathy secondary to diabetes is being prepared for discharge. The client has an ulceration on his foot, which must be soaked in warm water three times per day. Due to the neuropathy, the client cannot sense the temperature of the water with his extremities. What instructions should be given to this client?
    a. Check the temperature of the water with a thermometer before soaking your foot.
    b. Avoid placing your foot in steaming water.
    c. Assess the temperature of the water with your hand before inserting your foot.
    d. Always have someone else evaluate the temperature of the water.

23. Your client is sleepy but arouses to touch and the call of his name. His state of awareness is best described as:
    a. confused.
    b. disoriented.
    c. semicomatose.
    d. somnolent.

True or False

Read the following statements to determine if they are true or false. If a statement is false, alter the statement to make it true.

24. A client may experience cultural deprivation if he is isolated from his family, peers, or support persons of his own culture.
True False

25. As part of the nursing assessment, the client should be evaluated for vision and hearing and for olfactory, gustatory, tactile, and kinesthetic status. Mental status should also be evaluated when assessing a client for sensory perceptual process.
True False

Completion

26. When conducting a nursing history, what sensory perceptual aspects should be evaluated?

27. Identify the types of clients who are most likely to experience social isolation.

28. Identify at least one health promotion activity in each area to prevent sensory deficits.
vision
hearing
taste

Case Study

29. Marla Nicholson is an 87-year-old widow with severe osteoporosis. Her numerous compression fractures and recent fractured hip limit her activities. Marla rarely ventures out of the house. Her children and grandchildren live over 1000 kilometres away. Marla's daughter is concerned about her mother. On a recent visit, she contacts you, the nurse at the community geriatric program. She requests that her mother be evaluated for participation in an adult day health-care program. As part of your evaluation, you arrange to meet Marla at her home.

    a. Identify three areas that you would evaluate during your visit to Marla.
    Marla is interested in being part of the adult day health-care program. She realizes that she will be able to meet other seniors and engage in social activities while still living in her home. She eagerly agrees to participate. Approximately one month after joining the program, Marla falls and refractures her hip. She is hospitalized at the community hospital affiliated with the adult day program. You visit Marla two days after surgery. She appears tense, restless, and disoriented.

    ____

    ____

    ____

    ____

    b. What do you suspect is wrong with Marla? What interventions would you suggest?
    After a 10-day hospital stay, Marla is discharged to a rehabilitation centre. Marla is reluctant to enter the centre, but the orthopedic surgeon insists that she stay in the centre while receiving daily physical therapy. Two weeks after her admission to the centre, you arrange a visit to evaluate when she will be able to return to the adult day program. Marla yawns frequently and appears tired. She seems apathetic and depressed.

    ____

    ____

    ____

    ____

    c. What do you suspect is wrong with Marla? What interventions would you suggest?

    ____

    ____

    ____

    ____

CHAPTER 42

Rest and Sleep

This chapter discusses the roles of rest and sleep in health maintenance. It emphasizes your role in facilitating sleep for the client, particularly with nonpharmacological sleep aids.

KEY TOPICS

This study guide chapter reinforces the following topics discussed in the textbook chapter:

- physiology of sleep
- characteristics of NREM and REM sleep
- stages of sleep
- sleep assessment
- factors that affect sleep
- interventions to promote sleep

Matching

Match the following types of sleep with their descriptions:

a. NREM sleep
b. REM sleep

___ 1. this is often called paradoxical sleep
___ 2. it comprises four stages, each of which is progressively deeper sleep
___ 3. skeletal muscles are relaxed; muscle tone is depressed
___ 4. heart rate and respiratory rate are decreased
___ 5. heart rate and respiratory rate are often irregular
___ 6. active dreaming occurs

Match the following common sleep disorders with their definitions or characteristics:

a. hypersomnia
b. insomnia
c. narcolepsy
d. parasomnias
e. sleep apnea

___ 7. a sleep attack, a sudden wave of sleepiness that occurs during the daytime; controlled by CNS stimulants
___ 8. a cluster of waking behaviours that appear during sleep and interfere with sleep; includes somnambulism, bruxism, and nocturnal enuresis
___ 9. excessive sleep; may be related to medical conditions or serve as a coping mechanism to avoid feeling pressure or responsibility

___ 10. the most common sleep disorder; an inability to obtain an adequate amount or quality of sleep

___ 11. the periodic cessation of breathing during sleep; may be obstructive, central, or mixed

Multiple Choice

Circle the correct response for each question.

12. Rest is essential for health. Rest is characterized by:
    a. total body inactivity.
    b. calmness.
    c. being outside in fresh air.
    d. anxiety-provoking conditions for type A personalities.

13. Sleep is a basic need. Sleep is characterized by:
    a. a state of altered consciousness.
    b. a state of unconsciousness.
    c. increased perception and responsiveness to external stimuli.
    d. four stages of REM sleep interspersed with NREM sleep.

14. What effect does exhaustion have on the duration of REM sleep?
    a. As the client becomes more rested, the amount of REM sleep decreases.
    b. Fatigue and exhaustion have no effect on REM and NREM cycles.
    c. The duration of REM sleep is minimal.
    d. The duration of REM sleep is extended to counteract the fatigue.

15. The functions of sleep include:
    a. completion of digestion.
    b. restoration of normal levels of activity and balance among parts of the nervous system.
    c. provision of REM and NREM cycles.
    d. relaxation of the body.

16. As an individual moves from young adulthood to older adulthood, several changes in the sleep–wake cycle are evident. Which of the following is the true statement that characterizes these changes?
    a. The amount of sleep required decreases, but the amount of REM sleep increases.
    b. Stage IV sleep decreases over this time frame; as a result, restorative sleep declines.
    c. NREM and REM sleep cycles increase in length. The amount of time asleep also increases.
    d. Although restful sleep increases, the use of sleep medications also rises.

17. Assessment of a client's sleep involves several activities. What are the essential components of a sleep assessment?
   a. polysomnography, oximetry, and EEG
   b. EEG, EOG, and EMG
   c. history, physical, and treatment history
   d. sleep history, sleep diary, and physical examination

True or False

Read the following statements to determine if they are true or false. If a statement is false, alter the statement to make it true.

18. Providing a restful environment for clients is an important nursing function.
True False

____

____

19. A child's sleep–wake pattern does not approximate the pattern of an adult until the child is two years of age.
True False

____

____

20. Activity in the parasympathetic branch of the autonomic nervous system predominates during sleep.
True False

____

____

Completion

21. Diagram the adult sleep cycle in the space below.

____

____

____

____

____

____

22. Identify at least five factors that affect sleep.

23. When is it appropriate to ask a client to keep a sleep diary? What information should the diary contain?

24. Which diagnostic test is used to evaluate clients with sleep problems?

Case Study

Mahalia Winters is a 52-year-old client admitted to the community hospital for surgical repair of a bowel obstruction. She is admitted to your unit with the following orders:

Vital signs q2-4h

Bedrest with BRP (bathroom privileges)

Strict NPO

Lactated Ringers @ 125 mL/hr

Ancef 1.0 g q6h IV

Benadryl 50 mg @ HS

Demerol 50–100 mg IM q4h PRN pain

To be seen by anesthetist for preoperative evaluation

Scheduled for surgery in the A.M.

25. What factors might affect Mahalia's sleep pattern?

26. What information about sleep would be valuable for you to know when planning her care?

Mahalia has undergone a bowel resection for obstruction. Her clinical course has been rocky. Her unstable condition necessitated a six-day stay in the intensive care unit. She has now returned to your clinical unit. The nurse from ICU reports that Mahalia has had little sleep over the past six days.

27. What signs and symptoms of a sleep problem would you expect to find on physical examination?

28. Mahalia refuses to get out of bed. She complains to you that she is too exhausted to get up. On the basis of her history and current complaint, what is an appropriate nursing diagnosis?

29. Identify at least five nursing interventions that may help Mahalia achieve more sleep while hospitalized.

30. Mahalia asks you about the wisdom of using sleeping medications. How would you respond?

CHAPTER 43

Activity and Exercise

This chapter emphasizes safety and health promotion in moving, transferring, and exercising clients. It emphasizes good body mechanics to prevent injury and to ensure efficiency of effort. It also highlights the essential skills of range-of-motion exercises, ambulation, and transfer.

KEY TOPICS

This study guide chapter reinforces the following topics discussed in the textbook chapter:

- body alignment
- body mechanics
- exercise
- activity tolerance
- immobility
- interventions to prevent musculoskeletal problems and pressure areas
- techniques to move, turn, and transfer clients
- range-of-motion exercises

Matching

Match the following joint movement terms with their definitions:

a.	abduction	e.	inversion
b.	adduction	f.	pronation
c.	circumduction	g.	supination
d.	eversion		

___ 1. moving the bone toward the midline of the body

___ 2. turning the sole of the foot outward by moving the ankle joint

___ 3. moving the bones of the forearm so that the palm faces upward when the hand is held in front of the body

___ 4. moving the bone away from the midline of the body

___ 5. moving the distal part of the bone in a circle while the proximal end remains fixed

___ 6. turning the sole of the foot inward by moving the ankle joint

___ 7. moving the bones of the forearm so that the palm faces downward when the hand is held in front of the body

Multiple Choice

Circle the correct response for each question.

8. Body movement requires coordinated muscle activity and neurological integration. Which four elements are required for body movement?
   a. strength, coordination, intellect, balance
   b. balance, gravity, posture, support
   c. posture, joint mobility, balance, coordination
   d. body alignment, body mechanics, body strength, body fitness

9. Your client is involved in an exercise program. She states that she regularly walks around the track at the local high school. The speed of her walk allows her to speak to her exercise partner in short answers. What type of exercise is she engaged in?
   a. aerobic
   b. anaerobic
   c. isokinetic
   d. isometric

10. The major reason for using proper body mechanics is to:
   a. prevent injury.
   b. increase the amount of weight that can be moved.
   c. facilitate safe and efficient use of appropriate groups of muscles.
   d. increase physical endurance and stamina.

11. Which three elements are involved in body mechanics?
   a. posture, load, and centre of gravity
   b. line of gravity, centre of gravity, and base of support
   c. balance, gravity, and support
   d. synergistic muscles, postural tonus, and righting reflexes

12. Back injuries can happen to anyone. However, certain movements increase the risk for injury. Which of the following movements are high risk?
   a. lifting more than 22 kg and stooping over with knees locked
   b. jumping and bending with the knees locked
   c. twisting your neck and climbing stairs with your lower back curved
   d. twisting your mid-to-lower back and stooping over with your knees locked

13. Which factor do you *not* evaluate when you conduct an assessment of a client's activity and exercise patterns?
    a. inspection and palpation of the joints
    b. range-of-motion of joints
    c. ability to lift a 5 kg object
    d. muscle strength and mass

14. To avoid injury while lifting, you should:
    a. hold the lifted object close to the body.
    b. hold the lifted object out away from the body.
    e. straighten the legs while lifting.
    d. shorten the base of support.

15. Your client is positioned on his side with both his legs flexed in front of him. The upper leg is more acutely flexed than the lower. The lower arm is behind the client, and the upper arm is flexed at the shoulder and elbow. What position is your client in?
    a. Fowler's position
    b. lateral position
    c. orthopneic position
    d. Sim's position

16. Which of the following statements is true of active range-of-motion exercises?
    a. They are exercises in which the nurse puts the client's joints through the complete range-of-motion.
    b. They are conducted by having the client move each joint through its full range-of-motion.
    c. They involve out-of-bed activity.
    d. The client requires the assistance of a physical therapist in order to perform them.

17. An appropriately sized axillary crutch extends from the:
    a. floor to one to 3 to 5 cm below the axilla.
    b. floor to the height of the shoulder.
    c. anterior axillary fold to the base of the lateral malleolus.
    d. floor to the axilla.

18. Your client has been on prolonged bedrest and is very fatigued. Which of the following strategies will help to manage his fatigue?
    a. Schedule all activities for the early morning hours after he has had a full night's sleep.
    b. Have the client perform all activities rapidly to complete them as soon as possible.
    c. Intersperse rest and activity periods.
    d. Maximally assist the client in all activities until his strength has improved.

True or False

Read the following statements to determine if they are true or false. If a statement is false, alter the statement to make it true.

19. Posture, or body alignment, affects cardiovascular, respiratory, renal, and gastrointestinal functions.
True False

____

____

20. The broader the base of support and the higher the centre of gravity, the greater are the stability and balance.
True False

____

____

21. An immobilized client should be turned at least every two hours.
True False

____

22. Transfer belts should be used only when transferring a client from a bed to a stretcher.
True False

____

____

23. Passive range-of-motion exercises are useful in maintaining joint flexibility but have no value in maintaining joint strength.
True False

____

____

24. A client who has been in bed for several weeks will require assistance with getting out of bed and may need to be taught quadriceps exercises.
True False

____

____

Completion

25. What factors are involved in the coordination of body movements?

____

____

26. You must turn a 145-kg client who is unable to assist with movement. Describe the principles you will follow in order to prevent injury to yourself or the client.

____

____

____

____

____

27. What are the key factors that affect body alignment and mobility?

____

____

____

____

28. Complete the following table by identifying the hazards of immobility and benefits of exercise for each body system:

Body System	**Hazards of Immobility**	**Benefits of Exercise**
Musculoskeletal		
Cardiovascular		
Respiratory		
Metabolic		

Body System	Hazards of Immobility	Benefits of Exercise
Urinary		
Gastrointestinal		
Integumentary		
Psychoneurological		

29. What are the major components that must be addressed when designing a physical activity plan?

____

____

____

30. Review the textbook discussion on exercise programs. Evaluate your own exercise program for wellness. Does your program include a warm-up, a training period, and a cool-down phase? How often do you engage in physical exercise? Are the intensity and the duration of exercise sufficient?

____

____

____

____

31. Carmelita Medina, 48 years old, underwent abdominal surgery two days ago. She asks you to teach her how to sit on the side of the bed independently. What instructions will you provide her?

____

____

____

____

32. Before Carmelita begins to ambulate, what can you do to prepare her for safe ambulation?

____

____

____

____

____

33. While ambulating for the first time with you, Carmelita begins to fall and complain of faintness. What are the appropriate measures to take?

____

____

____

____

Enrichment Activities

1. Borrow a pair of crutches from your learning resource centre or physical therapy department. Practise each of the crutch-walk techniques described in the text.

2. Practise proper positioning and transferring with a fellow student. Talk to each other as you conduct this exercise. Feel for areas of pressure or discomfort and communicate this information.

CHAPTER 44

Clients Having Surgery: Promoting Healthy Recovery

This chapter examines the perioperative experience from the belief that surgery is a unique human experience that creates stress. It emphasizes your role in preparing the client for surgery and preventing postoperative complications.

KEY TOPICS

This study guide chapter reinforces the following topics discussed in the textbook chapter

- preoperative assessment
- preoperative care
- intraoperative care
- anesthesia
- postoperative care
- prevention of postoperative complications

Matching

Match the following terms with their descriptions:

a. conscious sedation
b. epidural anesthesia
c. general anesthesia
d. local anesthesia
e. patient-controlled analgesia
f. regional anesthesia
g. spinal anesthesia

___ 1. a temporary interruption of the transmission of nerve impulses to and from a specific region of the body

___ 2. injection of an anesthetic into the area inside the spinal column but outside the dura mater

___ 3. a subarachnoid block; injection of an anesthetic through a lumbar puncture

___ 4. minimal depression of level of consciousness with retention of the ability to respond verbally and physically and maintain a patent airway

___ 5. infiltration of an area with an anesthetic

___ 6. the loss of all sensation and consciousness

___ 7. IV pain management that is controlled by the client

Multiple Choice

Circle the correct response for each question.

8. Your client is scheduled for same-day surgery. You have assessed her preoperative status, knowledge of the planned surgery, previous experience with surgery and anesthesia, and emotional/psychological concerns. What other aspects must be assessed for this client?
   a. desire to be hospitalized
   b. availability of a responsible adult for after-care and safe transport home
   c. childhood history and developmental stage
   d. immunization history

9. What is the purpose of the preoperative assessment?
   a. to meet regulatory and legal requirements
   b. to determine the most appropriate anesthesia
   c. to establish a baseline to be used for further evaluation
   d. to inform the surgeon about the client's health status

10. There is always risk involved with any surgical procedure. Of the following clients, who has the highest surgical risk?
    a. an 81-year-old client with Alzheimer's disease and hypertension
    b. a 26-year-old graduate student on birth control pills
    c. a 14-year-old client with asthma
    d. an obese 40-year-old client

11. Preoperative teaching for a hospitalized client should include all of the following, *except* what?
    a. a general timetable for perioperative events
    b. the need to restrict food and fluids for at least 24 hours
    c. deep-breathing, coughing, turning and leg exercises
    d. any required physical preparation, such as bowel or skin prep

12. Surgical clients are usually instructed to fast for six to eight hours before surgery. The purpose of this fasting is to:
    a. keep the client from vomiting.
    b. decrease gas in the intestinal tract.
    c. decrease the need to urinate or defecate in the perioperative phase.
    d. reduce the risk of aspiration.

13. Obtaining legal, informed consent to perform a surgery is the responsibility of the:
    a. client.
    b. nurse.
    c. primary physician.
    d. surgeon.
14. The purpose of leg exercises and sequential compression devices is to:
    a. promote muscle strength.
    b. facilitate early ambulation.
    c. prevent thrombophlebitis.
    d. facilitate lung aeration.
15. Surgical nurses may function in either the scrub or circulating position. What is a key distinction between these roles?
    a. The circulating nurse assists the surgeon; the scrub nurse assists the anesthetist.
    b. The scrub nurse is responsible for sponge and instrument counts; the circulating nurse is responsible for medication and narcotic counts.
    c. The circulating nurse assists the surgeon and scrub nurse and is dressed in clean garb; the scrub nurse assists the surgeon and is dressed in sterile attire.
    d. The circulating nurse wears a sterile gown, gloves, and cap; the scrub nurse wears a sterile gown only.
16. The client is scheduled for cardiac surgery. In which position will the client most likely be placed for surgery?
    a. Fowler's
    b. lithotomy
    c. prone
    d. supine
17. The immediate postoperative position of choice for a client who has had spinal anesthesia is:
    a. flat.
    b. low-Fowler's.
    c. prone, with a pillow underneath the abdomen.
    d. side-lying with the head slightly elevated.
18. The purpose of splinting while coughing is:
    a. pain reduction, especially for the client with abdominal surgery.
    b. prevention of evisceration and dehiscence.
    c. prevention of thrombophlebitis.
    d. client security.

True or False

Read the following statements to determine if they are true or false. If a statement is false, alter the statement to make it true.

19. Surgery may be categorized according to degree of urgency, degree of risk, or purpose.
True False

____

____

20. With any of the types of regional anesthesia, the client loses sensation in an area of the body but remains conscious.
True False

____

____

21. Any client over the age of 55 is at increased risk for surgical complications.
True False

____

22. The nurse in the surgical suite is solely responsible for maintaining a sterile field.
True False

____

____

23. For the client scheduled to undergo abdominal, thoracic, or pelvic surgery, coughing and deep breathing exercises are not required.
True False

____

____

24. The client undergoing major surgery always receives an enema, shave, and sedative preoperatively.
True False

____

____

25. During the initial postoperative phase, maintenance of a patent airway is a major nursing priority, especially for the client recovering from general anesthesia.
True False

____

____

26. Unless otherwise indicated, the physician should be informed if the client has not voided within eight hours following surgery.
True False

27. Pain is usually greatest during the first eight hours after surgery.
True False

Completion

28. A postoperative client usually remains in the PARR until:

29. Which assessments should you perform when receiving a postoperative client from the recovery room?

30. Your postoperative client returns from surgery with a nasogastric tube. What is your role in managing the client who requires gastric suctioning?

31. What are your responsibilities when caring for a client with a closed wound drainage system?

32. Complete the following table by filling in the possible cause, clinical signs, and preventive interventions for the potential postoperative problems:

Problem	Possible Causes	Clinical Signs	Preventive Interventions
Pneumonia			
Postoperative Ileus			
Thrombophlebitis			
Wound Dehiscence			
Postoperative Depression			

Case Study

David Lipscomb is a 51-year-old client admitted to Mercy Medical Centre for abdominal surgery.

33. What preparation for surgery is required?

34. During your assessment, David states, "No one ever explained this surgery to me. The doctor told me I needed this surgery, but I don't understand why. I'm really not sure about all this." A signed consent form is on the chart, and the operating room transporter has just arrived to transport the client. How would you handle this situation?

35. Identify an appropriate nursing diagnosis for David.

36. As you prepare David for surgery, you note that his chest and abdomen are very hairy. He will undoubtedly need hair removal prior to surgery. What should you do?

37. David undergoes resection of a loop of bowel and returns to the unit later that evening. An NG tube is in place for 48 hours and then removed. On the third postoperative day, he asks you when he will be able to eat and drink again. What is your best response?

CHAPTER 45

Pain Management

This chapter presents current theories on pain and pain management. It stresses your role in assessing, diagnosing, planning care for, intervening in, and evaluating the client's pain experience. It also underscores the importance of understanding the uniqueness of pain perception.

KEY TOPICS

This study guide chapter reinforces the following topics discussed in the textbook chapter:

- pain syndromes
- physiology of pain
- factors affecting the pain experience
- pain assessment
- pain management
- nonpharmacological pain strategies

Matching

Match the following types of pain with their descriptions:

a.	acute pain	e.	phantom pain
b.	chronic pain	f.	radiating pain
c.	intractable pain	g.	referred pain
d.	neuropathic pain		

___ 1. This pain is resistant to relief despite therapeutic interventions.

___ 2. The client reporting this type of pain may appear restless and anxious. This pain is related to tissue injury and will abate with healing.

___ 3. This pain may be described as shooting or stabbing. It results from a disturbance of the peripheral or central nervous system.

___ 4. This pain is perceived at the source and extends to nearby tissues.

___ 5. This is a painful sensation perceived in a missing body part or in a paralyzed body part.

___ 6. This pain is felt in a part of the body that is considerably removed from the tissues causing the pain.

___ 7. This pain lasts longer than six months and often limits normal functioning.

Multiple Choice

Circle the correct response for each question.

8. Pain is a universal experience. Which of the following descriptions most accurately portrays pain?
   a. Pain should be evaluated through assessment of behaviour. Verbal reports of pain are not sufficient cause for treatment.
   b. Pain is highly subjective. It is whatever the client states it is.
   c. Caregivers should attempt to delay administration of pain medication to prevent development of drug dependence.
   d. Pain is always a signal that serious physiological problems exist.

9. Which of the following statements about pain is true?
   a. All pain sensations received by nociceptors pass the pain gate and are transmitted to the brain.
   b. Pain impulses may be transmitted to the brain through fast pain or slow pain pathways. Regardless of the pathway, the impulse is transmitted in the same fashion, although the speed of transmission is different.
   e. The cerebral cortex is thought to play a role in the interpretation and localization of pain.
   d. Fast pain fibres release substance P, which is slow to build up at the synapse and slow to be destroyed. This property is thought to play a role in the nature of chronic pain.

10. Your client is experiencing significant leg pain due to a recent injury. According to gate control theory, you could affect his pain perception by ascending modulation. Which method is consistent with this approach?
    a. massage
    b. relaxation
    c. education and emotional support
    d. use of options

11. Numerous factors affect the pain experience. Of the following list, which factor would be *least* likely to affect pain?
    a. age
    b. educational level
    c. ethnic and cultural values
    d. expectations of significant others

12. Pain assessments should be performed:
    a. only when the client states she is having pain.
    b. once per day.
    c. immediately after administration of IV morphine.
    d. and initiated by the nurse.

13. Pain may be acute or chronic. Chronic pain is often characterized by:
    a. overt behavioural responses, such as rocking, immobilization of a body part, or tossing and turning.
    b. absence of behavioural or physiological responses.
    c. elevation of blood pressure, pulse, and respirations.
    d. dull or piercing pain.

14. Pharmacological pain management involves a variety of drugs to treat symptoms. Which of the following statements about opioids is true?
    a. Addiction to opioids may develop even when they are given for acute pain.
    b. Clients with severe pain often experience diminishing effects of opioids with continued use.
    c. Physical dependence on a drug is a sign of addiction.
    d. Respiratory depression is the most serious side effect of opioid analgesia.

15. The preferred route of delivery for opioid administration is:
    a. oral.
    b. intramuscular.
    c. intravenous.
    d. transdermal.

16. Patient-controlled analgesia (PCA) may be used for acute and chronic pain. Which of the following clients would be the most likely candidate for PCA?
    a. a 22-year-old woman with severe neurological deficits
    b. an alert postoperative client in pain
    c. a postoperative client with Alzheimer's disease
    d. a three-year-old child with pain after a tricycle accident

17. Your client is experiencing severe postoperative pain. You have just administered an opioid by injection but wish to supplement pain relief with nonpharmacological pain management strategies. Which strategy can you implement independently?
    a. acupuncture
    b. immobilization
    c. massage
    d. TENS

True or False

Read the following statements to determine if they are true or false. If a statement is false, alter the statement to make it true.

18. Pain threshold and pain tolerance are similar among individuals.
True False

____

____

19. All clients who have undergone an appendectomy experience similar levels of pain.
True False

____

____

20. Pain intensity may be evaluated by use of a simple rating scale or through picture rating scales, verbal descriptions, or nonverbal cues.
True False

____

____

Completion

21. Patrick Mooney is a 13-year-old grade 9 student. During lunch period, he and another student argued and a fight ensued. Patrick has a "black eye" and an abrasion on his left cheek. The other child is without injury. As the school nurse, what independent nursing actions could you take to alleviate Patrick's pain? Provide rationales for your choices.

____

____

____

____

____

22. What are the collaborative nursing actions to reduce pain?

____

____

____

____

____

Case Study

Cassandra Thomas is a 24-year-old client complaining of abdominal pain. She locates her pain in the epigastric region. On a 0 to 10 scale, she rates her pain as a 6. She describes the pain as "constant throbbing" and says she feels nauseous.

23. What additional pain history information would help you plan your care for Cassandra?

On examination, Cassandra's vital signs are: BP 140/90, HR 112, RR 26, T 37.7C oral. Her skin is moist and warm to touch. She is mouth-breathing, and her oral mucosa appears pale and dry. She is lying on her side with her knees and hips flexed. She speaks only when asked a direct question.

24. Is Cassandra's pain acute or chronic?

25. Develop a pain management strategy appropriate for Cassandra.

26. If opioids are prescribed for Cassandra, what side effects would you anticipate?

27. Morphine via PCA pump is prescribed for Cassandra. Identify the benefits of this method.

28. How would you evaluate the effectiveness of your pain management strategies?

CHAPTER 46

Self-Concept

This chapter presents your role in maintaining and enhancing the client's perception of self. It emphasizes assessment of clients with altered self-concept and interventions to facilitate positive self-esteem.

KEY TOPICS

This study guide chapter reinforces the following topics discussed in the textbook chapter:

- self-concept
- self-esteem
- body image
- role
- personal identity
- strategies for promoting professional self-concept

Matching

Match the following terms with their definitions:

a. body image	d. role
b. global self	e. self-concept
c. personal identity	f. self-esteem

___ 1. how a person perceives the size, appearance, and functioning of the body and its parts

___ 2. how we feel about ourselves; a judgment of our own worth

___ 3. how we see ourselves; the cognitive component of the self system

___ 4. a set of expectations of how the person occupying one position relates to a person in another position

___ 5. the collective beliefs and images one holds about oneself

___ 6. what distinguishes self from others; the conscious sense of individuality and uniqueness that is constantly evolving throughout life

Multiple Choice

Circle the correct response for each question.

7. When asked about how she sees herself, your client states that she has been told by others that she is bright, articulate, and attractive. She is unable to voice a personal opinion about herself. Which of the statements most accurately depicts this client?
   a. She is very me-centred. Her self-knowledge and insights are focused on how she can create the best image.
   b. She is very other-centred. This may inhibit her ability to attain a positive self-concept.
   c. She has limited self-expectations.
   d. She has not successfully negotiated Erikson's stage of Integrity versus Despair.

8. Your client has a large discrepancy between his ideal self and perceived self. His ideal self is unrealistic. What can you conclude?
   a. He should be seen for counselling services on a regular basis.
   b. His perceived self is most likely inaccurate.
   c. He should be assessed for low self-esteem.
   d. He will be motivated to improve.

9. Which of the following statements about role is correct?
   a. Each person usually has several roles over a lifetime, but holds only one role at a time.
   b. As you gain confidence in your nursing abilities, you will begin to feel role strain, indicating that your behaviours meet social expectations.
   c. When you believe you practise competently, you have achieved role mastery.
   d. Role ambiguity occurs when expectations are unclear and the individual does not know what is expected.

10. Which four criteria do people use to form their concept of self?
   a. role performance, body image, personal identity, and self-esteem
   b. age, beauty, intelligence, and social status
   c. money, beauty, power, and significance
   d. comfort, status, role, and power

11. Which of following statement(s) about self-esteem is correct?
   a. Significant others are important in the development of self-esteem. A significant other takes on importance at a particular stage in life but there is limited carryover of effect into the next stage of development.
   b. People are strongly influenced by societal expectations during adolescence and adulthood only.

c. Ideally, an individual will successfully achieve all developmental tasks as he or she progresses through life. However, as long as an individual successfully achieves the developmental tasks associated with young adulthood, he or she may continue to be productive in later life.
d. Having a repertoire of coping styles and communication techniques is important so that an individual can adapt to situations and maintain or enhance self-esteem.

12. Which cluster of behaviours may indicate low self-esteem?
    a. avoiding eye contact, self-deprecating remarks, the tendency to recognize shades of grey in performance and thinking, frequent pessimistic statements
    b. hesitant speech, minimizing the positive in a situation, statements that focus on personal shortcomings
    c. optimistic attitude, socially active, upright posture, seeing mistakes as learning opportunities
    d. maximizing the negative, minimizing the positive, socially interactive, a tendency to overgeneralize

13. You are assessing your client's self-concept. You have identified the client's age, developmental level, health history, and family and cultural values. What other aspects must be evaluated?
    a. stressors, resources, and history of success and failure
    b. body image, personal identity, and perceived self
    c. evaluation of role and others' point of view
    d. psychiatric history and level of education

14. You are conducting a psychosocial assessment of a client. Of the following descriptions, which depicts ideal behaviour during this assessment?
    a. You ask directed questions, record quotes from the client, and involve family in the assessment.
    b. You give the client a list of questions you need answered and allow the client to answer verbally or in writing depending on his/her comfort level.
    c. You ask open-ended questions, demonstrate interest, and are aware of your own biases that could influence the assessment.
    d. You interview the client and family together and verify client responses with the family.

True or False

Read the following statements to determine if they are true or false. If a statement is false, alter the statement to make it true.

15. Body image develops partly from others' attitudes and responses to your body and partly from your own exploration and attitude toward your body.
    True False

    ____

    ____

16. A person with an adequate self-esteem is able to carry out a role despite feeling depressed about inadequacies.
True False

17. Rapport and a trusting relationship are prerequisites to an effective assessment of self-concept.
True False

18. You can assist your clients in developing enhanced self-evaluations by modelling positive self-statements, providing helpful feedback, and assisting them to verbalize positive self-statements and to visualize strong positive images.
True False

Completion

19. What is the nurse's role in dealing with self-concept and self-esteem?

20. Evaluate your own self-concept. Are you me-centred or other-centred?

21. Using the "Framework for Identifying Personality Strengths" as presented in the textbook, identify your own personality strengths.

22. Phillipa Jonas is a seven-year-old child with myopia and astigmatism. Corrective glasses have been prescribed, but Phillipa does not wear them in school because many of the other children make fun of her. Phillipa's mother believes her daughter has low self-esteem and cannot tolerate the other children's taunting. As the nurse, what advice would you give the mother?

____
____
____
____

Case Study

You are working in a long-term care facility. The majority of residents are elderly. You note that the facility is very institutional: the walls are bare, the rooms and floor are beige, and the hallways are dark.

23. What changes would you make in the setting to enhance the self-esteem of the residents?

____
____
____
____
____
____
____

24. What suggestions would you make to encourage professional self-concept among the staff?

____
____
____
____
____
____
____

25. What suggestions would you make to enhance client self-esteem?

____
____
____
____
____
____
____

CHAPTER 47

Stress and Coping

This chapter introduces you to multiple views on stress and its various manifestations. It emphasizes your role in minimizing client stress and presents numerous tips on how to control your professional stress.

KEY TOPICS

This study guide chapter reinforces the following topics discussed in the textbook chapter:

- models of stress
- manifestations of stress
- anxiety
- anger
- coping strategies
- interventions to minimize and manage stress

Matching

Match the following terms with their definitions:

a. alarm reaction
b. coping mechanism
c. stage of exhaustion
d. stage of resistance
e. transactional stress theory

___ 1. This is the second phase of the general and local adaptation syndromes. It is characterized by attempts to cope with the stressor and limit the stressor to the smallest area of the body that can deal with it.

___ 2. This term encompasses a set of cognitive, affective, and adaptive responses that arises out of person–environment interaction.

___ 3. This is the initial reaction of the body to a stressful event. It comprises two parts: the shock phase and the countershock phase. The shock phase is associated with a fight-or-flight response. In countershock, the effects of the shock phase are reversed.

___ 4. The ways to cope with the stressor have been exhausted. Rest must occur if the individual is to continue.

___ 5. This refers to an innate or acquired way of responding to a changing environment or specific problem.

Multiple Choice

Circle the correct response for each question.

6. Tomorrow is your first clinical day as a nursing student. How might this event relate to stress?
   a. You will experience a developmental stressor for which there are no coping responses.
   b. This new event may trigger stress. Your reaction may be dependent on your perception of the event and your developmental stage.
   c. This is a negative stressor. Successful negotiation of this stressor will require mobilization of coping strategies.
   d. The first clinical day is a planned event for which you have prepared. It should not trigger a stress response.

7. Research demonstrates that people with a high level of stress are more prone to:
   a. display nervous anxiety.
   b. use drugs to cope with the stress.
   c. develop illness or be less able to cope with illness.
   d. reject relaxation methods.

8. Which of the following are body responses to stressors?
   a. increased cardiac output, bronchial dilation, increased blood clotting, and increased fat mobilization
   b. decreased myocardial contractility, decreased blood clotting, decreased glucose metabolism, and increased blood pressure
   c. increased blood pressure, increased heart rate, increased appetite, and increased urine output
   d. decreased energy, increased need for rest, increased appetite, and increased metabolism

9. Anxiety is a common reaction to stress. Anxiety is characterized as:
   a. having an identifiable source.
   b. related to the present.
   c. being related to definite concerns and beliefs.
   d. the result of psychological or emotional conflict.

10. Your client is experiencing depression related to recent loss of a loved one. If this depression continues unabated for a full year, how must you proceed?
    a. Depression for this length of time is not surprising. You must continue to offer support and encouragement.
    b. Depression is an uncommon reaction to a stressful event. This client should be assessed for signs of psychiatric dysfunction.

c. Prolonged depression may require treatment. This client should be referred for further evaluation.

d. Situational depression is very common. This client requires no intervention.

11. Which stage of anxiety actually enhances perception and abilities?

a. mild anxiety

b. moderate anxiety

c. severe anxiety

d. panic

True or False

Read the following statements to determine if they are true or false. If a statement is false, alter the statement to make it true.

12. Death of a spouse is a highly stressful event and always produces a significant amount of anxiety.
True False

____

____

13. Psychological manifestations of stress include anxiety, fear, anger, and depression.
True False

____

____

14. Problem solving, fantasy, and prayer are the only cognitive indicators of stress.
True False

____

____

15. Crisis intervention assists clients through long-term adaptation to stress.
True False

____

____

Completion

16. What are two examples of short-term coping strategies?

____

____

17. In the space below, draw and label a scale illustrating the four levels of anxiety. Record your current level of anxiety.

18. Identify at least five ways in which you can successfully manage your stress.

19. Reflect on your most recent experience with stress. What were your verbal and motor manifestations of stress?

20 Jeff Drew is a 20-year-old client with insulin-dependent diabetes. During his first month at college, Jeff has had trouble controlling his blood sugars. He attributes this difficulty to a hectic college schedule, erratic eating, and a dislike for dormitory food. By the second month, he requires hospitalization for control of his diabetes. What factors must be considered when evaluating Jeff's level of stress?

Case Study

Jose Rojas is a 41-year-old mechanic, who sustained a partial amputation of his left index finger while operating a machine at work. He is admitted to your unit after surgical repair of the injury. Jose is quite concerned about future use of his hand. He also voices concern about the length of time he must be off work.

21. How can you help minimize his anxiety?

22. What are the goals of nursing care for Jose?

23. On the third day of hospitalization, Jose becomes very angry and threatens to leave the hospital against medical advice (signing out AMA). How would you respond to Jose?

24. What independent nursing actions could you take to help Jose relax?

CHAPTER 48

Loss, Grieving, and Death

This chapter discusses the processes of loss and grief. It presents coping with death, the ultimate loss, as an example of handling loss. The chapter emphasizes your role in assisting clients with successful transition through the grieving process. To facilitate personal growth, you are encouraged to evaluate your own beliefs about death and grief.

KEY TOPICS

This study guide chapter reinforces the following topics discussed in the textbook chapter:

- grief
- death
- nursing of the dying
- loss and grief responses

Matching

Match the following terms associated with loss and grieving with their definitions:

a. bereavement c. loss

b. grief d. mourning

___ 1. subjective experience of a surviving loved one after the death of a significant other

___ 2. total response to loss; manifested in thoughts, feelings, and behaviours

___ 3. behavioural process through which grief is eventually resolved or altered

___ 4. actual or potential situation in which something that is valued is changed, no longer available, or gone

Multiple Choice

Circle the correct response for each question.

5. Which type of loss may be viewed as a developmental crisis and can be anticipated to some extent?
   a. loss of one's job
   b. loss of a home due to fire
   c. death of a parent
   d. death of a child

6. Which of the following clients is exhibiting dysfunctional grief?
   a. a wife who believes that her husband's death is a blessing as he is no longer in severe pain
   b. a recently widowed woman who loses five pounds and is unable to concentrate
   c. a child who would like to get another pet right away after the death of the family cat
   d. a 35-year-old woman who is still angry at her mother for dying and thus abandoning her when she was 12

7. Your client has recently been notified that he has metastatic colon cancer. The physician believes that he has less than 12 months to live. When you enter the room, he is cheerful and smiling. He tells you that he has decided that the physician must have gotten someone else's test results. He says, "I'm healthy and happy. He made a mistake. I'm not going to worry about things." According to Kubler-Ross, what stage of grieving is the client experiencing?
   a. acceptance
   b. anger
   c. bargaining
   d. denial

8. What is the most effective way to help the client presented in Question 7?
   a. Offer spiritual support.
   b. Support the client, but do not reinforce his beliefs.
   c. Encourage his beliefs, since they are his way of coping.
   d. Confront his refusal to accept the truth.

9. On the oncology unit, you provide care for many middle-aged adults with life-threatening illnesses. When working with this age group, you realize that they:
   a. may have learned to cope with loss through previous loss, availability of support, and personal strength.
   b. need assistance with regaining the normal continuity and pace of emotional development.
   c. usually experience the greatest number of losses.
   d. are prone to regression if they feel threatened, afraid, or abandoned by loss.

10. A client in the intensive care unit has been unresponsive to verbal or tactile stimuli for over three weeks; has shallow, spontaneous respirations; and relies on a pacemaker to sustain an adequate blood pressure. This client could be described as:
    a. experiencing cerebral death.
    b. clinically dead.
    c. critically ill.
    d. legally dead.

11. Which of the following is true of closed awareness of death?
    a. It implies that the client, family, and health personnel know the prognosis but choose not to talk about it.
    b. It may present an ethical dilemma for the nurse.
    c. It most frequently occurs in extended families who choose to handle their grief within the family network.
    d. It occurs when the client suddenly deteriorates physically.

12. Palliative care has been ordered for your client. You recognize that this means that:
    a. your client should not be resuscitated in the event of a respiratory arrest.
    b. the focus of care is symptom control and compassion.
    c. in the event of death, the client has agreed to donate organs and tissue.
    d. death is not anticipated; care should be aggressive.

13. Your client is a devout Christian. As his condition deteriorates, his family requests that you immediately contact the hospital chaplain for spiritual support. You, however, are an atheist. How should you respond?
    a. You should contact the chaplain for spiritual support.
    b. You should attempt to negotiate switching clients with a fellow nurse who has religious values that parallel the views of the client.
    c. You should explain to the family that you do not agree with their views and ask them to contact their own spiritual advisor.
    d. You should determine the client's current status in order to assess the need for spiritual support.

14. The physician has written a Do Not Resuscitate order for a client. In the event that this client experiences a cardiopulmonary arrest, you should:
    a. notify the physician immediately and ask the family if they would like heroic efforts.
    b. perform CPR until the order has been verbally verified by a physician.
    c. provide care and comfort but do not initiate CPR.
    d. provide oxygen and emergency medications but no CPR.

15. Your client was pronounced dead five minutes ago. The client's family is en route to the hospital. Your goal is to prepare the body before the family arrives in one hour. You realize that:
    a. livor mortis will appear quickly, so you must close the eyes and replace the dentures immediately.
    b. algo mortis must be offset to produce a natural appearance of the individual.
    c. rigor mortis immediately sets in, so you must rush to prepare the body.
    d. rigor mortis develops in two to four hours, and preparing the body before the family arrives in one hour should be adequate.

True or False

Read the following statements to determine if they are true or false. If a statement is false, alter the statement to make it true.

16. An actual loss can be perceived by others, but a perceived loss is only evident to the person who has experienced the loss.
True False

____

____

17. Nursing skills in situations of loss include attentive listening, silence, open and closed questioning, clarifying and reflecting feelings, advising on ways to handle the situation, summarizing, and evaluating the client's handling of the situation.
True False

____

____

____

18. Impending death is heralded by loss of muscle tone, slowing of the circulation, changes in vital signs, and sensory impairment.
True False

____

____

Completion

19. What are the factors that determine how an individual deals with a loss?

____

____

20. What are the major goals of dying clients?

____

____

21. Shelli Jenkins is terminally ill with breast cancer. You are coordinating Shelli's care. Identify at least five appropriate nursing actions.

____

____

____

____

____

22. Have you ever experienced the death or loss of a significant other? If so, identify the relationship of this person to you and the effect this loss had on you.

____

____

____

23. React to the following statement: "Death is always a negative experience, and health professionals should strive to forestall death at all costs."

____

____

____

24. You are caring for an 11-year-old boy with leukemia. While you are giving him his morning medications, he asks you, "What happens when you die?" How would you respond to him?

____

____

____

25. Your terminally ill client asks you what happens after death. How would you respond?

____

____

____

Case Study

Anna Bradley is a healthy 71-year-old woman. Anna race-walks five miles three times per week, does not smoke, consumes limited alcohol, and consistently eats a low-fat, low-salt, high-fibre diet. She keeps active in the community by volunteering as a teacher's aide at the elementary school. Anna is known in the neighbourhood as a model of healthy aging.

Anna's husband recently died suddenly due to a lethal cardiac dysrhythmia (altered cardiac rhythm). He had no history of cardiac disease and had been pronounced "in excellent health" at a recent physical examination.

Anna is devastated. She tells you she no longer has "the strength to go on." She cannot imagine living without her spouse of 50 years.

26. How would you respond to Anna's statements?

____

____

____

____

____

____

Answer Key

Chapter 1 Answer Key

1. d
2. c
3. b
4. a
5. c
6. b
7. e
8. a
9. d
10. b
11. a
12. b
13. d
14. a
15. f
16. e
17. c
18. a
19. c
20. d
21. a
22. b
23. e
24. c
25. b
26. (a) caregiver
    (b) communicator, case manager
    (c) counsellor and communicator
    (d) client advocate, case manager, counsellor, and communicator

Chapter 2 Answer Key

1. e
2. b
3. c
4. a
5. d
6. c
7. d
8. a
9. a
10. c
11. b
12. d
13. to keep nurses abreast of new knowledge and techniques; to help nurses attain expertise in a specialized nursing practice; and to provide nurses with essential information for nursing practice.
14. Registered Nurse (RN), Registered Psychiatric Nurse (RPN), Licensed Practical Nurse (LPN).
15. (a) Licensed Practical Nurse
    (b) Registered Nurse
    (c) RN
    (d) 10 to 18
    (e) diploma program
    (f) baccalaureate degree
    (g) graduate education at the master's or doctoral level
    (h) inservice programs
    (i) continuing education
16. Your answer should incorporate a summary type of programs that he can apply for: Practical Nursing or Baccalaureate Degree Programs. Include suggestions for him to consult with his high school Career Counsellor, do volunteer work at a hospital, clinic, or community health centre as applicable, recommend books to read or Web sites to explore, and audit some classes at the local college or university.

Chapter 3 Answer Key

1. c
2. d
3. a
4. b
5. e
6. a
7. b
8. a
9. a
10. c
11. c
12. d
13. right not to be harmed, right to full disclosure, right of self-determination, right of privacy and confidentiality
14. insert *Select a research design* between the fourth and fifth step
15. abstract
16. tables, figures
17. False Research is the systematic inquiry that uses orderly scientific methods to solve problems. Problem solving is a series of steps designed to solve problems, but it does not employ orderly scientific methods.
18. True
19. True
20. Obtaining informed consent is the responsibility of the principal investigator. The participants have to be informed of the consequences of participating. Because the participants are minors, a legally authorized representative, such as a parent or guardian, may sign the consent. The person consenting for the child must be able to judge whether there is a reasonable balance between the potential benefits and the risks of participating. The consent must be voluntary and not coerced. Furthermore, the child's representative must be told that refusal to participate will not jeopardize the quality of care received by the child.

Chapter 4 Answer Key

1. e
2. c
3. f
4. d
5. g
6. a
7. b
8. f
9. a
10. d
11. b
12. h
13. e
14. i
15. j
16. c
17. g
18. b
19. c
20. c
21. d
22. (Examine your program's philosophy or interview faculty or administration.)
23. (See discussion and tables in the text.)
24. Nursing theory offers a framework for generating knowledge, and research investigates the questions. Research findings may be developed into theories for nursing.
25. A question that you would want to ask of each of the presenters is: "Why did you select that theory?" Other questions would be: how they assess clients, how the theory helps with the identification and application of nursing care, how they explain to clients their philosophy of care, how they evaluate their care, and how they reflect on their nursing practice.

Chapter 5 Answer Key

1. a
2. e
3. b
4. f
5. d
6. g
7. c
8. b
9. d
10. c
11. b
12. True
13. False Coping patterns may change due to demands.
14. True
15. False When planning nursing care, the client condition and client evaluation of needs will determine the order of priority.
16. a stable physical environment, a stable psychological environment, a social environment with healthy role models, a life experience that provides satisfactions
17. Knowledge of human needs helps the nurse set priorities for care, identify ways to assist the client to relieve distress, and understand potential client needs.
18. (a) physiological needs
    (b) safety and security needs
    (c) love and belonging needs
    (d) self-esteem needs
    (e) self-actualization
19. (See the text for discussion on internal and external resources.)
20. (See text for specific examples.)
21. (Refer to the chapter for assistance with your example.)
22. (Your answers will depend upon the cultural beliefs of the clients in your care. For assistance, refer to the table in the text.)
23. Assess both internal and external resources. For internal resources, explore her knowledge, skills, and communication patterns, problem solving skills, sense of purpose, and previous experiences. External support systems, such as family, religious affiliation, health-care workers, or other connections in the community, are important resources.

Chapter 6 Answer Key

1. d
2. a
3. b
4. c
5. d
6. b
7. d
8. a
9. b
10. False Canadian families are characterized by high mobility. Between 1991 and 1996, almost half of the Canadian population moved to another location.
11. True
12. True
13. commendation
14. engaging in a collaborative relational stance

    asking reflective questions

    enabling access to the patient

    eliciting illness narratives

    commending family and individual strengths

    offering information

    creating and encouraging family support

    suggesting respite from caregiving
15. (See the text for discussion of the different types of families.)
16. (Refer to the chapter.)
17. (a) (Check the chapter for assistance with your ecomap drawing.)

    (b) Find out if there are any other community agencies that might be helpful — include self-help, church, and other groups. Ask who might be most helpful for any particular challenges, for example: Who can Marla rely on best for daily activities? Inquire as to which relationships are supportive and which ones are stressful.

Chapter 7 Answer Key

1. f
2. d
3. a
4. c
5. e
6. b
7. b
8. c
9. a
10. d
11. a
12. g
13. c
14. e
15. b
16. f
17. a
18. c
19. c
20. True
21. False A code of ethics is a formal statement of a group's ideals and values.
22. True
23. False Advocacy in nursing is focused on protecting the public's rights and advancing the profession through informing, supporting and mediating.
24. strong commitment to service, belief in the dignity and worth of each person, commitment to education, professional autonomy
25. (Check with your facility. You may need to contact the administrative department to gather this information.)
26. (Consider your own views on abortion as well as how you feel about Catherine's views and use of health care.)
27. (Examples of questions are found in the discussion entitled "Clarifying Client Values.")
28. (a) 1. How can this situation be explored by using ethical principles? Which principles are applicable?

2. How does a focus on relationship assist our ethical understanding of the situation?

3. How would everyone be affected by the decision?

    (b) (The chapter presents the CNA Code of Ethics, which outlines the values and responsibilities.)

    (c) Consult the text for Storch's ethical decision-making framework. The first step is: *Information and Identification. Clarification and Evaluation* is the next stage. *Action and Review* is the third step where the range of actions and anticipated consequences are explored. Here are a few options. You may want to look at the option of calling a client care conference to discuss your knowledge of a living will. With this approach you could gather support and advice from colleagues. Explore the possibility of what would happen if you directly confronted the family. Look at what would happen if you did nothing and did not make it known that there is a living will.

Chapter 8 Answer Key

1. d
2. g
3. b
4. c
5. e
6. f
7. a
8. g
9. h
10. c
11. e
12. a
13. f
14. b
15. d
16. c
17. b
18. c
19. d
20. e
21. b
22. d
23. b
24. a
25. d
26. a
27. False Nurse–client communication is not always protected as a privileged communication. The exceptions are in cases where harm might result to the client or others or when law requires disclosure. In Canada, confidentiality of information is incorporated as an ethic.
28. False On the basis of the legal doctrine of *respondent superior,* the employer is responsible for the conduct of the employee in most cases, but this doctrine does not prevail if the employee's actions are extraordinarily inappropriate.

29. True

30. True

31. Do not give the medicine. If the nurse administers the medication, he will be responsible for his own action as this is an unusually high dosage and should be questioned by the nurse. Notify the charge nurse of the apparent error in the order. In most cases, the nurse will place a call to the physician to discuss the order.

32. (Examine your own beliefs about collective bargaining. You may wish to have a class or small group discussion about collective bargaining for nurses.)

33. (Consider how you would feel if you did cross the picket line and how you would feel if you did not cross the line.)

34. (a) breach of duty on the part of the nurse

    (b) a relationship exists between the injury to the client and the breach of duty

35. medication error, incorrect sponge or needle count in the OR, burning a client, a client fall, ignoring a client's complaints, incorrectly identifying the client

36. The consent must be given voluntarily, the consent must be given by someone with the capacity and competence to understand, and the client must be given enough information to be the ultimate decision maker.

37. (You may wish to conduct a values clarification exercise.)

38. (Check with your instructor or investigate this question in the library.)

39. Implied consent exists when the person's nonverbal behaviour indicates a willingness. For example, when an individual keeps returning to attend group sessions or have physiotherapy.

40. (Check with your faculty or administration. You may wish to invite a nurse attorney to speak to your class.)

41. You may wish to consult with your clinical instructor about what you have witnessed. Be very objective, report only what you know, and avoid making assumptions.

Chapter 9 Answer Key

1. e
2. d
3. b
4. c
5. a
6. a
7. b
8. b
9. a
10. b
11. a
12. c
13. b
14. d
15. a
16. b
17. (See the text for the World Health Organization's and nursing theorists' definitions of health. Your own personal definition of health may be unique or a blend of ideas from many sources. "Developing a Personal Definition of Health" provides a list of questions that may help you formulate your personal definition of health.)
18.

Determinant that influences Health	Example
Income and Social Status	More people in high-income brackets rate their health as very good or excellent compared with the lowest-income group.
Education	People who have low literacy skills are more likely to suffer from poor health.
Social Environment	Family violence influences the health of mothers and children, and this is shown by the number of women who suffer from psychological and physical problems due to the violence.
Physical Environment	Air pollution has been associated with a higher number of asthmatic attacks and allergic reactions, especially in children.
Personal Health Practices	Diet, especially consumption of fat, has been linked to multiple diseases, such as heart conditions and cancer.
Social Support Network	The more social contacts people have, the lower are their premature death rates.

19. (a) a state of feeling unhealthy or ill

 (b) an alteration in body function resulting in a reduction of capacity or shortening of the normal lifespan

 (c) causation

20. Provide explanations about necessary adjustments, make arrangements to accommodate client's lifestyle, encourage other health professionals to support healthy aspects of client's lifestyle, and reinforce desirable changes in lifestyle.

21. Assess if Fanny is experiencing other factors that may be contributing to her distress. Encourage expression of feelings and thoughts. Assist her in problem solving. Establish support systems for her, if necessary. Demonstrate caring and compassion.

22. (a) socio-psychological

 (b) knowledge

23. Possible client responses include, but are not limited to, increased stress due to anxiety about the outcome, task reassignments, role changes, potential financial issues related to being out of work, and loneliness.

Chapter 10 Answer Key

1. c
2. a
3. e
4. d
5. b
6. c
7. d
8. b
9. c
10. a
11. True
12. False Both the nurse and the client review the data and summarize the information.
13. True
14. (To answer this question you will need to examine your community and its resources. Look at billboards, information presented on grocery store bags, newspaper or television health reports, and local health fairs for information dissemination programs. Health appraisal and wellness assessment services may be offered by area health centres, hospitals, or fitness clubs. Appraisal tools may be found on the Internet. Lifestyle and behaviour change programs may be advertised in local newspapers, phone books, shopping centres and hospitals, medical centres, and doctors' offices. Environmental control programs are often offered by community groups or by local political and environmental groups that are working to improve the quality of air, food, water, and other resources.)
15. (a) (Utilize the assessment tool in text Figure 10.3 to evaluate your personal health risks.)

    (b) (Your answer will be dependent on the results of your self-evaluation.)

    (c) (Your answer will be dependent on the results of your self-evaluation.)
16. (a) There is incomplete assessment information. For example, no data are supplied about Jack's diet, stress level, safety habits, or use of nonprescription or illegal drugs. You will need to use one of many health risk appraisal tools presented in the chapter to evaluate Jack's health.

    (b) Health-seeking behaviour (annual screening exam)

    (c) Praise existing positive health behaviours, identify areas that may require change, role model healthy lifestyle behaviours and attitudes, educate Jack to be an effective health-care consumer, serve as an advocate in the community for changes that provide a healthy environment.

Chapter 11 Answer Key

1. m
2. j
3. h
4. e
5. f
6. d
7. g
8. o
9. l
10. i
11. n
12. k
13. b
14. c
15. a
16. b
17. c
18. d
19. d
20. b
21. True
22. True
23. True
24. to understand the biopsychosocial-spiritual approach to care that facilitates the client's growth and holism and to provide for self-care in a manner that reveals the nurse's healing power
25. (Your answer will depend upon your own experiences with alternative treatment modalities.)
26. (Your answer will depend upon your own experiences with self-healing.)
27. Your answer will depend on how you feel about humour and laughter. It may be helpful to reflect on what your positive and negative experiences were when humour was used in different nursing situations. For example, did you see it as a way of coping, as a way to release anger, or as a way to facilitate learning?

Chapter 12 Answer Key

1. d
2. a
3. e
4. c
5. b
6. a
7. c
8. b
9. f
10. d
11. e
12. c
13. b
14. a
15. b
16. c
17. a
18. d
19. c
20. d
21. c
22. a
23. False Clients with heart disease, diabetes mellitus, joint disease, and chronic pain have physiological conditions that may affect their sexuality.
24. False Breast self-examination for women and testicular self-examination for men should be conducted monthly.
25. True
26. elf-knowledge and comfort with sexuality, acceptance of sexuality as an area for nursing intervention, a willingness to work with clients expressing their sexuality in a variety of ways, knowledge of basic sexuality communication skills, an ability to recognize the need of the client and family to have the topic of sexuality introduced
27. To maintain, restore, or improve sexual health; to increase knowledge of sexuality and health; to prevent the occurrence of STIs; to prevent the spread of an existing STI; to increase satisfaction with the level of sexual function; to increase sexual self-concept

28.

Level	*Example*
P Permission giving	Ask an open-ended question, such as, "What questions do you have about. . ."
LI Limited information	Provide basic and specific information on sexuality and the identified sexual health problem or issue.
SS Specific suggestions	Offer suggestions to help the client adapt sexual activity to promote optimal functioning.
IT Intensive therapy	Therapy provided by a clinical nurse specialist or sex therapist is used when the first three levels of counselling have been ineffective.

29. (a) How you would handle this situation depends on many things, including your relationship with the client, the nature of the advances, and your level of discomfort. See the box "Nursing Strategies for Inappropriate Sexual Behaviour" for specific suggestions.

(b) Possible causes include misinterpretation of your behaviour, need for reassurance that he is still sexually attractive, fear over future ability to perform sexually, need for attention, need for control or power, and inaccurate belief that this is appropriate behaviour.

Chapter 13 Answer Key

1. a
2. e
3. d
4. f
5. g
6. b
7. h
8. c
9. c
10. a
11. a
12. a
13. a
14. True
15. False Parish nurses work with a congregation's ministry team, where they combine nursing and health expertise with theological concepts.
16. False A holy day is a day dedicated for special religious observance.
17. Spiritual health and beliefs may be assessed in the general history, through a nursing history, and by clinical observations of the client's environment, behaviour, verbalization, and mood.
18. There are many possible responses including the following: sit with her and allow her to express her thoughts and emotions, ask her if she would like to see a clergy member or a significant other, discuss how she feels about her illness and the meaning of the illness.
19. (a) You will want to observe Joseph's environment for evidence of sacred writings, pictures or icons, or other religious items. If you observe these items, you may wish to use these as launching points for your discussion. In addition, you will want to observe his behaviour and verbalizations related to religion and spirituality. Questions about his attitude about his disease may also yield information. In addition, you can use such questions as those in the "Assessment Interview" to aid you in your assessment.

    (b) Provide presence through open discussion with the client or with the client and his significant others. Support the client's religious practices by assisting the client to have desired devotional materials or by working with the family to have comforting literature read or visits made by clergy. Assist with prayer by praying with client, remaining quiet while he prays, or facilitating quiet time so the client may pray. A referral for spiritual care may also be made by contacting a local religious person.

(c) There are many possible responses, including: inform the client you are uncomfortable and offer to obtain a clergy person, indicate you are uncomfortable praying with him but offer to stay with him while he prays, acknowledge that you respect the client's desire to pray but that you are unable to pray with him.

Chapter 14 Answer Key

1. g
2. c
3. b
4. f
5. d
6. e
7. h
8. a
9. a
10. b
11. a
12. b
13. True
14. True
15. False This is an example of cultural assimilation or acculturation.
16. True
17. False Racism is a hostile feeling toward an individual who is a member of a race that you feel is inferior to your own. Discrimination occurs when there is differential treatment of an individual or group based on race, ethnicity, gender, social class, or exceptionality.
18. True
19. False When caring for a client who speaks a different language, it is best to utilize an objective individual for translation services.
20. False To provide safe and effective care, nurses who work consistently with clients from specific cultural groups should increase their knowledge about cultural behaviour and communication patterns within those cultures.
21. True
22. Culture is learned, taught, social, adaptive, satisfying, difficult to articulate, and present on many levels.
23. (Review the discussion in the text for clarification.)
24. (Your response will depend upon your culture and the culture of your prospective client.)
25. (Examine your own knowledge and experience.)
26. The magico-religious health belief view suggests that health and illness are controlled by supernatural forces. These forces can be identified as a higher power or God or an evil spirit. Consequently, the treatment for illnesses consists of magical or religious

treatments. In the scientific or biomedical health belief view, life and life processes are controlled by the physical and biochemical processes that can be influenced by people. Illnesses are caused by germs, bacteria, or viruses or a breakdown of the human body, and treatments consist of medicines or surgery. The holistic health belief view suggests that forces of nature must be in balance or harmony. For example, the First Nations members teach the Medicine Wheel, that the physical, mental, emotional, and spiritual aspects of human nature must be in balance to be healthy.

Chapter 15 Answer Key

1. g
2. k
3. l
4. a
5. p
6. b
7. j
8. i
9. f
10. c
11. o
12. e
13. n
14. h
15. m
16. d
17. b
18. c. Choice “c” is incorrect because a client may refuse a treatment at any time. A second opinion is not required.
19. b
20. c
21. False Hospitals provide a variety of health-care services, including inpatient and outpatient care, specialized diagnostic and treatment services, and health promotion and disease prevention programs.
22. True
23. False Long-term care facilities are intended for people who require personal services, some regular nursing care, and occasional medical attention.
24. False Hospice care is dedicated to improving or maintaining the quality of life until death.
25. True
26. True.
27. False Home care services are appropriate for acute, short-term care as well as long-term monitoring of clients with chronic illness.

28. True

29. (a) community centres, hospitals, weight control classes, stop smoking programs, stress reduction activities

(b) hospitals, physician's offices, community clinics

(c) hospitals, skilled nursing facilities, physical therapy offices, occupational therapy offices or departments

31. (You will need to contact your instructor, and the health facility of classmates further along in the program to determine the nursing model(s) used in your local facilities.)

31. inadequate rest and privacy, poor physical environment, questionable personal safety, inadequate health care, poor access to facilities for personal hygiene, poor compliance with treatment plans, substance abuse, exposure to elements, lack of social support, improper nutrition, few personal resources

Chapter 16 Answer Key

1. f
2. a
3. b
4. e
5. g
6. c
7. d
8. c
9. d
10. a
11. b
12. a
13. True
14. False Referral processes in health care are a systematic problem solving approach that involves knowledge of resources, solving problems, setting priorities, coordinating, and collaborating.
15. True
16. (See the box, "Pew Commission Competencies for Future Practitioners." Also, note that Barnes, et al. (1995) believe that nurses will need to be prepared for multiple levels of practice and need increased clinical preparation in and with communities as well as with elderly and vulnerable populations.)
17. Nurses should aim to collaborate with clients, peers, other health-care professionals, professional nursing organizations, and legislators.
18. initiate discharge planning upon admission to any health-care setting, include the client and family in the planning process, and collaborate with other health professionals, as needed, to ensure that all needs are met
19. (a) Ms. Roberts' personal and health data; her ability to perform activities of daily living; identification of any physical, cognitive, or functional limitations; presence (or absence) of a caregiver and this person's abilities; adequacy of Ms. Roberts' financial resources; the home environment; and the potential need for home care assistance

    (b) Ms. Roberts will require information about medications, dietary or activity restrictions, signs of complications that need to be reported, follow-up appointments and telephone numbers, and where any needed supplies can be obtained.

Chapter 17 Answer Key

1. b
2. a
3. c
4. d
5. c
6. a
7. d
8. b
9. c
10. False Documentation of care is a legal requirement, and data must be recorded on the client's medical record.
11. True
12. True
13. The home setting is intimate, and intimacy fosters familiarity, sharing connections, and caring among the clients, family, and nurse. Behaviours are more natural, cultural beliefs and practices are more visible, and multigenerational interactions tend to be displayed.
14. advocate, caregiver, educator, case manager, coordinator of services
15. (a) You will need to gather information from the chart or referring physician and contact Diane to schedule a home visit. During the pre-entry stage, your goals are to establish rapport and collect as much data about the client as possible.

    (b) While in the home, you will need to continue to develop rapport, assess the infants and the family, determine the plan of care and desired outcomes in conjunction with Diane and her family and delineate what care will be provided.

    (c) Determine if your home health agency employs a security firm that may accompany you on this visit; if not, determine the best mechanism to receive a security escort. Avoid taking personal belongings on the visit. Inform others at your agency about your concerns and develop a plan to signal for help, if needed.

    (d) Due to the immunocompromised status of her parent and the presence of three premature infants and a toddler, you will need to focus your efforts on health teaching, especially handwashing and disposal of wastes. You will also need to assess Diane for caregiver role strain.

Chapter 18 Answer Key

1. c
2. b
3. a
4. d
5. a
6. a
7. b
8. c
9. False Because of the migration of rural youth to the urban areas, there is a resultant increase in the proportion of elderly who remain in the rural communities.
10. True
11. True
12. depression, substance abuse, changing family and economic dynamics, cultural changes, declining religious affiliations, and Western society's views of suicide as a terminal way of solving problems
13. highly visible members of the community, greater autonomy, greater knowledge of client's home and family conditions, closer interface with other health-care professionals, and greater opportunity to affect health policies and health planning
14. Your agenda needs to include topics on prevention of hearing loss as well as preservation of residual hearing. For children and adolescents, place emphasis on wearing proper hearing-protection equipment during skeet shooting, decreasing length of exposure to harmful noise, for example, listening to loud music. For adults, include topics on how they might isolate the sound by erecting barriers or surround the source of the sound with sound-dampening enclosure.

Chapter 19 Answer Key

1. d
2. e
3. c
4. a
5. b
6. f
7. a
8. e
9. f
10. b
11. g
12. c
13. j
14. i
15. d
16. h
17. c
18. b
19. d
20. a
21. b
22. True
23. False Morality refers to the requirements necessary for people to live together in society, while moral behaviour is the way a person perceives those requirements and responds to them.
24. True
25. to assess the client's growth and development using the standards proposed in the major theories, to identify and report any problem areas, to plan and implement nursing strategies that will maintain or promote the client's development
26. *Six months*: This is a period of rapid physical growth. Nursing care must be designed to meet physical and psychological needs. Infant safety is paramount. *Thirty months*: This is a time of increasing autonomy and physical mobility. Psychosocial skills are on the rise. Nursing care must permit the toddler to explore and develop, but not at the expense of safety. A balance between risk taking and safety is required. *Five years*: This is a period

of slower physical growth but expanding social development. When a five-year-old child is hospitalized, the nurse must facilitate play time and social activity. *Twelve years*: The 12-year-old child must be evaluated for the appropriate stage of development. Some children of this age will have the issues of school-aged children, while others have moved into adolescence. The 12-year-old experiences rapid physical growth as well as social growth. Peer groups take on extreme importance. Nursing care will be directed toward the level of development at which the child is functioning.

27. (Review the chapter for assistance with this response.)

28. Stage 3—caring for self and others: The client needs to balance her needs and her son's. There is an interconnection between the self and others, and so, neglecting herself may lead to negative consequences for the son.

Chapter 20 Answer Key

1. c
2. a
3. e
4. b
5. d
6. g
7. b
8. f
9. d
10. e
11. a
12. c
13. c
14. b
15. a
16. d
17. c
18. d
19. a
20. d
21. b
22. c
23. a
24. b
25. a
26. c
27. False An infant's basic task is survival, which requires breathing, sleeping, sucking, eating, swallowing, digesting, and eliminating.
28. True
29. False The ability to creep and crawl is usually developed by the age of nine months. However, depth perception does not usually develop until 12 months of age.

30. False Starting school is significant because it allows the child to compare his or her own skills with those of the peer group. The child also receives impressions of how his or her skills are perceived by the teacher, the school nurse, and peers.

31. True

32. (a) three times

    (b) four times

33. (a) by overriding of the sutures or junction lines of the skull bones

    (b) nine to 18 months

    (c) from four to eight weeks after birth

34. using the Apgar scoring at birth and the Denver Developmental Screening Test for evaluation of development; teaching parents to wash hands before handling the infant; instructing about and/or administering immunizations; encouraging health promotion visits; teaching accident prevention and child-proofing information; teaching skin care; explaining nutritional needs and usual progression of diet; teaching expectations regarding elimination; explaining usual patterns of rest, sleep, and crying; encouraging stimulation through play

35. identification, introjection, imagination, and repression

36. Moral behaviour is learned through modelling.

37. The preschooler has greater verbal and motor skills and more autonomy than the toddler. This results in greater involvement of the child in health promotion. At the preschool level the child can assist with screening for vision and hearing problems. The preschool child is more active and can be taught safety skills, such as how to cross the street and bicycle safety, and can be involved with taking responsibility for some hygiene.

38. The nurse can promote cognitive development by screening for vision, hearing, and learning problems. The nurse is also active in promoting health, thereby helping develop a child who can learn.

39. continued need for health maintenance visits and immunizations; instructions on safety and hygiene education; nutritional information to ensure an appropriate diet; education about physical fitness and exercise; menstruation education for girls and sexuality education for both sexes; information on the hazards of smoking, alcohol, and drugs

40. (a) Express willingness to discuss her concerns. Listen attentively. Provide accurate information in response to questions.

    (b) Gather further data about Martin's general state of health, eating patterns, sleeping patterns, and elimination. Physically assess the child. Explain that crying periods lasting one to two hours per day are normal in infants.

    (c) Encourage health maintenance visits and immunizations, stress the need for adequate supervision to prevent accidents, encourage use of safety-tested car seats, ask caregivers for evidence of activities that may indicate visual problems, begin dental hygiene and regular dental care, alert parents to the need to encourage adequate nutrition, encourage potty training when the child shows interest and readiness, provide freedom to play within the limits of safety, encourage cognitive stimulation through play and caregiver interaction.

(d) By age 5, most children can easily separate from parents and enjoy playing with other children. Scott may be delayed. Further evaluation employing the Denver Developmental Screening Test and physical and psychosocial assessment of the child and family appears warranted.

(e) The start of adolescence is marked by the onset of puberty. Strong interest in school, peers, and outside activities is common among school-age children.

Chapter 21 Answer Key

1. e
2. a
3. b
4. c
5. g
6. d
7. c
8. g
9. c
10. f
11. d
12. b
13. d
14. b
15. c
16. c
17. a
18. True
19. True
20. False Elderly persons are more susceptible to respiratory infections due to decreased ciliary activity and decreased capacity to cough effectively.
21. (See the discussion in the chapter on "Adulthood and Maturity" for common measures of adulthood.)
22. *Vision:* degenerative changes in the eye, resulting in relative inflexibility of the lens, or *presbyopia*; increased opacity of the lens, frequently resulting in cataracts; decrease in pupil size with increased sensitivity to glare and decreased ability to adjust to darkness

    Hearing: diminished hearing ability, or *presbycusis*

    Taste: decreased number of taste buds, resulting in decreased sense of taste, especially sweet

    Smell: atrophy of the olfactory bulb, resulting in decreased sense of smell

    Touch: gradual reduction in skin receptors, leading to an increased threshold for pain and touch and diminished capacity to distinguish temperature and pressure

23. The nurse practitioner should advise Matilda on health promotion activities. These activities should include routine health maintenance visits with appropriate screening and assessments; immunizations; safety measures to avoid injury; dietary assessment for adequacy of nutrients and fluid and prevention of constipation; development of a regular, moderate exercise program; discussion of sleep patterns and methods to facilitate rest encouragement related to maintaining independence (the nurse practitioner may choose to support Matilda's decision to stay active by working independently); discussion of her support network and counselling on appropriate use of drugs and alcohol.

24. (Reflect on your own experiences as a nursing student or your interactions with elderly friends or relatives.)

25. (Look through community listings of senior services and discuss with discharge planners.)

Chapter 22 Answer Key

1. e
2. h
3. d
4. a
5. c
6. g
7. b
8. f
9. c
10. a
11. d
12. b
13. d
14. True
15. False Critical thinkers are very independent people.
16. True
17. False Critical thinkers show perseverance when working out solutions.
18. True
19. False The intuitive method of problem solving may be used by nurses with a broad knowledge base and extensive clinical experience.
20. False Creative thinkers are flexible and quick to generate ideas.
21. rational, reflective, constructively sceptical, autonomous, creative, fair and unbiased, focused on what to believe or do.
22. trial and error, intuition, the nursing process, the scientific method/research process, and the modified scientific method
23. (See the text discussion of the 10-step scientific method and the seven-step modified scientific method, as well as Table 22.4.)
24. (See the text section on critical thinking and the box, "Standards for Critical Thinkers.")

25.

Attitude That Fosters Critical Thinking	Example of Strategy
Independence of Thought	Try to avoid just using your past experiences as a basis for helping the client. Broaden your experience by using Socratic questioning.
Fair-mindedness	Be open to the client's points of view.
Insight into Egocentricity and Sociocentricity	Examine your own biases and prejudices, social pressures, customs, and values.
Intellectual Humility and Suspension of Judgement	Be aware of the limits of one's knowledge. Admit what you do not know.
Intellectual Courage	Recognize that some of your beliefs may be false or wrong.
Integrity	Apply the same rigorous standards to your own knowledge and beliefs as you apply them to others.
Perseverance	Resist the temptation to come up with a quick and easy answer. Critical thinkers show determination in seeking effective solutions.
Confidence in Reason	Have confidence in the reasoning process and look at emotion-laden arguments using standards of evaluating thoughts or ideas.
Interest in Exploring Both Thought and Feelings	Acknowledge that both thoughts and feelings are integral in individuals' decision making. Deal with negative emotions by not making hasty decisions.
Curiosity	Ask questions, and be inquisitive.
Contextual Awareness	Try to find out the unique experiences and circumstances contributing to the client's situation. Challenge assumptions about people.

Chapter 23 Answer Key

1. d
2. a
3. e
4. b
5. c
6. a
7. b
8. a
9. a
10. c
11. b
12. c
13. M
14. N
15. M
16. C
17. N
18. C
19. c
20. a
21. b
22. k
23. c
24. l
25. e
26. d
27. i
28. g
29. j
30. h
31. s

32. o
33. f
34. m
35. n
36. p
37. q
38. d
39. c
40. b
41. a
42. b
43. a
44. b
45. c
46. a
47. c
48. d
49. d
50. c
51. c
52. c
53. b
54. c
55. b
56. True
57. False "When did you last eat?" is an example of a closed question.
58. True
59. False "Who are the people you can count on for support?" is an example of a neutral question.
60. True
61. False Goals and desired outcomes provide direction for planning nursing interventions and enable the nurse and the client to determine if and when the problem has been resolved.

62. True

63. True

64. (a) conversation

 (b) specific information

 (c) nurse

 (d) gather information

 (e) build rapport

 (f) client

 (g) problem solve, counsel, evaluate the client's response to the treatment plan

65. establish rapport and orient the client to the purpose and nature of the interview

66. to gather information through the various uses of questions

67. to maintain the rapport and trust established in the interview and to facilitate future interactions

68. (Compare the tool with frameworks in the text.)

69. (a) Registered Nurses

 (b) other nursing personnel

70. verify data with the client and the family; apply knowledge from supporting disciplines; acquire clinical experience; know population norms; consult resources; consider patterns of behaviour, rather than isolated incidents; improve critical thinking skills

71. client's health values and beliefs, client's priorities, resources available to the nurse and the client, urgency of the health problem, medical treatment plan

72. Independent nursing interventions are those activities that nurses are licensed to initiate on the basis of their knowledge and skills. Examples include instituting fall precautions or taking vital signs qlh on a client who is believed to be unstable.

73. Dependent nursing interventions are those activities carried out under the physician's order or supervision. Some examples are administering medications ordered by the physician or following wound care orders.

74. Collaborative nursing interventions are actions that the nurse carries out in collaboration with other health team members. Some examples include teaching use of a walker in collaboration with physical therapy or monitoring a client's response to medication.

75. A standing order is a written order that gives nurses the authority to carry out specific actions under certain circumstances.

76. Correct

77. Incorrect (This outcome needs a time frame and a measurable distance of ambulation.)

78. Incorrect (This outcome is not possible to achieve; if weight loss is a goal, the goal must be realistic. Either the time frame must be changed for the 10-kilogram weight loss, or the amount of weight loss for one week must be more realistic, such as 0.5 kilogram).

79. Incorrect (This outcome must be modified to contain only one specific client response or behaviour, and it must be specific and measurable and possess a time frame.)

80. Correct

81. Retrospective audit, concurrent audit, peer review

82. (a) objective data BP 158/98, P 104 regular, RR 26, T 36.8C oral, client is short of breath and appears fatigued, wife is teary-eyed

(b) subjective data: Client states, "I am dying. Let me rest. I will sleep and die." Wife states, "My husband had a heart attack four months ago. Over the last month, it has been harder and harder for him to breathe. He is so short of breath he sleeps sitting up in a chair."

(c) Anxiety, fear of illness as life-threatening, and acute illness may impede data collection. Attempt to reduce anxiety and fear, and ask close-ended questions to obtain essential data. Because the client is fatigued and short of breath, you may need to defer full interview until the client is more rested or not so short of breath. Culture and gender will need to be considered when planning the interview and exam. Consider asking the wife some questions in order to conserve the client's energy.

(d) the client, family, old and current charts, other health professionals, the literature

83. (Nursing diagnoses may be written in many forms; they may be single statements or multi-part statements. See your text for details on how to formulate nursing diagnoses.)

(a) Potential diagnoses may include Anxiety related to impending surgery, as evidenced by elevated blood pressure and heart rate, and Potential for Infection.

(b) Pain related to recent mastectomy, as evidenced by patient statement, Anticipatory Grieving related to recent mastectomy.

84. (a) The desired outcome must include the subject, action verb, condition/modifiers and the criterion of desired performance. For example, "By the end of today's teaching session, the client will be able to correctly demonstrate use of the prescribed metered-dose-inhaled bronchodilator."

(b) Nursing orders must be clear instructions on how to carry out the intervention to meet the client goals. For example, explain to the client the actions of the bronchodilator at the first teaching session.

Chapter 24 Answer Key

1. g
2. j
3. f
4. d
5. l
6. b
7. k
8. a
9. i
10. e
11. h
12. c
13. b
14. a
15. d
16. c
17. b
18. d
19. b
20. True
21. False The client may read his or her own chart.
22. False All charting must be timed, dated, and signed. Entries must be made in dark-coloured ink.
23. False The frequency of charting is based on agency policy and the client condition.
24. True
25. False A telephone order must be countersigned by the physician within the time frame specified by the agency.
26. (a) serving as the central location for client data from all health professionals
    (b) fragmentation, repetition, delays in client care
    (c) educational purposes
    (d) quality assurance purposes
    (e) future health-care needs

(f) ensure that the facility is meeting their standards

(g) identification of agency needs

27. (Check with your institution, faculty or preceptor.)

28. Possible responses include, but are not limited to:

(a) advantages: all nurses educated to write this form of care plan, care plan is individualized to client; disadvantages: time-consuming to write, no standard nomenclature (see text for more details)

(b) advantages: save time, ensure that key interventions are not missed; disadvantages: must be individualized, may not recognize subtleties of individual client situation, may not recognize cultural variations (see text for more details)

(c) advantages: goal-oriented, all health-care providers working toward same goals, clear pattern of care; disadvantages: must be individualized, may be driven by financial concerns versus client concerns (see text for more details)

29. graphic record, fluid intake and output record, medication record, daily nursing care record

30. to ensure continuity of care for the client by transmitting pertinent information about the client, client condition, and plan of care

31. A nursing conference is a meeting to discuss possible solutions to a client care problem. The meeting may be multi-disciplinary. Nursing rounds occur at the bedside. The client is encouraged to participate in the discussion.

32.

	Abbreviation	***Term***
a.	NPO	nothing by mouth
b.	OOB	out of bed
c.	hs	at bedtime (hour of sleep)
d.	STAT	immediately
e.	bid	twice daily
f.	q6h	every 6 hours
g.	BRP	bathroom privileges
h.	ADL	activities of daily living
i.	DAT	diet as tolerated
j.	po	by mouth

33. (a) Avoid general words, such as "good." Instead, chart what the client ate or the percentage of the meal that was consumed.

(b) Problems with this charting include: nurse did not sign name and left a blank space at the end of all entries; nurse skipped lines before beginning charting.

(c) Charting should be brief, accurate, and devoid of inferences or personal judgement.

Chapter 25 Answer Key

1. d
2. b
3. g
4. c
5. e
6. a
7. f
8. c
9. a
10. b
11. a
12. a
13. True
14. True
15. True
16. To search the literature, you may need to visit the library at your school or college or log on to the Internet from a personal computer. Next, you will need to determine the appropriate bibliographical database(s) for the topic you have chosen. Once in the database system, you will need to follow instructions specific to the database system; however, in general, you will need to enter keywords that describe your area of interest.
17. (You will need to discuss the variety of clinical sites used by your program with your faculty and peers.)
18. Some of the possible uses for computers in a hospital unit include ordering client supplies and lab work, tracking client locations, staffing of nursing units, and analyzing quality and cost of care. Computer chips are present in tympannic thermometers, IV pumps, medication dispensing systems, supply dispensing systems, controlled access devices to medication rooms, client-controlled analgesia machines, specialized beds for pressure sore prevention, and nurse alert systems. Did you find others?
19. Your answer will be based on what you know the computer can do at present and your imagination. It may include the following possibilities: use of voice recognition to dictate and word process your nursing reports and care plans; use of simulated and virtual labs for practising nursing skills, such as changing IV tubings or inserting nasogastric tubes; and digital technology being able to give a bed bath or a massage.

Chapter 26 Answer Key

1. a
2. d
3. c
4. b
5. a, c, d
6. a
7. d
8. a
9. c
10. a
11. d
12. b
13. I
14. F
15. F
16. I
17. I
18. c
19. b
20. c
21. c
22. c
23. a
24. b
25. d
26. b
27. True
28. False Attentive listening requires energy and concentration.
29. True
30. True
31. age, gender, appearance, diagnosis, education, values, ethnic and cultural background, personality, expectations, setting

32. be honest, listen attentively, help him identify how he feels about his asthma and the required medications, identify his developmental level and speak to him at the appropriate level, be genuine, openly discuss his lack of adherence to the medical regimen, ask him to be part of the planning of medication administration times

33.

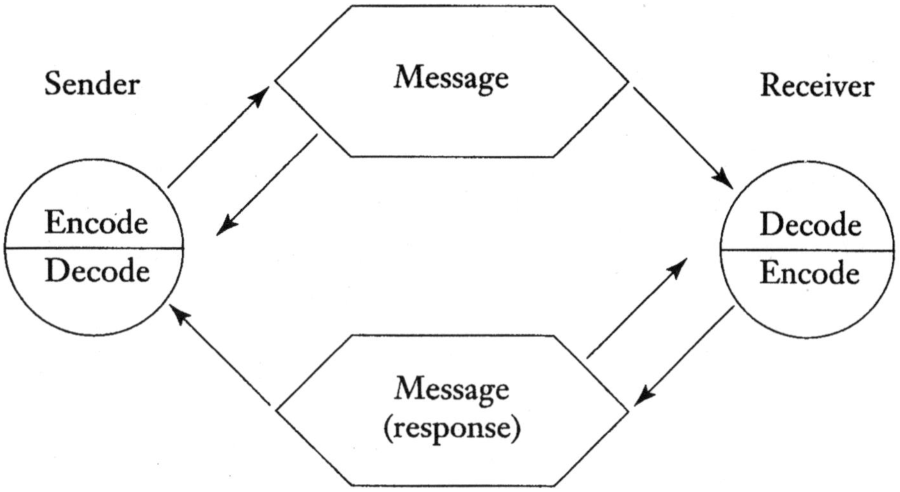

34.

Intimate:	bathing a client, changing a dressing, conducting a physical assessment, feeding a baby
Personal:	taking a history, checking an IV, discussing an issue with the client
Social:	making rounds, having group discussions
Public:	leading a class, such as new parenting skills

35. accomplish its goals, maintain cohesion, develop and modify structure to improve effectiveness

36. a

37. d

38. d

39. b

40. Bob needs to convey caring and compassion. Several possible responses are: Sit quietly with her allowing her to regain composure. Tell Jean, "I'm so sorry. I see this is very painful for you." Hold her hand, and allow her to cry. When she has regained composure, Bob may wish to explore with her who her key support people are so that he may help her enlist additional support.

41. d

Chapter 27 Answer Key

1. e
2. i
3. b
4. h
5. a
6. c
7. g
8. d
9. f
10. c
11. k
12. b
13. f
14. a
15. h
16. g
17. l
18. e
19. j
20. i
21. d
22. c
23. c
24. b
25. a
26. d
27. b
28. a
29. b
30. a
31. c

32. a

33. d

34. c

35. True

36. True

37. False When assessing the vascular system, it is important to palpate pulses on both sides of the body simultaneously to determine symmetry of the pulse volume, except when evaluating the carotid pulses.

38. True

39.

Technique	Description	Example of Use
Inspection	visual examination, assessment by use of sight, possible use of naked eye or lighted instruments	refers to inspection of skin, funduscopic examination of eyes, inspection of a wound
Palpation	examination of the body using the sense of touch, light or deep; examiner primarily uses pads of fingers	may be used to determine texture, temperature, distention, presence of pulse, tenderness or pain, size, consistency, or mobility
Percussion	a striking of the body to elicit sounds that can be heard or vibrations that can be felt	used to determine the size and shape of internal organs; may be used to delineate a liver margin or fluid in the lungs
Auscultation	a way of listening to sounds produced within the body; may be direct—use of the unaided ear—or indirect through a stethoscope	used to assess breath sounds, bowel sounds, heart murmurs, or joint movement

40. location, distribution, configuration, colour, shape, size, firmness, texture, and characteristics of individual lesions

41. (a) extremely dull sound produced by percussion over very dense tissue, such as muscle or bone

(b) a thud-like sound produced by percussion over dense tissue, such as the liver, spleen, or heart

(c) a hollow sound produced by percussion over the lungs

(d) a booming sound present only over abnormal tissue, such as an emphysematous lung

(e) a musical or drum-like sound produced by percussion over an air-filled organ

42.

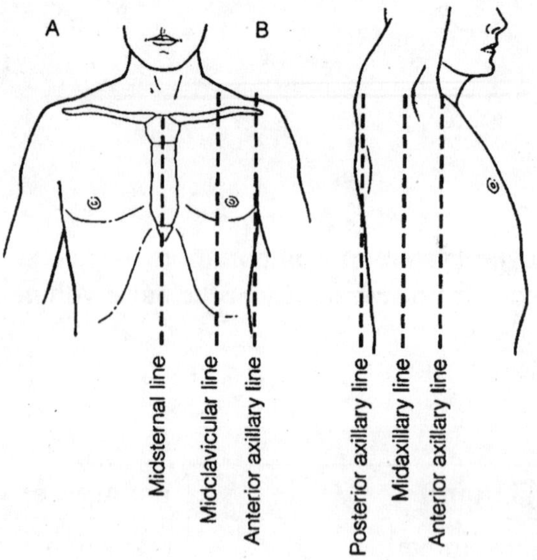

43.

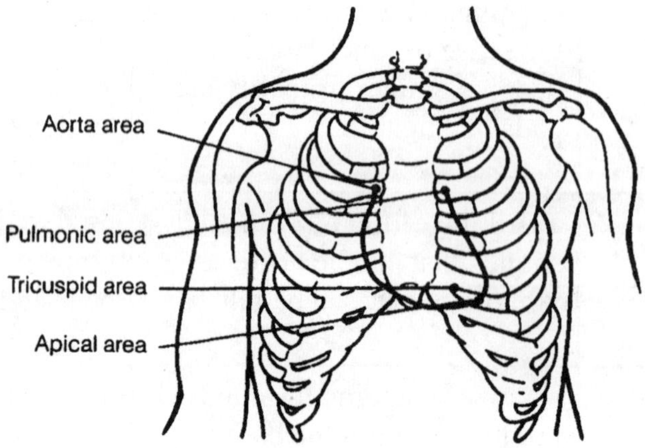

44. Ask the client to walk, and observe his/her gait. Questions to ask might include: Do you have any muscle or joint pain? Have you ever broken a bone? What has been your tallest height? Have you lost height?

45. (See chapter discussion of required skills, and evaluate your comfort level.)

46.

Name of Nerve	*Type*	*Assessment*
I: Olfactory	S	ask client to close eyes and identify common smells
II: Optic	S	check visual acuity and visual fields; conduct an opthalmoscopic examination
III: Oculomotor	M	assess six ocular movements and pupillary reaction
IV: Trochlear	M	assess six ocular movements
V: Trigeminal	B	check sensation of cornea, skin of face, and nasal mucosa; ask client to clench teeth
VI: Abducens	M	assess directions of gaze
VII: Facial	B	ask client to perform a variety of facial expressions and check taste on anterior tongue
VIII: Auditory	S	assess ability to hear spoken word and vibrations of tuning fork
IX: Glossopharyngeal	B	check gag reflexes, evaluate taste on posterior tongue, and assess tongue movement
X: Vagus	B	assess with cranial nerve IX; check speech for hoarseness
XI: Accessory	M	ask client to shrug shoulders against resistance and turn head side to side
XII: Hypoglossal	M	ask client to protrude tongue and move from side to side

47. (a) You will need to assess the client's functional and cognitive status, underlying conditions, and sensory function. You may need to allow extra time for the client to answer your questions and assume the required positions.

(b) Rather than assume a head-to-toe approach, you will need to alter your approach so that you proceed from least invasive or least uncomfortable to the most invasive procedure.

Chapter 28 Answer Key

1. d
2. c
3. h
4. b
5. a
6. g
7. f
8. e
9. c
10. g
11. d
12. b
13. f
14. e
15. a
16. d
17. c
18. b
19. c
20. b
21. a
22. d
23. a
24. b
25. c
26. d
27. d
28. d
29. b
30. b
31. a

32. False In an intradermal injection, the syringe is held at a 15-degree angle to the skin with the bevel of the needle upward.

33. False The speed of absorption of a drug given by intramuscular injection is faster than injection via the subcutaneous route.

34. True

35. True

36. Percutaneous absorption of a medication may be altered by lacerations, burns, or other skin irritations.

37. True

38. age, pregnancy, gender, ethnicity, culture, diet, environment, psychological factors, illness and disease, and time of administration

39. client's full name, date and time the order was written, name of the drug to be administered, drug dosage, route of administration, frequency of administration, signature of the person writing the order

40. (a) 3000 mg

    (b) 90 kg

    (c) 0.5 mg

    (d) 1500 mL

    (e) 2 mL

41. 2 tablets

42. 0.7 mL

43. Dispose of sharps in appropriate containers only. Never bend or break needles before disposal. Avoid recapping needles. If a needle must be recapped or removed, use a safety mechanical device or a one-handed technique.

44.

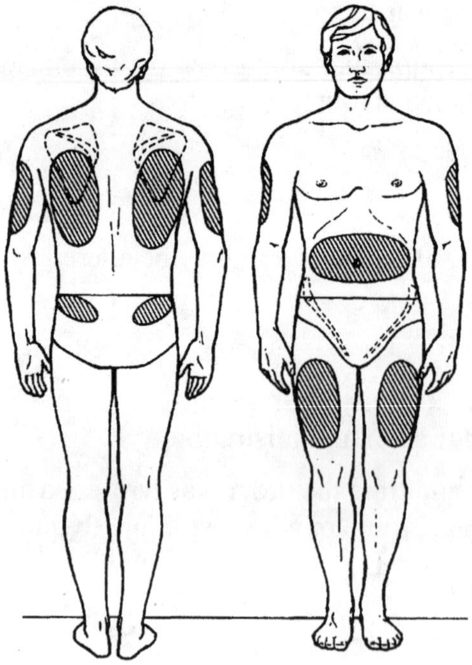

45. the right client, the right drug, the right dose, the right route, and the right time

46. Assess the client before administering the medication to obtain baseline data. (You will need to check the apical heart rate prior to giving Digoxin.) Follow the five rights when preparing and administering the medication. Be sure to verify the identity of your client. Name bands should be checked! Inform the client about the medication. Assist the client in taking the medication. You may need to provide water or help the client to a sitting position. Observe the client taking the medication. Settle the client. Record your assessment, and document that the medication has been given per agency policy. Provide ongoing assessment of the client.

47. 1 mL

48. Break the ampule at its constricted neck. Use a filter needle when withdrawing the medication from the ampule into a syringe. After withdrawing the medication, replace the filter needle with a regular needle. You may wish to review Procedure 28.2 for a more thorough discussion of this process.

49. dorsogluteal, ventrogluteal, vastus lateralis, and rectus femoris sites; possibly the deltoid if the client is well developed

50. (Review Procedure 28.9 for assistance with your response.)

51. IV medications may be added to the IV fluid container, administered through an additive set or a volume-control administration set or by IV Push route.

Chapter 29 Answer Key

1. d
2. c
3. e
4. a
5. b
6. I
7. E
8. E
9. E
10. b
11. a
12. a
13. c
14. d
15. c
16. c
17. a
18. a
19. True
20. False Motivation can be enhanced by letting the client succeed. Break the skill down into small tasks and provide positive reinforcement as the client masters each of the steps.
21. False When implementing client teaching you should always address any areas that are causing anxiety at the beginning of the teaching session.
22. True
23. False Cognitive learning may be evaluated by direct observation of behaviour, written measurements, such as tests, oral questioning, or self-reports.
24. True
25. (Refer to the discussion in the text on reading level and apply the SMOG index as presented in the box in Chapter 29.)
26. The information must be accurate; current; based on learning objectives; adjusted for the learner's age, culture, and ability; consistent with the information the nurse is teaching; and selected with consideration for how much time and resources are available for teaching.

27. diagnosed learning needs, learning objectives, topics taught, client outcomes, need for additional teaching, and resources provided

28. The teaching plan must include assessment of the learner, diagnosis of a learning need, development of a teaching plan, strategies for implementing the plan, and ways to evaluate the outcome and effectiveness of your teaching.

    You will need to begin by assessing Sarah's knowledge of personal care and body mechanics. Include an assessment of her anxiety level about providing this care. Write a nursing diagnosis based on your assessment. The teaching plan must include learning objectives that are measurable and time-oriented. Describe how you will teach Sarah. The teaching plan should include discussion of bathing, hygiene, and proper body mechanics. Consider having Sarah give her mother a bed bath in the hospital so that she can have her questions answered and receive immediate feedback. Explain how you will evaluate Sarah's progress toward her learning objective, as well as how you will record your teaching and the necessary documentation on the client's chart.

29. (a) There are many possible ways to encourage Elsa's learning, including encouraging the development of readiness by explaining the value of self-care, having her actively involved in her learning process, providing feedback and encouragement throughout the teaching, organizing the teaching plan from simple to complex, providing ample time for the teaching session and allowing her to give a return demonstration, arranging continued follow-up so that repetition of teaching material is possible, having the teaching session in a quiet environment that is well lighted and comfortable in temperature, and teaching at the client's cognitive level and when the client is well rested and comfortable.

    (b) Possible responses include: elevated anxiety levels, lack of interest, pain or discomfort, hypoglycemia or markedly elevated blood sugars, a language barrier, inadequate psychomotor ability, and a difference in values about the importance of learning diabetes self-management.

    (c) You must assess Elsa's desire or willingness to learn and her ability to learn at this time. Pain and other distractions must be addressed so that she is ready to learn.

Chapter 30 Answer Key

1. a
2. b
3. b
4. a
5. a
6. f
7. a
8. d
9. c
10. b
11. e
12. d
13. a
14. c
15. b
16. a
17. b
18. c
19. a
20. b
21. d
22. c
23. False Scott Fortier is an informal leader in his nursing unit. This role is acquired through seniority, age, ability, or charisma.
24. True
25. False Planned change requires problem-solving, decision-making, and interpersonal skills. It is a purposive attempt to influence the status quo. Unplanned change is haphazard. Drift and natural change are examples of this type of change.
26. a charismatic leader
27. (Examine your own experience with leadership.)
28. (See the section on mentors and preceptors in the chapter.)
29. (See Table 30.3 for a concise presentation of the four planned change models.)

30. There are many possible responses, including: emphasizing the positive consequences of the change and how each group will benefit, involving each group of resisters in the change process, actively listening to each side, and redirecting resistance by diverting attention to another issue.

31. (a) There are many possible answers to this question. This scenario is currently an area of concern in many health-care facilities. You might consider exploring how numerous units have actually handled this dilemma. As the manager, however, you are responsible for managing resources effectively and efficiently enhancing employee performance; building and managing the teams; managing conflict; delegating, and initiating, and managing change. To accomplish these functions, the nurse manager must communicate well and think critically.

To mediate this conflict, you will need to determine what the concerns of each group are. You will also need to explain the financial constraints that have prompted this change. You might also consider using the "Guidelines for Delegating Tasks and Procedures" presented in a box in this chapter to determine what, if any, additional tasks may be delegated to the Nurse's Aides, to develop a plan to safely provide client care with the new staffing mix, or to justify rejection of the new staffing mix.

(b) Each group is affected differently by the proposed change. RNs and LPNs will lose positions or hours, whereas Nurse's Aides will gain positions or hours and take on new challenges. The manager has received a mandate to cut the budget. See the box "Common Driving and Restraining Forces" in the text.

Chapter 31 Answer Key

1. i
2. l
3. m
4. h
5. c
6. g
7. f
8. k
9. d
10. b
11. e
12. j
13. a
14. c
15. a
16. d
17. b
18. c
19. b
20. c
21. d
22. c
23. a
24. b
25. a
26. c
27. d
28. True
29. False Nursing goals for the client with a fever are designed to support the body's normal physiological processes, provide comfort, and prevent complications.
30. False For an accurate oral temperature measurement, the thermometer should be left in place two to three minutes for a glass thermometer. If you are using an electronic

thermometer, listen for the sound that indicates the maximum temperature has been reached.

31. False For an accurate rectal temperature measurement, the thermometer should be held in place three minutes or for the length of time specified by your agency when using a glass thermometer. For neonates the length of time is usually five minutes. If you are using an electronic thermometer, listen for the sound that indicates the maximum temperature has been reached.

32. True

33. False Normally, the apical and radial pulse rates are identical.

34. True

35. basal metabolic rate, muscle activity, thyroxin output, epinephrine, norepinephrine and sympathetic stimulation, and fever

36. Is there a reason for my client to be hypothermic? Has my client had a cold drink in the last 30 minutes? Was the thermometer left in place for the appropriate amount of time?

37.

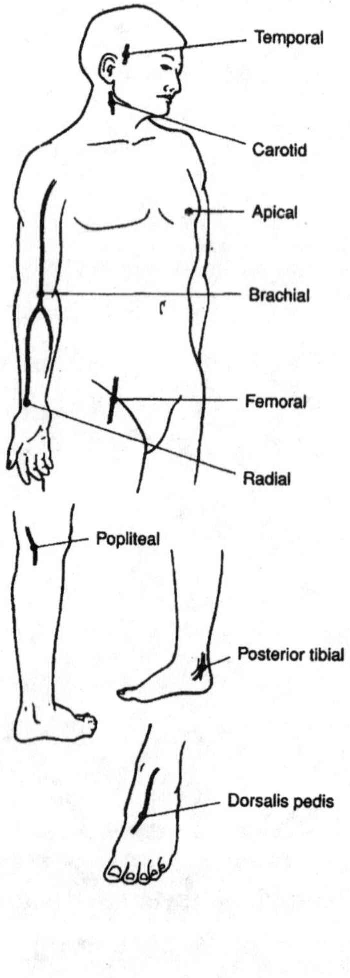

38. age, exercise, stress, race, obesity, gender, medications, diurnal variations, and disease process

39. (a) Susan's temperature and pulse rate are elevated. It is not unusual for a person with a fever to experience tachycardia. Susan's respiratory rate is at the upper limit of normal. Her initial blood pressure reading is within normal limits; however, this reading should be evaluated against prior readings, if they are available.

 (b) On admission, Susan should have her vital signs assessed to establish a baseline. Her vital signs should be checked again before and after administration of any drugs that affect the cardiac and respiratory systems or any procedure. She should be reassessed any time she has a change in condition.

 (c) regularly assess vital signs; monitor lab work ordered by the NP; remove excess covers if she feels warm, or apply blankets if she feels chilled; measure intake and output; provide oral hygiene; provide a tepid sponge to increase heat loss through conduction; provide dry clothing and linen

 (d) pulse rate, rhythm, volume, arterial wall elasticity, and presence of bilateral equality

Chapter 32 Answer Key

1. d
2. h
3. g
4. e
5. b
6. c
7. f
8. a
9. h
10. b
11. a
12. f
13. i
14. e
15. g
16. c
17. d
18. c
19. a
20. b
21. c
22. a
23. b
24. d
25. c
26. b
27. c
28. b
29. d
30. b
31. d

32. c

33. a

34. True

35. False During the nursing history, the nurse should assess the degree to which a client is at risk for infection and any client complaints that may be consistent with an acute infection.

36. False A fever accompanies a systemic infection.

37. True

38. False Asepsis is the freedom from infection or infectious material. In medical asepsis, objects are referred to as clean or dirty, but in surgical asepsis, sterile technique is used.

39. False Clients who are placed in isolation may experience sensory deprivation, feelings of inferiority, or decreased self-esteem.

40. pain, swelling, redness, heat, and—if the injury is severe—impaired function of the part

41.

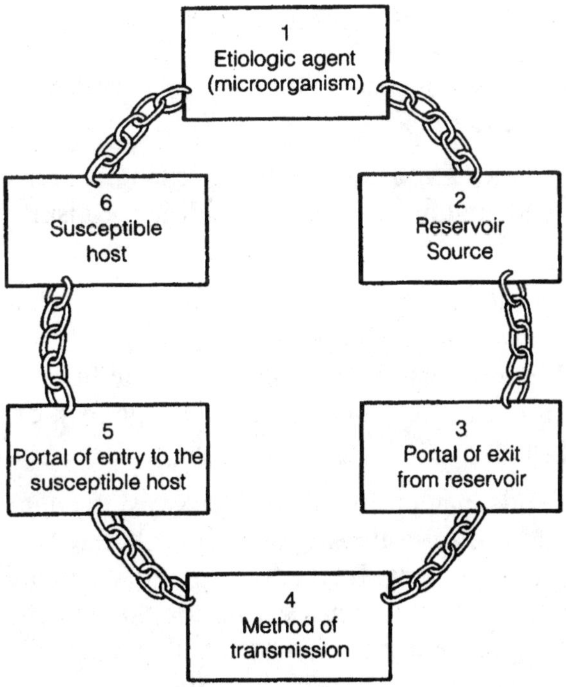

(See Table 32.6 in the textbook chapter for a detailed list of interventions to break the chain of infection.)

42.

Type of WBC	*Normal Range As a Percentage of Total WBC*
Neutrophils	55% to 75%
Lymphocytes	20% to 40%
Monocytes	2% to 8%
Eosinophils	1% to 4%
Basophils	0.5% to 1%
Total WBC	100% or 4500 to 11, 000/cu mm

43. standard precautions plus airborne precautions

44. standard precautions

45. You must follow standard precautions and wash your hands before and after all client care.

46. Encourage the parents to provide regular bathing, shampooing, and dental care. All children should be immunized. The children need a balanced diet. Parents should communicate with staff about skipped breakfasts or any problems with meals. Similarly, the preschool staff should inform the parents of the child's food and fluid intake while at school. Children also need adequate rest and sleep in order to remain healthy. Sick children should not attend school.

47. See "Steps to Follow after Exposure to Bloodborne Pathogens" for detailed guidelines on how to handle an accidental needle stick. In addition, consult your school policy on needle sticks.

48. Hand washing is considered a major prevention strategy for nosocomial infections. For routine care, a vigorous hand washing under a stream of water for at least 15 seconds using antimicrobial liquid soap is recommended. In addition to hand washing, environmental controls and identification and management of clients at risk for infection should also be instituted.

49. The LCDC recommends that antimicrobial hand washing agents be used in this circumstance as well as in the following situations: before invasive procedures, in special care units, in caring for clients with GI and respiratory wound infections colonized with multi-drug–resistant microbes, or when caring for clients with enteric infections that are known to have prolonged environmental survival. (see Research Note and Clinical Guidelines on Recommendations on Handwashing.)

50. gloves and gown; eye wear if body substances could splatter in your face

51. Handle the linen as little as possible and with the least amount of agitation. Place the soiled linen in the appropriate laundry bag, and tie the bag closed before sending it to the laundry.

52. Place the needle in a puncture-resistant container. Do not detach the needle or recap the syringe.

53. You will need to evaluate his ability to perform hygiene activities and to self-administer medications. You will need to assess the client's support system and their ability and resources to provide care, if needed. In addition, you must teach infection control techniques to the client and family.

Chapter 33 Answer Key

1. b
2. c
3. e
4. d
5. a
6. c
7. b
8. a
9. d
10. b
11. a
12. c
13. d
14. a
15. c
16. b
17. b
18. c
19. a
20. a
21. True
22. True
23. False Restraints may be used only when necessary for the client's health and safety.
24. (Answers will vary.)
25. This tool could be used as part of an admission assessment to an acute care facility. It could also be used as part of discharge planning. This also would be an excellent addition to data collection in ambulatory or clinic-based practices, as part of health curriculum in schools, in employee health promotion programs, or even as a public service announcement on billboards or in ads on mass transit.

26. light, arrangement of furniture and equipment, presence of disease-producing microorganisms, use of grounded electrical equipment only

27. First, protect and evacuate clients who are in immediate danger. Second, report the fire. Third, contain the fire. Finally, extinguish the fire.

28. Assign nurses to work as "buddies," place clients at risk in an area that is closely supervised, stay with clients who are sedated or confused or who have gait disturbances while they are using commode or bathroom, monitor clients' medications, position bed at the lowest level from the floor; consult the text for additional responses.

29. Each response will be individualized. As a nursing student, it is important for you to recognize your own beliefs and biases that you have about this controversial topic.

30. Ensure a safe workplace by increasing knowledge and skill regarding the issue of violence, being proactive by refusing to tolerate violence and harassment, providing health promotion strategies to support nonviolent interactions in families, and carrying out nursing services with respect.

31. (Compare your response with the examples given in the textbook.)

32. Elevate side rails to prevent falls, position client appropriately in bed, provide adequate lighting, assess balance and gait when client is out of bed and provide assistance as required, place a skid-free slipper on the noncasted foot, keep the floor dry and free of obstacles, use appropriately grounded electrical equipment only.

33. (See home hazard appraisal in chapter.)

34. Assess her risk factors for falls and institute preventive measures (see Table 33.1).

Chapter 34 Answer Key

1. b
2. d
3. g
4. e
5. c
6. a
7. f
8. d
9. c
10. c
11. a
12. b
13. d
14. d
15. b
16. a
17. b
18. a
19. True
20. False Bathing removes accumulated oil, perspiration, dead skin cells, and bacteria. Bathing also produces a sense of well-being, stimulates the circulation, and provides an excellent opportunity to assess the client.
21. True
22. False Clients with diabetes mellitus or peripheral vascular disease are particularly prone to infection if skin breakage occurs. These clients should have their nails filed instead of clipped. In some agencies, these clients must be seen by a podiatrist or physician for foot care.
23. True
24. False Brushing and flossing teeth removes food particles that can harbour and incubate bacteria and also stimulates the gums.
25. True
26. True
27. True

28. False Ears may be cleaned during the bath. Cotton-tipped applicators should never be used to remove cerumen.

29. True

30. True

31. False When providing perineal care to a man, wash the shaft of the penis and retract the foreskin of an uncircumcised man to clean the glans penis. Replace the foreskin after cleaning, and wash and dry the scrotum.

32. conducting a nursing history to determine the client's skin care practices, self-care abilities, and past or current skin care practices; conducting a physical assessment of the skin; identifying clients at high risk for developing skin impairment

33. Limit bathing to once or twice per week and apply lotion or cream to skin to prevent dryness and itching.

34. prompt skin care to prevent irritation

35. visual impairment, inability to use or coordinate the hands, inability to sense or perceive pressure, pain or discomfort in the feet, physical or psychological problems that impede self-care in general, lack of access to hygiene facilities (e.g., homelessness)

36. Keep the room at the most comfortable temperature for him. Assure adequate ventilation and lighting of the room. Pay close attention to the effect of noise on Bryan. Provide periods of uninterrupted rest for him.

37. Assess his usual hygiene practices and customs. Ask his family to bring in personal items, such as a comb, brush, or toothbrush. Plan routine hygiene to be consistent with his previous habits. Maintain conversation with Bryan while providing care. Encourage him to vent his fears and concerns. Carefully drape his body while providing care.

Chapter 35 Answer Key

1. d
2. a
3. b
4. e
5. c
6. b
7. d
8. d
9. c
10. b
11. d
12. a
13. c
14. b
15. c
16. d
17. a
18. False The frequency of defecation is highly individual, varying from several times per day to two to three times per week.
19. True
20. True
21. False Establishing a colostomy irrigation schedule will result in regular evacuation of the bowel and free the client from wearing a pouch or appliance.
22. inadequate fluid intake, repeated ignoring of the defecation reflex or inhibiting defecation by conscious contraction of the external sphincter, a diet low in fibre, immobility or inactivity, impaired neurological functioning, depression, lack of privacy, barium used for diagnostic purposes, general anesthesia, discomfort with defecation, regular use of laxatives or enemas, some medications, muscle weakness and poor sphincter tone, disease processes that affect peristalsis
23. stress; medications (especially antibiotics, iron preparations, and cathartics); allergies to foods, fluids, or drugs; diseases of the colon; imbalance of intestinal flora
24. Fibre is found predominantly in carbohydrates. Examples of high-fibre foods are fruits and vegetables, whole-grain products, and bran. Food that is minimally processed has the highest fibre content. Hence, fresh fruit is higher in fibre than canned fruit.

25. You will need to assess the client. Your assessment should include normal bowel patterns, a description of usual characteristics of stool, and any past or present problems with elimination. You will also need to investigate his diet to determine if he has been eating enough to create stool. Questions you might ask include: "Has he been eating?" "What type of diet is he receiving?" "Was he NPO for a lengthy period of time due to his surgery?"

26. immobility, awkward position for elimination due to bedrest and traction, potential embarrassment or concerns about lack of privacy

27. Constipation related to bedrest and hospitalization as evidenced by complaints of feeling bloated.

28. Attempt to re-establish his normal elimination pattern by offering the bedpan at this time and providing privacy and adequate time for elimination. Since Earl is on a regular diet, encourage him to increase his fluid intake and increase the fibre in his diet. Additional water, juices, or hot beverages should be offered. Foods high in fibre, such as prunes, raw fruit, bran, and whole-grain products, should be included in the diet. Earl must remain in bed due to skeletal traction. However, you may need to speak with his physician about positioning and bed exercises. To encourage defecation, the head of the bed should be elevated as much as his condition permits. If possible, the hips should be flexed. Bed exercises, particularly of the upper body and abdomen, will prove helpful.

Chapter 36 Answer Key

1. b
2. d
3. f
4. a
5. g
6. c
7. e
8. b
9. d
10. c
11. b
12. c
13. a
14. c
15. d
16. b

17. c

18. False In the male only, the urethra serves as a passageway for reproductive fluid as well as urine.

19. True

20. True

21. circumstances that counter the client's accustomed conditions; inadequate fluid intake; some medications; poor muscle tone; any conditions that impair flow of urine from the kidneys to the bladder or urethra; febrile conditions or conditions that create excessive fluid loss through perspiration, feces, wound drainage, or other outlet; hypotension; and exposure to spinal anesthetics

22. a nursing history, which contains data about voiding patterns and habits, past or present problems involving the urinary system, and any problems that may affect urination along with a physical assessment of the genitourinary system, hydration status, examination of the urine, and relating data obtained from the results of any diagnostic tests and procedures

23. drink eight 8-ounce glasses of water per day; void every two to four hours; avoid use of harsh soaps, bubble bath, powder, or sprays in the perineal area; avoid clothes that fit tightly in the perineal area; wear cotton underclothes; and wipe the perineal area from front to back

24. Begin Ethel on a bladder training program and teach her Kegel exercises. Throughout the process, provide substantial positive reinforcement. You will also need to discuss maintenance of skin integrity. Skin that is constantly moist is prone to breakdown. Until greater control of urinary urge is accomplished, Ethel will need to scrupulously clean and dry her genitalia after an episode of incontinence. Some women utilize absorbent pads to soak up leaked urine. (See Boxes on Clinical Guidelines and Client Teaching in the text for specific bladder training and Kegel exercise instructions.)

25. Wash the perineal-genital area before catheter insertion. Use strict sterile technique. Do not force the catheter. Passage may be facilitated by elevating the penis to a position perpendicular to the body. Use a closed system, if possible. If the client is uncircumcised, replace the foreskin after catheter insertion. Suspend the drainage bag below the level of the bladder.

26. If not contraindicated, increase fluid intake to decrease the likelihood of urinary stasis and potential infection. Provide routine hygiene care. Maintain drainage bag below the level of the bladder. Avoid kinks in the tubing system.

27. Remove the tape attaching the catheter to the client. Don disposable gloves. Insert a sterile syringe into the injection port of the catheter and withdraw fluid from the balloon. Gently withdraw the catheter after the balloon has deflated. Dry the perineal area. Measure the urine in the drainage bag. Instruct the client that you will need to monitor his first voiding. Record the time of removal and the amount, colour, and clarity of the urine, along with instructions to the client.

Chapter 37 Answer Key

1. l
2. c
3. j
4. k
5. f
6. h
7. e
8. b
9. d
10. i
11. a
12. g
13. c
14. c
15. d
16. a
17. c
18. a
19. d
20. a
21. b
22. c
23. b
24. False Avoid massaging over bony prominences as this may lead to deep tissue trauma.
25. True
26. True
27. True
28. False During the proliferative phase of wound healing, new tissue begins to fill in the wound.
29. False Wound cleaning is usually undertaken to remove debris from wounds.
30. True
31. True

32. True

33. immobility and inactivity, inadequate nutrition, fecal and urinary incontinence, decreased mental status, diminished sensation, excessive body heat, advanced age

34. Postoperative hemorrhage is an emergency. Don sterile gloves and apply a pressure dressing to the wound. Monitor the client's vital signs and call the physician. You may need to prepare the client to return to surgery. Preparation for the operating room (OR) is often facilitated by notifying the OR team of the current situation.

35. Modify the client's position so that his knees are bent to decrease pull on the incision. Quickly apply a large sterile dressing soaked with normal saline over the wound. Immediately notify the physician as surgical repair may be necessary. This is a frightening experience. You will need to reassure the client and provide comfort measures while managing the above tasks.

36. Begin by assessing the client's overall condition. Check vital signs along with his tolerance of the injury. Assess the size and severity of the wound. Evaluate the amount of bleeding. Inspect the wound for foreign bodies. Determine if there are any associated injuries. Inquire about the timing of the last tetanus toxoid injection.

37. All of these signs and symptoms are associated with the normal healing process.

38. to protect the wound from mechanical injury, to protect the wound from microbial contamination, to provide or maintain a high humidity, to provide thermal insulation, to absorb drainage and/or débride a wound, to prevent hemorrhage when applied as a pressure dressing, to splint or immobilize the wound site, to provide psychological comfort

39. Confirm the type and strength of the irrigant. Ideally, the solution will be isotonic. If an antimicrobial solution is used, it should be well diluted. Warm the solution to body temperature. Use sterile technique. If using a catheter, do not force it into the wound. Dry the skin around the wound when you have completed the irrigation.

40. Heat is usually applied to a wound to cause vasodilation and promote soft tissue healing and suppuration. Cold is usually applied to a wound because it causes vasoconstriction and helps control bleeding after an injury.

41.

Colour	*Goal of Wound Care*	*Intervention Examples*
Red	protect	cleanse gently, avoid the use of dry dressings, apply a topical antimicrobial, apply a transparent or hydrocolloid dressing, change the dressing infrequently
Yellow	cleanse	irrigate the wound, apply wet-to-dry dressings, use absorbent materials, consult with physician about topical antimicrobial
Black	débride	perform sharp, mechanical, chemical, or autolytic débridement

42. Martin is on bedrest as a result of his injury. In addition, he has diminished sensation. A healthy 19-year-old should move frequently, even when confined to bed. However, Martin cannot move and does not feel pain or pressure. He also has an elevated temperature, which will raise the metabolic rate of his body cells and make him more prone to tissue damage. Martin requires fluids and nutrients to remain healthy. Due to his acute injury, his caloric requirements are elevated. His current poor nutritional intake places him at added risk for pressure ulcer formation. The Foley catheter will provide a drainage route for urine and protect his skin from urine. It is not uncommon for spinal injury clients to be constipated or impacted. Therefore, fecal incontinence is also not a current risk factor.

43. Your charting should contain the following information: location, size, and stage of the ulcer; condition of the wound bed, wound margins, and surrounding skin; evidence of any clinical signs of infection; when the pressure ulcer was first detected and any previously used treatments.

44. Explain the need for adequate fluid and nutrition in order to heal the current pressure ulcer and avoid development of further pressure ulcers. Provide scrupulous hygiene care to keep Martin's skin clean, dry, and free of irritation. If Martin's temperature remains elevated, hygiene care will need to be administered more frequently. Keep pressure off the wound. Institute a turning schedule. Avoid skin trauma while turning and repositioning. Consider use of an overlay mattress or specialty bed. Discuss your treatment and prevention plan with Martin.

45. transparent adhesive, polyurethane foam, a hydrocolloid dressing, or a hydrogel dressing (see Table 37.8 in the textbook to determine the appropriate forms of dressings for each pressure ulcer stage)

46. There are many potential nursing diagnoses for Martin including:

    Impaired Skin Integrity related to recent C-15 fracture, poor nutritional intake and febrile state as evidenced by Stage II pressure ulcer

    Body Image Disturbance related to quadriplegia as evidenced by despondent behaviour

    Altered Nutrition: Less Than Body Requirements related to refusal to eat as evidenced by 5 kg weight loss

Chapter 38 Answer Key

1. c
2. a
3. d
4. f
5. g
6. e
7. b

8. b
9. a
10. d
11. a
12. c
13. b
14. a
15. d
16. True
17. False In general, metabolic rates decrease in the elderly. Vitamin, mineral, and most other nutrient requirements remain unchanged. However, psychosocial factors may affect appetite.
18. True
19. False Ingestion of a low-calorie diet coupled with increased physical activity is the most effective way to lose weight and maintain weight loss.
20. False The nurse recognizes that all of these clinical signs may indicate a nutritional problem.
21. to provide energy for body processes and movement, to provide structural material for body tissues, and to regulate body processes
22. (See the text for *Canada's Food Guide for Healthy Living*. Compare your own diet to these recommendations.)
23. developmental stage, beliefs about food, personal preferences, religious practices, lifestyle, health status, advertising, psychological factors, ethnicity and culture, economic status, and peer groups
24. (Review Procedure 38.1 for insertion guidelines.)
25. Several methods may be used to verify placement of a large-bore tube. These methods are aspirating gastrointestinal secretions, measuring the pH of aspirated fluid, and injecting air while auscultating over the epigastric area.
26. Nursing responsibilities include verification of tube placement at regular intervals, adequately securing the tube, determining any food allergies, checking the expiration date of the feeding, administering the feeding at room temperature, regularly checking residual volumes, providing daily nasogastric tube care, and documenting all care.

Chapter 39 Answer Key

1. g
2. c
3. a
4. d
5. b
6. f
7. e
8. c
9. b
10. c
11. b
12. a
13. b
14. d
15. a
16. d
17. d
18. b
19. c
20. b
21. d
22. c
23. a
24. False In the healthy individual, respiration is largely controlled by chemoreceptors in the medulla oblongata, which respond to increases in carbon dioxide concentration. However, in individuals with a pulmonary disease, such as emphysema, oxygen levels, not carbon dioxide, play a major role in regulating respirations.
25. True
26. False Cough suppressants are medications that suppress or stop the cough reflex. Codeine is a common constituent of these medications.
27. False Endotracheal suctioning removes secretions from the deeper airways, such as the trachea and bronchi. Oropharyngeal or nasopharyngeal suctioning removes secretions from the upper respiratory tract.

28. True

29. False An oropharyngeal airway stimulates the gag reflex and, therefore, is not used in clients who are alert.

30. False Nasopharyngeal intubation may be conducted by a nurse. Endotracheal intubation is only performed by nurses with special preparation.

31. The nose warms, moistens, and filters the air. Cilia propel irritants and foreign particles so that they can be removed. Mucus entraps foreign particles. The cough reflex helps clear the lower respiratory passageways of irritants and foreign particles. The sneeze reflex helps clear the nasal passageways.

32. Position the client to allow for maximum chest expansion. Encourage or provide frequent changes of position. Encourage ambulation or activity, such as getting out of bed. Ensure comfort through pharmacological and nonpharmacological means.

33. Maintain a patent airway. Prevent skin breakdown around the tracheostomy stoma. Prevent infection at the tracheostomy site.

34. The pulse, respiratory rate, and temperature are elevated. Oxygen saturation is below normal limits. The crackles are adventitious breath sounds.

35. Arrange to collect the sputum sample in the morning or after postural drainage, if possible. If this is not possible, the client may be suctioned. Provide mouth care, and ask the client to breathe deeply and expectorate sputum into a sterile container. The client will need to be advised of the difference between sputum and saliva. Gloves should be worn while collecting the sample. To obtain a chest x-ray, the client must be taken to the x-ray department or a portable exam must be ordered. The client should remove all jewellery and clothing above the waist. To obtain a CBC, a venous blood sample must be drawn. A CBC measures hemoglobin, hematocrit, RBC count, WBC count, and a differential of red cell and white cell count.

36. There are two deep-breathing exercises: abdominal breathing and pursed-lip breathing. See the textbook section on deep breathing and coughing for a full description of each of these exercises.

37. Linda's sleep-wake schedule and meal times will have to be considered when planning the schedule. The sequence of each session will be: positioning, percussion, vibration, and removal of secretions by coughing or suctioning. A session should last 30 minutes or less.

38. Select a sensor on the basis of the client's size. Select and prepare the site for monitoring. Apply the sensor. Determine proper functioning by examining the waveform or the audible beep with each arterial pulsation. Set safety alarms. Check the site on a regular basis. Normal oxygen saturation is 95 percent to 100 percent. Note: Linda is receiving supplemental oxygen at 5 l pm. In the healthy individual, this would raise saturation to the upper limit.

39. A nasal cannula is an inexpensive low-flow device that does not interfere with the client's ability to eat or talk.

Chapter 40 Answer Key

1. d
2. a
3. e
4. c
5. b
6. f
7. b
8. a
9. d
10. b, f
11. d, e
12. c
13. f
14. e
15. a, b
16. d
17. a, d
18. a
19. b
20. c
21. a
22. c
23. d
24. b
25. a
26. d
27. c
28. d
29. False A colloid is a protein or large molecule that does not readily dissolve into true solution; a crystalloid is a salt that readily dissolves into true solution.
30. False Each kilogram of weight gained or lost is equivalent to one litre of fluid gained or lost.

31. True

32. False Chvostek's sign is commonly used to assess imbalances of calcium and magnesium. A positive response may occur in clients with hypocalcemia or hypomagnesemia.

33. True

34. True

35. urine, insensible loss through the skin as perspiration and the lungs as water vapour in the expired air, noticeable loss through sweat, and loss through the intestines in feces

36. age, climate, diet, stress, illness, medical treatments, medications

37. An isotonic imbalance occurs when water and electrolytes are lost or gained in equal proportions. An osmolar imbalance occurs when a loss or gain of only water alters the concentration or osmolality of serum.

38. Dependent edema is found in the lowest body parts. Pitting edema is edema that leaves a small depression or pit after finger pressure is applied to the swollen area.

39. Take a nursing history. Be sure to include questions about fluid and food intake, fluid output, presence of abnormal loss or retention of fluid, signs and symptoms of electrolyte imbalance, general state of health and current health problems, medications and treatments (see the Assessment Interview, "Fluid, Electrolyte, and Acid-Base Balance," for a detailed list of potential interview questions). Obtain clinical measurements of weight, vital signs, and I & O. Assess skin turgor and neuromuscular irritability, perform a physical examination, and review pertinent lab results.

40. The nurse is responsible for administering and maintaining the therapy.

41. (Check with your facility, instructor, or preceptor.)

42. (a) 250 mL/hr

    (b) 125 mL/hr

43. (Ask your physician or inquire when you donate blood.)

44. Always use surgical asepsis when changing solutions, tubing, dressings, and filters; closely monitor infusion rates to prevent hyperglycemia (too rapid administration) or hypoglycemia (infusion too slow); do not abruptly stop TPN administration.

45. (See the text chapter to complete the table.)

Electrolyte	**Role/Location**	**Signs/Symptoms of Hypo-**	**Signs/Symptoms of Hyper-**
Sodium (Na^+)	functions in the control and regulation of body fluids; helps maintain blood volume and interstitial fluid volume; works with K^+ to maintain ICF and ECF electrolyte balance via active transport; involved in transmitting nerve impulses and contracting muscles; is the principal cation in ECF	confusion, pitting edema over bony prominences, lethargy, muscle cramps, anorexia, nausea, vomiting, postural hypotension, seizures, coma	extreme thirst; dry, sticky mucous membranes, if severe: agitated behaviour, restlessness, fatigue, disorientation, hallucinations
Chloride (Cl^-)	works with sodium to help maintain the osmotic pressure of the blood; involved in regulating acid-base balance of the body; involved in buffering oxygen and carbon dioxide exchange in RBCs; is the principal anion of ECF	hypochloremia in conjunction with hyponatremia; similar signs	hyperchloremia in conjunction with hypernatremia; similar signs
Potassium (K^+)	affects the functions of most body systems; active in acid-base balance of the body; plays a major role in the transmission of electrical impulses to the heart, muscles, lung tissue, and intestines; is the major cation of ICF	muscle weakness, leg cramps, fatigue, anorexia, nausea, vomiting, decreased bowel sounds and motility, cardiac arrhythmias, depressed deep tendon reflexes	GI hyperactivity, diarrhea, irritability, apathy, confusion, cardiac arrthymias, bradycardia or cardiac arrest, muscle weakness, areflexia, paresthesias, and numbness in extremities

Electrolyte	Role/Location	Signs/Symptoms of Hypo-	Signs/Symptoms of Hyper-
Calcium (Ca_2^+)	functions in bone formation and in transmission of nerve impulses, muscle contraction, blood coagulation, and activation of certain enzymes; constitutes only 1% of ECF, most in ICF	tingling sensation in fingers and around mouth, abdominal and skeletal muscle cramps or tremors, cardiac arrhythmias, positive Trousseau's and Chvostek's signs; if severe: tetany and convulsions	flank pain, lethargy; reduced muscle tone, anorexia, nausea, vomiting, depressed deep tendon reflexes, constipation, polyuria; if severe: cardiac arrest
Magnesium (Mg^{2+})	maintains neuromuscular activity; metabolizes carbohydrates and proteins; activates many intracellular enzyme systems; is located in the ICF	neuromuscular irritability, increased reflexes, positive Trousseau's and Chvostek's signs, tachycardia, elevated BP disorientation, confusion, vertigo	peripheral vasodilation, lethargy; drowsiness, coma, impaired respirations, nausea, vomiting, muscle weakness, paralysis, hypotension, bradycardia, depressed deep tendon reflexes; if severe: respiratory and cardiac arrest
Phosphate (PO_4-)	works with calcium in bone and tooth formation; involved in many chemical actions of the cell, is essential for functioning of muscles, nerves, and RBCs; involved in metabolism of protein, fat, and carbohydrate; located in both the ICF and ECF	acute hypophosphatemia: confusion, seizures, coma, muscle pain, decreased muscle strength, positive Chvostek's sign; chronic hypophosphatemia: memory loss, fatigue, bone pain and joint stiffness, respiratory failure	tetany, circumoral paresthesias, anorexia, nausea, vomiting, hyperreflexia, tachycardia

46.	Hematocrit	40% to 54% (males)
		37% to 47% (females)
	Serum osmolality	275 to 300 mOsm/kg
	Urine osmolality	500 to 800 mOsm/kg
	Urine pH	4.6 to 8.0
	Urine specific gravity	1.005 to 1.030
47.	pH	7.35 to 7.45
	$PaCO_2$	35 to 45 mm Hg
	PaO_2	80 to 100 mm Hg
	HCO_3	22 to 26 mEq/L
	Base excess	-2 to +2 mEq/L

48. uncompensated metabolic acidosis
49. partially compensated respiratory acidosis with moderate hypoxemia
50. uncompensated metabolic alkalosis with mild hypoxemia
51. uncompensated respiratory alkalosis
52. Ensure that the correct solution is infusing, observe the rate of flow and compare with the scheduled rate, inspect the patency of the IV tubing and needle, check for kinks or obstructions or leakage, inspect the insertion site for infiltration of fluid, phlebitis, and bleeding.
53. The following factors influence the rate of IV flow: position of the forearm, position and patency of the tubing, height of the infusion container/bottle, possible infiltration or fluid leakage, and relationship of the size of the angiocath to thc vein. (See the box in the text on "Factors Influencing Flow Rate," for specific examples.)
54. Trace the source of the leakage. If the leak is at the catheter connection, tighten the tubing into the catheter. If the leak cannot be stopped, slow the infusion as much as possible and replace the tubing with a new one. Estimate the amount of solution lost.
55. All IV bags should be changed every 24 hours to prevent contamination, and IV tubing should be changed every 48 to 72 hours depending on the institution's protocols and manufacturer's recommendation.

Chapter 41 Answer Key

1. b
2. g
3. d
4. f
5. e
6. a
7. c
8. a, b
9. a
10. b
11. b
12. a
13. a
14. b
15. a
16. c
17. b
18. a
19. d
20. c
21. b
22. a
23. d
24. True
25. True
26. the client's present sensory perceptions, usual functioning, sensory deficits, and potential problems ("The Assessment Interview" in Chapter 41 provides a list of interview questions that may help you evaluate the client's status)
27. Numerous answers are possible, including: elders who are confined to the home, clients who have recently relocated, recently widowed individuals, and clients confined to bed.
28. *vision*: have regular vision screening; *hearing*: have a hearing test; *taste*: maintain good oral hygiene and hydration

29. (a) assess for sensory deprivation; assess for current sensory/perceptual functioning; assess for the presence of other support systems, such as neighbours, church, or social networks; evaluate the client's activity level (Does she read? Watch television? What activities does she enjoy?)

(b) Marla suffers from sensory overload. Introduce yourself, and call her by name; speak in a low tone, and avoid a hurried manner; attempt to keep noise levels down; explain hospital routines and noises to Marla; dim lights during rest or sleep; ensure appropriate analgesia; and organize nursing care so that she has rest intervals free of interruptions; if possible, provide a private room.

(c) Marla suffers from sensory deprivation. Address her by name, and touch her hand while speaking to her; arrange for her to get the newspaper, watch television, or engage in activities in the unit; provide a calendar and clock; if possible, arrange her room so that she has access to a window; encourage friends or family to visit.

Chapter 42 Answer Key

1. b
2. a
3. a, b
4. a
5. b
6. b
7. c
8. d
9. a
10. b
11. e
12. b
13. a
14. c
15. b
16. b
17. d
18. True
19. False A child's sleep-wake patterns begin to approximate the pattern of an adult by the end of the fifth or sixth month.
20. True
21.

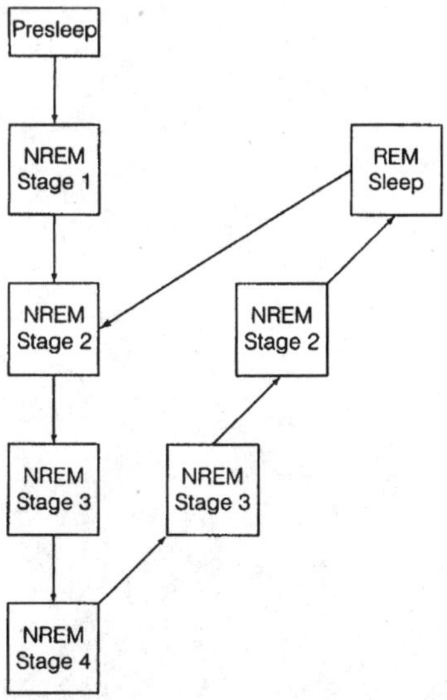

22. age, illness, environmental factors, such as noise and level of familiarity, fatigue, lifestyle (especially shift work), emotional stress, alcohol and stimulants, diet, smoking, motivation, and use of medications

23. It is appropriate for a client to keep a sleep diary when a sleeping problem exists. However, occasional sleeplessness does not warrant a diary. Similarly, if the diary produces undue anxiety, it may exacerbate the sleeping problem, and therefore, it is not appropriate. A sleeping diary should contain information about activities performed before bedtime, bedtime rituals, time of going to bed, trying to sleep, actual sleeping, and awakenings. The presence of any worries or concerns that may affect sleep should be recorded as well as any factors the client believes affect sleep.

24. polysomnography

25. noise level of the hospital unit, unfamiliar surroundings, anxiety about impending surgery, use of Benadryl @ HS, discomfort from bowel obstruction, use of Demerol for pain, NPO status

26. usual sleeping patterns, bedtime rituals, whether she regularly uses any sleep aids, any recent problems with sleep

27. puffy eyes, red conjunctiva, dull-appearing eyes, limited facial expressions, irritability, inattentiveness, yawning, confusion, lack of energy; or lack of coordination

28. Activity Intolerance related to sleep deprivation as evidenced by refusal to get out of bed

29. dim lights, close client's door, unplug the phone, adjust room temperature for comfort, attempt to institute any routine bedtime rituals if they are not contraindicated by her condition, offer a back massage before sleep, schedule medications to avoid night-time awakenings, provide analgesia, listen to any of her concerns

30. Mahalia should be instructed that use of sleep medications while hospitalized is appropriate. However, long-term use of sleeping medications should be discouraged.

Chapter 43 Answer Key

1. b
2. d
3. g
4. a
5. c
6. e
7. f
8. c
9. a
10. c
11. b
12. d
13. c
14. a
15. d
16. b
17. a
18. c
19. True
20. False The broader the base of support and the lower the centre of gravity, the greater are the stability and balance.
21. True
22. False Transfer belts allow the nurse to control the movement of a client during a transfer. They may be used when assisting the client out of bed to ambulate or to a wheelchair, commode, or sitting position in bed.
23. True
24. True
25. a properly functioning cerebral cortex, cerebellum, and basal ganglia
26. Ensure that you have adequate personnel to assist with the move. Keep client safety uppermost in your mind. Keep a wide base of support and stand as close to the client or bed as possible. Raise the bed to waist level to avoid stretching or reaching. If you will be pushing the client over, enlarge the base of support by moving your front foot forward. If you will be pulling the client over on his side, enlarge the base of support by moving the rear leg back. Use the major muscle groups to avoid back strain.
27. age, musculoskeletal and nervous system development, physical health status, mental health status, nutritional balance, lifestyle, personal values, stress level, energy level, climate, availability of recreational activities, and prescribed limitations

28.

Body System	Hazards of Immobility	Benefits of Exercise
Musculoskeletal	decrease in muscle strength, disuse osteoporosis, muscle atrophy, contractures, stiffness and pain in the joints	improved muscle size, shape, tone, and strength; maintenance of joint mobility and bone density
Cardiovascular	diminished cardiac reserve, increased use of the valsalva manoeuver, postural hypotension, venous vasodilation and stasis (especially in the leg veins), dependent edema, and increased risk of thrombus formation	increased cardiac output and efficiency and improved circulation
Respiratory	decreased respiratory movement, pooling of respiratory secretions, atelectasis, and hypostatic pneumonia	increased ventilation, improved diaphragmatic excursion, decreased effort of breathing, and improved clearance of secretions
Metabolic	decreased metabolic rate, negative nitrogen balance, anorexia, and negative calcium balance	increased metabolic rate, reduced serum triglyceride levels, and increased caloric needs
Urinary	urinary stasis, increased risk of renal calculi, urinary retention, and increased risk of urinary infection	improved efficiency in waste excretion, decreased urine stasis
Gastrointestinal	constipation and increased effort to evacuate stool	improved appetite, increased GI tract tone, and improved digestion and elimination
Integumentary	reduced skin turgor, increased risk of skin breakdown, and pressure ulcer formation	improved skin and hair condition
Psychoneurological	increased dependence, lowered self-esteem, and decreased social and cognitive interaction	improved tolerance of stress, improved body image, improved sleep, and increased energy

29. frequency, duration, intensity, and type of exercise

30. (Review the textbook section on physical fitness and apply the information to your personal situation.)

31. You instruct her to: roll to the side and lift far leg over the near leg, grasp the mattress edge with the lower arm and push the fist of the upper arm into the mattress, push up with arms as the heels and legs slide over the mattress edge, and maintain sitting position by pushing both fists into the mattress behind and to the sides of the buttocks.

32. Encourage her to perform ADLs, maintain good body alignment, carry out range-of-motion exercises to the maximum degree possible. For example, while in bed, she can start doing quadriceps drills by consciously tensing the muscles, drawing the kneecap upward and inward, and pushing the popliteal space of the knee against the bed surface, then relaxing the muscles.

33. Quickly assist her into a nearby chair, and help her lower her head. Stay with her, and when the weakness subsides, assist her back to bed. If there is no chair available, assist or lower her to the floor, assume a broad stance with one foot in front of the other, bring her backward so that your body supports her, and allow her to slide down your leg and lower her down gently, making sure her head does not hit the floor.

Chapter 44 Answer Key

1. f
2. b
3. g
4. a
5. d
6. c
7. e
8. b
9. c
10. a
11. b
12. d
13. d
14. c
15. c
16. d
17. a
18. a
19. True
20. True
21. False All clients should be evaluated for surgical risk factors. Age alone does not predict risk.
22. False The nurse in the operative suite confirms the client's identity and verifies physical and emotional readiness. In addition, the nurse assesses the response to preoperative medicines, treatments, or procedures; positions the client for surgery; performs skin preparation; assists in preparing and maintaining the sterile field; provides medications and supplies for the field; monitors the environment; manages catheters, tubes, drains, and specimens; performs sponge, sharp and instrument counts; and documents the care and the client's response to care.
23. False For the client scheduled to undergo abdominal, thoracic, or pelvic surgery, coughing and deep breathing exercises are especially important to prevent atelectasis and pneumonia.
24. False The client undergoing major surgery usually does not receive a preoperative enema unless bowel surgery is planned. Shaving of body hair prior to surgery is limited. Clipping of hair is preferred. Use of preoperative sedation is no longer a routine practice.

25. True

26. True

27. False Pain is usually greatest 12 to 36 hours after surgery.

28. The client is conscious and oriented and able to maintain a patent airway, vital signs have stabilized, protective reflexes have returned, movement of all four extremities is possible (if this was a preoperative condition), and urine output is adequate. In addition, the client should be afebrile or the febrile state has been attended to and the dressing is dry and intact.

29. Evaluate level of consciousness and orientation. Take the client's vital signs and compare initial readings with PARR data. Frequently monitor vital signs until stable or in accordance with agency policy. Check skin colour and temperature. Assess fluid balance. Position the client appropriately. Inspect the IV site, the dressing, and the condition of any drains or tubes. Assess the client's level of comfort. Review and institute the surgeon's postoperative orders.

30. You will be responsible for initiating the suction and maintaining the apparatus in proper working order. You will need to periodically measure and evaluate the drainage from the tube as well as assess the client and the suction system regularly. To ensure the tube's proper function, you may need to irrigate the tube. Mouth care and nose care should be given every three hours, as needed, to promote comfort. You must also document all of your care. Review Procedure 44.3 for additional details.

31. As the nurse caring for the client with a closed wound drainage system, you are responsible for maintaining patency of the tube and for ensuring proper functioning of the system. You must also measure and record the type and amount of drainage. Any abnormalities should be reported to the physician.

32.

Problem	**Possible Cause**	**Clinical Signs**	**Preventive Interventions**
Pneumonia	infection, toxins, irritants causing inflammatory process (aspiration of food, gastric contents or other substances, related to loss of gag reflex)	elevated temperature, cough, dyspnea, chest pain, expectoration of blood-tinged or purulent sputum	deep-breathing exercises, coughing, moving in bed, early ambulation, positioning to prevent aspiration
Postoperative Ileus	handling the bowel during surgery, anesthesia, electrolyte imbalance, wound infection	abdominal pain and distention, constipation, absence of bowel sounds, vomiting	IV fluids until peristalsis returns, gradual re-introduction of oral feeding as ordered, early ambulation

Problem	Possible Cause	Clinical Signs	Preventive Interventions
Thrombophlebitis	slowed venous blood flow due to immobility or prolonged sitting; trauma to vein resulting in inflammation and increased blood coagulability	aching, cramping pain; absent peripheral pulse, edema, cool extremity, decreased sensation, affected area is swollen, red, and hot to touch, vein feels hard	early ambulation, leg exercises, anti-embolism stockings, sequential compression devices (SCD), adequate fluid intake
Wound Dehiscence	malnutrition (obesity, emaciation), poor circulation, excessive strain on suture line	increased incision drainage, tissues underlying skin become visible along parts of the incision	adequate nutrition, appropriate incisional support and avoidance of strain
Postoperative Depression	weakness, surprise nature of emergency surgery, news of malignancy, severely altered body image, maybe a physiological response to some surgeries	anorexia, tearfulness, loss of ambition, withdrawal, rejection of others, feelings of dejection, sleep disturbances (insomnia or hypersomnia)	adequate rest, physical activity, opportunity to express negative feelings or anger, client teaching

33. a nursing history; physical, psychological, and social assessment; assessment of surgical risk; verification of informed consent; preoperative teaching

34. David's statements indicate that he does not understand the surgery and/or has not freely given his consent. You must immediately notify the surgeon of the events and request that he speak to the client. In order for the client to give informed consent, he must be conscious, mentally competent, and not sedated. In addition, the information provided must be given to him in a comprehensible fashion. The transporter must be notified that David is not ready for surgery.

35. There are several potential nursing diagnoses, including Knowledge Deficit regarding abdominal surgery and Fear.

36. Verify with the surgeon that hair removal will be required. His hair removal should be done as close to the time of surgery as possible to reduce time for microbial growth. Usually, electric clippers are required to remove body hair.

37. Your response should be similar to the following:

    "Anesthesia and manipulation of the intestines affect function of the intestinal tract. Your surgeon and I are monitoring return of function by listening to your abdomen. You will be able to eat again when function returns. You will feel rumbling or pass gas when function returns."

Chapter 45 Answer Key

1. c
2. a
3. d
4. f
5. e
6. g
7. b
8. b
9. c
10. a
11. b
12. d
13. b
14. d
15. a
16. b
17. c
18. False Pain threshold is similar among individuals. However, pain tolerance varies greatly among people.
19. False Pain is a highly subjective experience. Therefore, all clients who have undergone an appendectomy will not experience pain in a similar fashion.
20. True
21. Independent nursing actions to reduce Patrick's pain include: massaging the back or stroking the head (stimulates touch fibres), applying ice (increases sensory stimulation), establishing imagery, providing music or alternative stimulation, such as a video game (provides distraction), and discussing that his injury will heal (reduces anxiety and fear). All of these actions apply knowledge from gate control theory to alter the pain response.
22. administration of analgesics, liniments or ointments, assistance with use of a TENS unit, and, in some cases, assistance with acupuncture
23. (Use the Assessment Interview on pain history as a guide.)
24. acute
25. Pharmacological and nonpharmacological strategies are appropriate for Cassandra. Nonpharmacological strategies include acknowledging her pain, assisting support persons, reducing fears and misconceptions about pain, providing distractions and

positive imagery, administering cutaneous stimulation (e.g., back rubs), or providing contralateral stimulation. Pharmacological strategies might include opioids, NSAIDs, and adjuvant analgesics. Given the pain description, opioids are the most likely choice for treatment.

26. drowsiness, respiratory depression, nausea, vomiting, and constipation

27. Cassandra will have control over her pain. She will not be dependent on the nurse to administer medication. Her analgesic blood level will be stable, and she will probably require less medication to remain comfortable.

28. Pain management may be evaluated through direct questioning of the client, through physical assessment, and through flowsheet records or a client diary.

Chapter 46 Answer Key

1. a
2. f
3. e
4. d
5. b
6. c
7. b
8. c
9. d
10. a
11. d
12. b
13. a
14. c
15. True
16. False A person with adequate self-esteem accepts himself or herself despite mistakes, defeats, and failures.
17. True
18. True
19. The nurse's role is to identify persons with a negative self-concept or low self-esteem and to assist them in developing a more positive view of themselves.
20. (See the discussion on self and self-esteem in the textbook chapter.)

21. (Use the information provided in “Framework for Identifying Personality Strengths” to conduct a self-evaluation.)

22. Provide a loving and secure environment. Provide positive feedback. Set long-term expectations that are realistic and enhance motivation. Provide opportunities for the child to succeed, and offer frequent encouragement.

23. Encourage resident involvement in changing the appearance of the facility. Let them be part of the planning and implementation. Suggest that clients keep photographs and personal belongings around them. Strive to create a more home-like environment.

24. Recognize and reward accomplishments. Praise excellence, and encourage a professional appearance and demeanour. Ask staff to set goals and develop a plan to achieve goals. Encourage staff to take personal responsibility for their care and the work environment.

25. Encourage clients to participate actively in their care. Be respectful of their wishes, and ask permission before moving their personal effects. Take time to listen to the clients. Allow plenty of time for the residents to complete a task. Allow the residents to be as independent as possible. Encourage participation in social events. Graciously accept thanks.

Chapter 47 Answer Key

1. d
2. e
3. a
4. c
5. b
6. b
7. c
8. a
9. d
10. c
11. a
12. False Death of a spouse is a significant life event. The degree of stress experienced by this event is highly individual.
13. True
14. False Problem solving, structuring, self-control, suppression, and fantasy are cognitive indicators of stress.
15. False Crisis intervention assists clients through short-term adaptation to an acute, time-limited state of disequilibrium.
16. using alcohol or drugs, daydreaming, and relying on a belief that everything will work out
17. ____

Mild Anxiety	Moderate Anxiety	Severe Anxiety	Panic

(Reflect on your current level of stress and anxiety to determine your current anxiety level.)

18. (Review the textbook chapter for assistance with this response. The section on stress management for nurses may prove helpful for dealing with school/work-related stress.)
19. (See the section in the text on verbal and motor manifestations of stress for assistance in answering this question.)
20. the nature of the stress, Jeff's perception of the stress, the number of simultaneous stressors, duration of exposure to the stressors, experiences with comparable stress, age and availability of support people
21. Orient the client to the unit and hospital environment. Encourage significant others to visit. Support the client by offering care and understanding. Provide factual information to questions about his injury. Repeat any information he has difficulty remembering. Encourage Jose to participate in his care, and provide ample time to ventilate his feelings.

Assess Jose's usual coping strategies, and help him to mobilize them. Allow him to be as independent as possible within the constraints of his injury.

22. Goals focused on anxiety include: decrease or resolve his anxiety, increase his ability to manage or cope with this stressful event, improve his role performance.

23. There are many possible responses. However, the chief objective is to offer support and understanding and focus on the feeling words of the client. An example of an appropriate response is: "It must be frustrating to be here." You will need to convey that it is essential to adhere to activity restrictions and to the surgeon's recommendations in order to ensure optimum function of his finger and hand.

24. Independent nursing actions that may help Jose relax include massage and guided imagery. Other relaxation techniques that could be employed include breathing exercises, progressive relaxation, meditation, music therapy, humour, and laughter. Nurses who have received additional training in biofeedback and therapeutic touch techniques may wish to utilize these methods.

Chapter 48 Answer Key

1. a
2. b
3. d
4. c
5. c
6. d
7. d
8. b
9. a
10. c
11. b
12. b
13. a
14. c
15. d
16. True
17. False Nursing skills in situations of loss include attentive listening, silence, open and closed questioning, clarifying and reflecting feelings, and summarizing.
18. True
19. stage of development, culture, spiritual beliefs, gender, socioeconomic status, support system, and cause of loss or death
20. The major goals of the dying client are to maintain physiological and psychological comfort and to achieve a dignified and peaceful death.
21. Assess Shelli's awareness of her condition and her concerns and fears. Determine where she would like to be cared for (for instance, at home or at the hospital), and provide care in this setting, if possible. Provide physical, psychosocial, and spiritual care. Offer support to Shelli's support system. Ensure dignity and respect before and after death. Provide postmortem care per agency policy.

22–26. *Completion and case study questions:* Take time to think about your answers to these questions. Use these exercises to get in touch with your own feelings about death and loss. You may wish to discuss the study questions in a small group. The answers to these questions are based on your personal experiences and feelings. However, you must always avoid forcing your own views upon the client and strive to use your best communication skills.